INDIA IN 1858

INDIA IN 1858

A SUMMARY OF THE EXISTING ADMINISTRATION
POLITICAL, FISCAL AND JUDICIAL OF
BRITISH INDIA
TOGETHER WITH THE LAWS
AND PUBLIC DOCUMENTS
RELATING THERE TO
FROM THE EARLIST
TO THE PRESENT TIME

ARTHUR MILLS, M. P.

GYAN PUBLISHING HOUSE
New Delhi - 110002

INDIA IN 1858

ISBN : 9788121200233

Published in 2015 in India by
Gyan Publishing House
23, Ansari Road, Daryaganj,
New Delhi - 110002
Phones : 23261060, 23282060 Fax : 23285914
e-mail : books@gyanbooks.com
website : gyanbooks.com

Laser Typesetting at : Vinayak Printers, Delhi
Printed at : Salasar Imaging System, Delhi

PREFACE.

THE announcement of contemplated changes in the Government of India, has naturally given rise to various suggestions as to the policy to be adopted in the future Administration of that portion of the British Empire.

The object of the following pages is not to multiply these suggestions, or to scrutinize the causes of those calamitous events, which have riveted the interest of all classes of the community in England, on India and its destinies.

Valuable as are the speculations of thoughtful and earnest men, on a question so momentous as that which affects the loss, or the maintenance of British authority in India, it is yet too evident that those speculations have in the present case often rested on a basis of actual knowledge of the past and present circumstances of our Eastern Empire, too slender for the superstructure of theories which it has been called upon to bear.

If Indian taxation, law, and judicial procedure are to become the battle-field of English Parliamentary warfare, it is, at all events, important, that we should know what Indian taxation, law, and judicial procedure *now are*. If the Civil Government and Military defence of India are to be re-organized, it is well that we should know what is the actually-existing system on which India now depends for its Civil Government and Military defence.

Those who have no personal knowledge of Asiatic character and institutions depend necessarily for their guidance in their practical dealings with these momentous questions, on those who possess such knowledge. There is, nevertheless, a certain stock of facts which is, or ought to be, accessible to all.

Buried in the folios in which repose minutes of evidence, obtained by Parliamentary Committees, and in those well-known histories of India, and treatises on its government, which are familiar to all students of Indian politics, all, and more than all, that it is necessary to know is, doubtless, to be found. But it is difficult sometimes to extricate this information from the mass of criticisms and controversies in which it is imbedded. To disentangle *facts* from the opinions in which they are, generally, interwoven, is the purpose of this volume. Simply to present, as faithfully and concisely as possible, the machinery of the Anglo-Indian Government, *as it now exists*, together with its fiscal and judicial apparatus.

The object to be attained being rather accuracy of statement than originality of language, the extracts of public documents, from which information is drawn, have been copied verbatim. Of those chapters which relate to the Home Government and the "Services" in India, the analysis of the evidence, taken before the Parliamentary Committees of 1852 forms, with slight alterations, the chief substance. For such portions of the table, appended to the Revenue Map, as are not contained in the territorial accounts, laid before Parliament, as well as for other valuable information, I am indebted to the Statistical Department of the East India House.

The Revenue Map is intended to afford data for a fair comparison of the various systems under which the Land Revenue of India is now collected. In classifying the Revenue Systems, the arrangement presented by the Government returns has been in all cases followed. Those Provinces, for instance, which are directly under the administration of the Governor-General in Council, are included in the Bengal accounts: the only exception being the Cis-Sutlej States, which are, for revenue purposes, classified with the North-West Provinces. It will be observed that in the Punjaub, the boundaries of the Collectorates are not marked, the survey for this purpose being as yet incomplete. The "Village System" which there exists cannot be said to fall strictly under either of the two great divisions of Indian tenures; the peculiarities of this system are described in the fifth chapter.

In order to form a satisfactory estimate of the relative productiveness of the systems under which the Land Revenues of India are now assessed, accurate data as to the comparative fertility of the various soils, the localities of culturable and unculturable, irrigated and unirrigated lands, are manifestly essential. In the absence of such data, the *areas* of the Collectorates can only be compared.

The brief chronological summary of the legislative changes and annexations which have marked the rise and progress of our Eastern Empire, contained in the first chapter, seemed an almost essential introduction to those which follow.

The leading events of Anglo-Indian history, and the various systems of policy through which it has passed, are associated, not so much with the successive Charters granted to the East India Company, as with the names of those men to whom the local government of that empire has been, from time to time, committed; from the days when peaceful traders presided over our earliest factories, to be afterwards succeeded by the warriors, who expelled the French and crushed the Mahrattas, and the diplomatists who were to absorb, one by one, under British supremacy, nearly all the ancient feudatories of the Mogul Empire.

The following are the names of those who have held Office as Governors-General and Administrators of India, with the Dates of Appointment; those prior to the Act of 1773 having been styled "Administrators;" those between 1773 and the Act of 1833 "Governors-General of Fort William;" those from 1833 to the present time "Governors-General of India in Council."

Alexander Dawson, January 27, 1748.
William Fytche, January 8, 1752.
Roger Drake, August 8, 1752.
Colonel Robert Clive, March 25, 1758.
Henry Vansittart, November 23, 1759.
John Spencer, November 26, 1764.
Lord Clive (second time), June 1, 1764.
Harry Verelst, January 26, 1767.
John Cartier, December 16, 1769.
Warren Hastings, April 25, 1771.
John Macpherson (provisionally), February 1, 1785.
Lord Macartney, July 1785. (Declined Office.)
Lord Cornwallis, February 24, 1786.
Major-General W. Meadows, April 28, 1790.
Sir John Shore (Lord Teignmouth), September 19, 1792.
Sir Alured Clarke (provisionally), September 20, 1797.
Lord Mornington (Marquess of Wellesley), October 4, 1797.
Marquess Cornwallis (second time), January 9, 1805. Died October 6.
Sir George H. Barlow (appointment revoked by H.M.), February 19, 1806.
Lord Minto, July 9, 1806.
Earl of Moira (Marquess of Hastings), November 18, 1812.
George Canning, March 27, 1822. (Declined Office.)
William, Lord Amherst, October 23, 1822.
W. B. Bayley (provisionally), March 23, 1828.
Lord William Bentinck, March 13, 1828.
William, Lord Heytesbury (appointment revoked by H.M.), January 28, 1835.

Sir Charles Metcalfe (provisionally), March 20, 1835.
George, Lord Auckland, August 12, 1836.
Edward, Lord Ellenborough (revoked by Court of Directors, May 1, 1844), October 20, 1841.
W. W. Bird (provisionally), 1844.
Sir Henry Hardinge (Viscount Hardinge), May 6, 1844.
James Andrew, Marquess of Dalhousie, August 4, 1847.
Charles John, Viscount Canning, July —, 1855.

The following are the Names of those who have held the Office of President of the Board of Commissioners for the Affairs of India since its Constitution in 1784.

Thomas, Lord Sydney, September 3, 1784.
Right Hon. W. Wyndham Grenville, March 12, 1790.
Right Hon. Henry Dundas, June 28, 1793.
George, Viscount Lewisham, May 19, 1801.
Robert, Viscount Castlereagh, July 12, 1802.
Gilbert, Lord Minto, February 12, 1806.
Right Hon. Thomas Grenville, July 16, 1806.
Right Hon. George Tierney, October 1, 1806.
Right Hon. Robert Dundas, April 6, 1807.
Dudley, Earl of Harrowby, July 16, 1807.
Right Hon. R. Dundas (second time), November 13, 1809.
Robert, Earl of Buckinghamshire, April 7, 1812.
Right Hon. George Canning, June 20, 1816.
Right Hon. Charles Bathurst, July 16, 1821.
Right Hon. C. Watkin Williams Wynn, July 8, 1822.
Robert Dundas, Viscount Melville, February 7, 1828.
Edward, Lord Ellenborough, April 24, 1828.
Right Hon. Charles Grant, December 6, 1830.
Edward, Lord Ellenborough (second time), December 20, 1834.
Right Hon. Sir John C. Hobhouse, Bart., April 29, 1835.
Edward, Lord Ellenborough (third time), April 9, 1841.
W. F. Fitzgerald, Lord Fitzgerald and Vesci, October 28, 1841.
Frederic J., Earl of Ripon, May 23, 1843.
Sir J. C. Hobhouse, Lord Broughton (2nd time), July 10, 1846.
Right Hon. Fox Maule, February 5, 1852.
Right Hon. J. C. Herries, February 27, 1852.
Right Hon. Sir Charles Wood, Bart., December 28, 1852.
Right Hon. R. Vernon Smith, ———, 1855.

The Constitution and functions of the Home and Local Government, with those of its subordinate instruments, will be described in the second and third chapters of this volume. It may be sufficient here to remark that the original establishment of the Board of Control appears to have arisen from the circumstance that at the time when by common consent it had become necessary that the Crown should be in some form represented in the Government of our Eastern dependencies, the department to which that authority would have been naturally committed had ceased to exist.

The expansion of British dominion in India at the close of the eighteenth century, precisely concurred in point of time with the loss of those American Provinces which had theretofore formed the bulk of our Colonial Domain.

The Imperial Parliament which, at the suggestion of Burke in 1782, had broken up as useless the Board of Plantations, and the Colonial Department, and the whole existing framework of Colonial Administration, was compelled only two years afterwards, at the suggestion of Pitt in 1784, to devise an entirely new machinery for the Home Government of India.

The political mechanism thus framed in 1784, which the successive modifications introduced by the statutes of 1813, 1833, and 1853, have left untouched in its leading features, is now on its trial.

Amidst the conflict of opinion on the past, present, and future of our Indian Empire we may yet derive hope and encouragement from the very concentration of the thought and intelligence of the country on those mighty problems which surround every department of a question, now once more, after the lapse of three-quarters of a century, thrown open to debate.

If our stock of knowledge on the subject we are called upon to discuss be confessedly meagre and inadequate, the progress of opinion and of events has in some respects fitted us for dealing more fairly and successfully than in former times with questions of policy affecting the remote dependencies of our Empire.

That cluster of affiliated States, which we still call Colonies, and which are still proud to call themselves the subjects of our Queen, have been endowed for the most part with the powers of self-government, and promoted to a rank very little removed from that of independent principalities. To retain for the longest possible period, at the smallest possible cost, with the greatest possible advantage to ourselves, the dependencies of our Empire, was once the problem which occupied the minds of British statesmen. To ripen those communities to the earliest possible maturity, moral and material, to qualify them by all the means within the reach of the Parent State for self-government and eventual independence is now the universally-admitted object and aim of our Colonial policy.

And though India may be as yet unripe for self-government, though its teeming population may be as yet incapable of appreciating or of exercising the privileges of freedom, to raise them to this standard, regardless of any political consequences to ourselves, will be the foremost object of all who rightly apprehend the duties and responsibilities of Imperial power. An inglorious and unlovely subjection to be maintained by force, when the functions of the Parent State are fulfilled, has no longer any charm for the Economist, the Philanthropist, or the Statesman. But a rude disseverance of those ties which bind us to those communities which still claim our protection, and still own a common sway, would be deprecated alike by all who have the foresight to anticipate the calamitous issues it would assuredly involve. And to those who regard vast empires, as permitted to exist and to expand for some higher purpose than the gratification of ambition, the exercise of State-craft, or the development of material wealth, the premature dismemberment of such empires seems nothing less than a wilful disorganization of a mighty machinery, which (however it may have been used by man) was designed by GOD for the civilization of mankind.

On the adoption of a policy involving the moral and material progress of India, the instincts of the country, though not as yet moulded into a presentable or practicable form, may, nevertheless, be said to be unanimous.

Whether this policy is to be carried out by the Anglo-Indian Government in its existing form, or by some other machinery differently contrived, to be substituted in its place,—whether under the present circumstances, and with the present resources of

India, such a policy can be carried out at all, are questions altogether foreign to these pages, the purpose of which is simply to contribute data for the formation of a correct opinion on these important subjects.

Integrity, intelligence, and courage have been, in past seasons of trial, conspicuous characteristics of the Anglo-Indian Service; let us hope, that, under whatever form of Government our Eastern Empire may eventually be placed, the same qualities may distinguish in an equal degree the *personnel* of its future administration.

CONTENTS.

CHAPTER I.

PAGE

INTRODUCTORY SKETCH OF THE POLITICAL HISTORY OF BRITISH INDIA 1

CHAPTER II.

EXISTING GOVERNMENT OF BRITISH INDIA.

Sect. I.—Home Government. Sect. II.—Local Government 30

CHAPTER III.

THE INSTRUMENTS OF INDIAN GOVERNMENT.

The Services—Civil (Covenanted and Uncovenanted), Military, Naval, Ecclesiastical 55

CHAPTER IV.

ADMINISTRATION OF JUSTICE IN BRITISH INDIA.

Sect. I.—Laws in Force in British India generally. Sect. II.—Laws and Judicial Procedure applicable to British-born Subjects—The Supreme Courts. Sect. III.—Laws and Judicial Procedure applicable to the Native Population of India—Civil Courts—Criminal Courts and Police. Sect. IV.—The Indian Law Commission 71

CHAPTER V.

EXISTING REVENUE SYSTEM OF BRITISH INDIA.

PAGE

Sources of Revenue.—Land—Salt—Opium—Customs —Miscellaneous 104

CHAPTER VI.

ADMINISTRATION OF NATIVE STATES.

Existing Relations with Native States: List of Treaties 135

CHAPTER VII.

EXISTING GOVERNMENT INSTITUTIONS AND PUBLIC WORKS IN BRITISH INDIA.

Sect. I.—Educational Institutions. Sect. II.—Public Works — Canals — Roads — Railways — Telegraphs. Sect. III.—List of Government Measures adopted to promote the Culture of Cotton. Sect. IV.—Measures adopted to promote the Working of Iron Ores . . 165

CHAPTER VIII.

LAWS AND PUBLIC DOCUMENTS RELATING TO BRITISH INDIA.

Sect. I.—Bengal Regulations, and Acts of the Governor-General in Council. Sect. II.—Orders in Council. Sect. III.—Acts of the Imperial Parliament. Sect. IV.—Parliamentary Reports, Accounts, and Papers . 181

APPENDIX A.

Mr. Fox's East India Bills 250

APPENDIX B.

PAGE

Draft of proposed Treaty between the East India Company and the King of Oude, and of Proclamation issued on its non-acceptance 282

APPENDIX C.

Regulations for the Examination of Candidates for the Civil and Military Services 290

INDIA IN 1858.

CHAPTER I.

INTRODUCTORY SKETCH OF THE POLITICAL HISTORY OF BRITISH INDIA.

THE British Empire in India may be divided politically into three classes of Territories, distinguishable by the degree and the form in which British authority is exercised over each.

I. The Territories which are subject to that system of administration, fiscal and judicial, which is embodied in the published Regulations and Acts of the Indian Government, as carried out exclusively by Members of the Civil Service, and known by the designation of "Regulation Provinces."

II. The Territories (consisting chiefly of the more recently acquired Districts) which are governed under such special and varying Instructions as have been from time to time issued for the guidance of the Functionaries, whether civil or military, to whom the administration of those Districts, which are called "Non-Regulation" Provinces, has been committed.

III. The Territories of Native Princes, with

B

whom relations have been established by various Treaties, differing in their stipulations, but generally entitling those States to British protection, on the condition either of payment of tribute, or cession of a portion of their Territory, or providing a Military Contingent.* These States are in various degrees under the political supremacy of the Anglo-Indian Government, exercised through Agents, called "Residents," stationed within their respective dominions; who act under instructions from the Governor-General in Council, to whom the management of these Territories is, generally, committed.†

British India, as thus defined, contains, according to recent returns, a population of about 180 millions, and an area of about $1\frac{1}{2}$ million of square miles; the detailed statistics of which are given in the following summary:—

* The territories of those Native Asiatic Princes who have simply entered into diplomatic relations with Great Britain, and who are therefore, except in matters in which they may have accepted British mediation, absolutely independent, cannot, of course, be properly included within the limits of British India.

† Some of the smaller Native States are associated for purposes of political communication, with the Presidencies to which they are geographically contiguous, as Travancore with Madras, and Kolapore with Bombay. *Vide* chap. vii. *infra*.

SUMMARY OF THE AREA AND POPULATION OF BRITISH INDIA.

	Area in Sq. Miles.	Total Area in Sq. Miles.	Population.	Total Population.
I.—Regulation Provinces.				
Under the Government of Bengal	126,133		37,262,163	
,, ,, North-west Provinces	72,052		30,271,885	
,, ,, Madras	119,526		20,120,495	
,, ,, Bombay	57,723		9,015,534	
		375,434		96,670,077
II.—Non-Regulation Provinces.				
Under the Governor-General of India in Council (comprising the Punjab, Oude, Berar, Pegu, the Tenasserim Provinces, and the Straits-Settlements	246,050		23,255,972	
Under the Government of Bengal	95,836		3,590,234	
,, ,, North-west Provinces	33,707		3,383,308	
,, ,, Madras	12,564		2,316,802	
,, ,, Bombay (comprising Sinde and Sattara)	73,821		2,774,508	
		461,978		35,320,804
III.—Territories of Native Princes under Subsidiary and Protective Treaties.				
Under the Governor-General of India in Council. Geographically contiguous to Bengal & North-West Provinces	515,533		38,702,206	
Madras	51,802		5,213,671	
Bombay	60,575		4,460,370	
		627,910		48,376,247
Total	....	1,465,322		180,367,148

India has been for nearly two thousand years the scene of successive warlike invasions and commercial enterprises, which have left almost unchanged the laws, religion, and general condition of the mass of its population.

During the thirteen centuries which intervened between the invasions of Alexander and that of Mahmoud of Ghuznee, India—comprising the two great districts of Hindostan and the Deccan—was split into a vast number of native kingdoms, alternately struggling for supreme power.

Of the northern portion, or Hindostan Proper, comprising the valleys of the Indus and the Ganges, from Kurrachee to Chittagong, the chief seats of power were Guzerat, Sinde, Malwa, Delhi, Benares, and Bengal.

Of the southern portion, or the Deccan, comprising the hill district and table-land between the Nerbudda and the Kistna, the chief dynasties were, during the same period, those which ruled over Kerala, Pandya, Chera, Carnata, Andra, Orissa, and Maharashta, or the Country of the Mahrattas.

The Indo-Mahommedan dynasties of Arab, Tartar, Turk, Affghan, and Mongol origin, which afterwards successively held sway at Ghuznee, Lahore, and Delhi, have left few more permanent traces of their power than the Indo-European Trading Companies, whose factories have been planted on the shores of India at various periods during the last three centuries, by subjects of Portugal, Holland, Denmark, Sweden, and France.

The government of British India, unlike those systems of polity which have gradually expanded with the advancing civilization of other countries, has consisted, for more than two centuries, of a sort of temporary machinery, contrived and modified from time to time to meet the necessities of successive conquests. Political powers, delegated, in the first instance, to a trading corporation for the limited purposes of their own commerce, were of course wholly insufficient for the government of a vast empire. Each succeeding change in the Administration of British India has been thus only the natural result of each succeeding conquest, which necessitated some fresh contrivance for strengthening the hands of the ruling power over the constantly-increasing area of the Imperial domain, and will be found on a review of those events in the order of their occurrence, to have been ordinarily preceded by an advance not so much in the power and resources of the country, as in its territorial boundaries.

16th Century.

During the whole of the 16th century attempts were made by Great Britain to extend, in the direction of India, the commerce which, at its commencement, had sprung up with the Levant. The efforts at Indian communication made successively by Sebastian Cabot in 1549, by Chancellor in 1553, by Drake in 1577, by the Turkey Company in 1581, by Cavendish in 1586, by Raymond and Lancaster in 1591, and by Sir Robert Dudley in 1596, were, however, attended with no permanent results. It was on the last day of the 16th century that Queen Elizabeth

First Charter.

17th Century. signed a Charter on behalf of about 220 gentlemen and merchants, constituting them "one bodie corporate and politique," by the name of "The Governor and Company of Merchants of London trading to the East Indies." Under this Charter, which was granted for fifteen years, revocable at any time at two years' notice, a capital was raised of 30,133*l.* 6*s.* 8*d.*, divided into 101 shares. Difficulties and delays having arisen, and the funds being inadequate, a subordinate Association, with a capital of 68,373*l.*, was formed, and the first expedition, consisting of five vessels, manned by 500 men, sailed from Torbay on April 22, 1601, to Acheen, in Sumatra, under Captain Lancaster.

In 1602 these adventurers established a factory at Bantam, in Java. In 1609 their Charter was renewed, and in the same year they launched, at Deptford, in the presence of King James and his son (afterwards Charles I.), a vessel of 1100 tons burthen, called the "Trade's Increase," afterwards lost in Bantam roads, and described by Sir William Monson as "the goodliest and greatest ship that was ever framed in this kingdom."

Up to 1613 the adventurers carried on their business on a system of separate risk and profit for each, but in that year it was commenced on a joint-stock account. In January, 1613, an Imperial firman was obtained from the Mogul, authorising the establishment of a British factory at Surat, and about the same time the embassy of Sir Thomas Rowe to Ajmere resulted in a nominal concession of liberty of trade to the British throughout the empire. On June 13, in the same year, an order in Council was passed "for regulating the trade to the East Indies." 17th Century.

In 1616, a new capital of a million and a half sterling was raised by about 950 persons, many of whom appear to have been of high rank.

In 1619, a treaty was signed at London, between Great Britain and Holland, for adjusting the rights and regulating the trade of the British and Dutch East India Companies, which, till the massacre of Amboyna, in 1622, was chiefly carried on with the Spice Islands. Up to that time (from 1600 to 1623) the British exports to India, including bullion, were about one million, and the imports therefrom about three millions altogether.

During this period—that is, through the first quarter of the 17th century—it appears, from the records of the Council Office, that the East India Company were made the occasional instruments of the Crown in the transportation of criminals to India.*

In 1626, notwithstanding objections raised to the drain of specie from Great Britain by means of the Company's trade, an Order in Council was issued, January 20, permitting them to export bullion.

In 1634, permission having been granted to the British by the Emperor to trade with Bengal, through the port of Piplee, in Orissa, a new Company, afterward, called "The Assada Merchants," obtained a

* *Vide* Orders in Council, *infra*.

17th Century. five years' licence from the Crown, and, under the auspices of Sir William Courteen, engaged in a competitive Trade. About ten years afterwards they were amalgamated with the original East India Company.

In 1640, by permission of the Rajah ruling that portion of the Coromandel coast, Fort St. George was erected as a depôt for the Company's muslins and wove-goods at Madras. For thirteen years Madras remained subject to the Company's station at Bantam; and when at the end of that time it was constituted a distinct Presidency, the British force there consisted of only ten soldiers and two factors.

About 1650 the Hooghly factory was erected under trading privileges granted by the then Mogul (Shah Jehan), which seem to have been obtained through the intercession of an English physician named Boughton.

In 1654, by a treaty with Holland, signed at Westminster, a mixed Commission of Dutch and English Members was appointed, under whose arbitration 85,000*l.* was awarded to the English East India Company, in adjustment of past differences, and compensation for losses.

In 1657, a Charter was granted by Cromwell, under which the rights of private adventurers were recognised, and a new subscription raised.

In 1661, Charles II. renewed the Company's Charter, by a clause of which the Island of St. Helena, of which they had taken possession ten years before, was confirmed to them. In the same year, the King married the Infanta Catherine of Portugal, and received as a portion of her dower the Island of Bombay. It appears, however, from the Records of Orders in Council, in the years 1660 and 1663, for sending munitions of war and money to Bombay, that this acquisition, not actually realised till 1664, was attended with considerable expense to the British Government; and in 1668 the Island was transferred to the East India Company, "to be held of the King in free and common socage, as of the Manor of East Greenwich, on the payment of the annual rent of ten pounds in gold." Bombay was expensively fortified by the Company, and the system of administration afterwards extended to the other Presidencies, with its gradations of writers, factors, and merchants, was adopted. 17th Century.

In 1676, letters patent were granted by Charles II. for the establishment of a Mint at Bombay, for the coinage of rupees and pice, a small copper coin.

In 1693, the Company's Charter was again renewed for a period of twenty-one years; but the public opinion then existing against its exclusive privileges was immediately afterwards expressed by a vote of the House of Commons, declaring it to be "the right of all Englishmen to trade to the East "Indies, or any part of the world, unless prohibited "by Act of Parliament." A system of corruption was at this time carried on by the Company, with the view of supporting their monopoly.

In 1693, more than 80,000*l.* appears to have been

17th Century. spent on "secret services," a large portion of which was known to have been applied in bribing members of Parliament: at the same time, the costly policy of the Childs' at Bombay, and the establishment in 1698 of the factory of Fort William in Bengal, was laying the foundation of further extravagance, the only obvious means for meeting which was to be found in increased territorial revenue, which last was only attainable by war.

The struggles at the same time with the Moguls in the person of Aurungzebe, and with the Mahrattas in that of Sevajee, and the jealous rivalry of other European powers, tended to aggravate the embarrassment of the British in India.

It was at this period that the Indian debt had its origin. At the time of the establishment of the Company at Calcutta, and the first purchase of land there, it amounted to 100,000*l.* It has now reached nearly sixty millions sterling.

In 1698, by Charter, dated Sept. 6, a competitive Company was incorporated under the title of "The General Society, trading to the East Indies;" and in the same year, by statute 9 & 10 Wm. III., cap. 44, interest at the rate of 8 per cent. was guaranteed on a loan of two millions to be raised by the new Association.

The rivalry between the two Companies having occasioned disastrous consequences to both, and the stock of the old Company having fluctuated in value during the three following years between 300 and

37 per cent.* a coalition became the only means of escape from ruin. 18th Century.

In 1702, by an indenture tripartite, to which the two Companies and the Crown were parties, and which was approved by Order in Council, dated June 11, 1702, provision was made for a full and complete union between the two Companies, under the designation of "The United Company of Merchants, trading to the East Indies."

In 1707, by statute 6 Anne, cap. 17, provision was made for legally amalgamating the two Companies; all differences to be submitted to Lord Godolphin (then High Treasurer), as Arbitrator, and his award to be binding. It appears that the "dead stock" brought into partnership by the two Companies, at the time of their union, was as follows:—By the old or "London" Company, the three Presidencies of Bombay, Madras, and Calcutta with their forts, factories, stores, and ammunitions, together with the rents and customs arising therefrom, and the firmans by right of which they were enjoyed; also the Island of St. Helena—three factories or trading posts in Persia, at Gombroon, Shiraz, and Ispahan, and certain settlements on the Island of Sumatra. The new Company brought in as their share (for which they were to be allowed 70,000*l.* in the united funds), factories at Surat, Masulipatam in the Bay of Bengal, Madupollam in Borneo, and Pulo Condore, on the

* *Vide* Anderson's History of Commerce, ii., p. 43.

18th Century. coast of Cochin China, with the stores and ammunitions belonging thereto.*

In 1711, by statute 10 Anne, cap. 28, the Corporate capacity of the United East India Company was recognised, and their privileges of trade continued.

The managing body of the East India Company at home, which had hitherto been styled the "Court of Committees," adopted, after the amalgamation, its present title of Court of Directors.

The Government of the three British Settlements in India was at this time committed to a President and Council appointed by the Company at each of the Stations; and its Civil affairs were conducted by subordinate functionaries sent out from England under covenants of service—the terms of which were, in general, that they should "obey all orders, that they should discharge all debts, and that they should treat the natives of India well." The Presidents were respectively Commanders-in-Chief of the military force stationed within the limits of their jurisdiction.

From existing records, it appears that the scale of salaries received by the Civil servants of the Company was extremely moderate. The highest appointment at Bombay did not exceed 300*l*. a year, the Governor of Madras had 200*l*. per annum, and of the six Councillors, the Chief had 100*l*., the Junior 40*l*. per annum. There were two Chaplains who re-

* *Vide* the "Quinque-Partite Indenture," in Charters of East India Company, pp. 316-344.

ceived 100*l*. per annum each. One Judge with a salary of 100*l*., and a staff of senior and junior merchants, factors, and writers, the lowest class of whom did not receive, besides their diet-money, more than 5*l*. per annum.* Each *employé* was, however, permitted to prosecute an independent traffic on his own account. 18th Century.

The garrisons were composed partly of recruits sent from England, partly of deserters from other European Settlements in India, partly of half-castes of Portuguese and Indian descent, called "Topasses," and partly of natives of pure Indian descent, Rajpoots and others employed by the Company, under the name of "Sipahies" (soldiers) or Sepoys.

In or about the year 1716 the authorities of the Company at Calcutta obtained from the Mogul, through the alleged influence of an English surgeon (Mr. Hamilton), who was sent with others on an Embassy to Delhi, a firman with certain privileges:

1. That the passport of the Company's President should exempt all British goods from examination by the Mogul Government Officers.

2. That the Officers of the Mint at Moorshedabad should give three days a week for the coinage of the Company's money there.

3. That all debtors of the Company should be delivered up on demand.

4. That the Company might purchase the lord-

* Lockyer's Trade of Bombay, p. 14.

18th Century. ships of thirty-eight towns in Bengal, with certain specified immunities.

It appears from dispatches addressed by the Directors to their servants at Calcutta, that these privileges, so far as they related to the cession of territory, were not valued or insisted on at that time.*

In 1744, by statute 17 Geo. II. cap. 17, the privileges of the East India Company were continued for a certain term, on conditions therein defined.

At this period internal weakness, and the invasions of Mahrattas, Persians, and Afghans, had well-nigh broken up the Mogul power in India. Cabool, Sinde, Moultan, and Cashmere, had been wrested from the empire by the invasions of Nadir Shah; Guzerat and Malwa had been lost by native intrigues.

The Deccan (the country between the Nerbudda and the Kistna, of which Hyderabad was the metropolis, and which had comprised six Mogul "soubahs," or provinces) was nominally under his deputy, the Nizam, but practically under the Mahrattas, under the leadership of the Peishwah, or Brahmin minister, of the effete Court of Sevajee at Poonah. Mysore had been seized by the Mussulman freebooter, Hyder Ali, who was destined, with his son Tippoo, to wage a long and chequered warfare with the British for the dominion of Southern India.

In 1746, war with the French began in the Carnatic, and continued with various alternations for fifteen years, when it was ended by the capture of

* *Vide* Auber's Rise and Progress, i. p. 25.

Pondicherry. In Bengal, in the meantime, the first-fruits of the battle of Plassey, fought in 1757, had been the addition of the district round Calcutta, and three years afterwards of Burdwan, Midnapore, and Chittagong, to the British dominions in that quarter.* It was at this time that the system, since so extensively adopted, of pensioning native Princes, through whom British rule was to be indirectly maintained, was first attempted in the cases of the Nabobs of the Carnatic and Bengal. 18th Century.

In 1765 Lord Clive was sent out with the supreme command, and in the same year, by the Treaty of Allahabad (August 12), the Dewannee, or Civil Government of Bengal, Bahar, and Orissa was granted to the East India Company, on payment of an annual tribute of twenty-six lacs, or 260,000*l.*, which was, however, only paid for five years. Administration of Lord Clive.

In the same year a district round Madras was obtained from the Nabob of the Carnatic; and in 1767 the Nizam granted to the Company the Northern Circars, on condition of military assistance.

In the same year, by statute 7 George III. cap. 57, the Territories and Revenues thus acquired were guaranteed for two years to the East India Company, on payment of 400,000*l.* per annum.

In 1769, by statute 9 George III. cap. 24, the provisions of the last-mentioned Act were continued for five years.

In 1772, the East India Company took the absolute Government of Bengal into their own hands,

* *Vide* Orme's Military Transactions in Hindostan, 1778.

18th Century. and pensioned the Nabob and his descendants with 160,000*l.* a-year.

In 1772 (April), a Select Committee of thirty-one Members was appointed to inquire into and report upon the State of India.

In 1773, this Committee was re-appointed; and another, called a Secret Committee, of thirteen Members, was likewise constituted; and in the same year, by statute 13 George III. cap. 63, the Imperial Parliament first made provision for the Government of British India. That statute enacted that the election of the twenty-four Directors of the East India Company (theretofore annual) should be thenceforward for certain terms prescribed in the Act. A Governor-General and four Councillors were also appointed for five years (their seat of government to be at Fort William, in Bengal), to administer the whole civil and military government of Bengal, Bahar, and Orissa, and the revenues thereof, and to have a general control over the subordinate Presidencies and Councils of Madras and Bombay. The Act empowered the Governor-General to frame ordinances and regulations, which must, in order to give them force, be registered in a "Supreme Court" constituted by the Act, and holding its sessions at Calcutta. In the same year (1773), another Act (13 George III. cap. 64) was passed, which, after reciting the financial difficulties of the East India Company, relieves them from their annual payment, and authorises the issue of 1,400,000*l.* in Exchequer Bills, to be applied in their relief. By the same Act, the Company were bound to export annually merchandise to the amount of 380,837*l.* (exclusive of naval and military stores), for two years. 18th Century.

Under the Act of 1773 (called the Regulating Act), Warren Hastings became Governor-General. Under his Administration, oppression gave rise to resistance—resistance to war—war to expenses—expenses to new oppressions. Administration of Warren Hastings.

In 1781, by statute 21 Geo. III. cap. 65, the privileges of the Company were continued for ten years, determinable thereafter on three years' notice. It was also enacted that the Company should pay 400,000*l.* in full satisfaction of all claims on them; that their dividends should be limited to eight per cent., and that after payment thereof, three-fourths of their surplus receipts should be paid into the Exchequer.

In 1782, a Select Committee of the House of Commons was appointed on Indian Affairs and Government.

In 1783, Mr. Fox introduced into Parliament (Nov. 18) two Bills * — 1. For vesting the affairs of the East India Company in the hands of seven Directors, to be aided by nine Proprietors named in the Bill, in which body all powers (subject to the authority of the Crown) were vested; 2. For the better government of the territorial possessions in India, the regulation of land tenures, and the abolition of monopolies. The Board to be created by the first Bill was to have in its gift all the

* Both Bills are printed at length in Appendix A.

18th Century. patronage of the Company. Neither of these Bills was passed. The first was rejected in the House of Lords, Dec. 17.

In 1784, by statute 24 Geo. III. cap. 25 (commonly called Pitt's Act), His Majesty was empowered to appoint six Privy Councillors as Commissioners for the affairs of India; three to form a quorum, and either the Chancellor of the Exchequer, or one of the Secretaries of State, to be President. By the same Act, appointments to vacancies in the office of Governor-General, and in the subordinate Governments at Fort St. George and Bombay, and of the Councillors, and all other functionaries at each Presidency; also the right to recall the Governor-General, and to declare war, were vested in the Court of Directors, from which body a Secret Committee was selected, invested with functions hereafter to be noticed. The Supreme Council at Calcutta constituted by the Act, consisted of the Governor-General and three Councillors, the Commander-in-Chief being second in authority.

Administration of Lord Cornwallis. In 1788, by statute 28 Geo. III. cap. 8, the Commissioners appointed by the last-cited Act, called the "Board of Control," were empowered to direct that the expense of raising, transporting, and maintaining such troops as might be required for the security of the British territories in the East Indies should be defrayed out of the territorial revenues. Lord Cornwallis became Governor-General. The chief act of his government was the permanent settlement of the Bengal land-revenue, by proclamation, dated March 22, 1793.

In 1793, by statute 33 Geo. III. cap. 52, the territorial possessions and revenues of India were further confirmed to the Company for twenty years, together with their commercial privileges. The powers of the Board of Control were also renewed and extended. The Governor-General of India was also invested with absolute powers in certain cases, and further provisions were made for the local government of the three Presidencies. 18th Century. Administration of Lord Teignmouth.

In the meantime, the Mysore and Mahratta Wars had brought vast accessions to the British dominions. Before the close of the eighteenth century, the power of Tippoo Saib had been annihilated by Lords Cornwallis and Wellesley, and his territory entirely subdued. The East India Company had taken in full sovereignty the Coast of Canara, the district of Coimbatoor, the passes of the Ghauts, and Seringapatam. A portion of Mysore had been placed indirectly, and Tanjore immediately, under British government. In 1801, the Carnatic was ceded by the Viceroy, and in the same year the Governor of Oude ceded half his territory, Allahabad, Rohilcund, and a portion of the Doab, while Great Britain assumed the protection of the whole. In 1802, war began again with the Mahrattas, who consisted of a cluster of Principalities, nominally feudatories of the Peishwah at Poonah, but really independent. Holkar at Indore, Scindia at Gwalior, the Rajah of Berar, and the Guickwar of Guzerat, were the chief of these, and they were aided by some predatory Northern Chieftains called Pindarrees. By force, or Administration of Lord Wellesley.

19th Century. fraud, they were all subdued, and brought into relations of dependence on British power.

In 1803, the Doab, or valley between the Jumna and the Ganges, Delhi, Agra, part of Bundelcund, and Cuttack, were added to our Empire; and by the battle of Assaye * (Sept. 23), the Mahratta power was broken, and the Great Mogul became a British pensioner.

Administration of Lord Hastings. In 1813, by statute 53 Geo. III. cap. 155, the Company were confirmed in the possession of all their past and lately-acquired territories for a further period of twenty years, together with their privileges of exclusive trade in tea with China; the cost of their establishments and payment of forces to be defrayed from their territorial revenues. By the 49th section, the first ecclesiastical provision was made for British India. A bishop and three archdeacons were to be appointed by the Crown, their salaries to be paid by the Company.†

In 1815 the Rajah of Nepaul, with whom war had arisen, signed a treaty accepting British mediation in certain events. In 1817, the Peishwah of Poonah was deposed, and the greater part of his territory was attached to the Presidency of Bombay.

In 1818, a district round Ajmere, which had

* Three years after the battle of Assaye, the first recorded mutiny of native Indian troops took place at Vellore, in Madras.

† Three dioceses have been since erected—at Calcutta in 1814; Madras, 1835; and Bombay, 1837.

formed a part of Scindia's dominions, was taken under direct British rule. 19th Century.

In 1824, Singapore, a settlement comprising one island and about fifty islets off the south point of the Malay peninsula, and which had formerly been the site of a Malay kingdom, was purchased in fee simple from the Sultan of Johore for 60,000 Spanish dollars, and an annuity of 24,000 in the same coin, for the natural lives of the proprietors. And in the following year Malacca, a settlement comprising an area of about 1000 square miles on the West Coast of the Malay peninsula, and which had been held by the Dutch, was by them exchanged with the British for Bencoolen in Sumatra. Administration of Lord Amherst.

These acquisitions, together with the Prince of Wales' Island, or Penang, have been since formed into a subordinate Government under the Presidency of Bengal, and called the "Straits Settlements."

At this period, the aggressions of the Sikh Chief Runjeet Singh having been successfully parried, the British dominion was extended over almost all Northern India from Calcutta to the Indus.

In the meantime, in consequence of a dispute respecting the Island of Cheduba on the Coast of Arracan, war was declared with the Birmese.

In 1826, by treaty of peace concluded at Yandabu, Feb. 24, the four Provinces of Arracan, Mergui, Tavoy, and Tenasserim on the Coast of Siam, were ceded to Great Britain, a British resident was established at Assam, and a payment of a million and a half sterling was exacted from the Birmese. In the

19th Century. same year Bhurtpore was taken under British protection.

Administration of Lord W. Bentinck.

In 1828, Lord W. Bentinck became Governor-General, and India enjoyed under his rule nearly six years of peace,* and under his auspices the system of employing natives in the subordinate offices of Government was, for the first time, generally introduced into India.

In 1833, by statute 3 and 4 Wm. IV. cap. 85, the possession of the British Territories in India was confirmed to the Company for a further period of twenty years; their privileges of exclusive tea trade to China, and their commercial business in general, was discontinued,—a fixed dividend of 10 guineas per cent. per annum was guaranteed to their Stockholders on conditions of the payment of two millions by the Company, to the Commissioners for reduction of the National Debt, the dividend being subject to a redemption by Parliament after April 1874, on payment of 200*l.* for every 100*l.* Stock; or if the Company should be previously deprived of the Government of India, on three years' notice at any time after 1854.

The Board of Commissioners for the affairs of India was remodelled, seven Cabinet Ministers being made ex-officio Members, and the Board was invested by the Act with powers of demanding copies of minutes of Courts of Proprietors and Directors, and of all

* The only forcible annexation which took place under Lord William Bentinck, was that of Coorg, in Southern India, in 1834.

material letters and dispatches proposed to be sent to India by the latter; and in the event of fourteen days' default on the part of the Court in preparing dispatches in pursuance of the Board's instructions, the latter was empowered to frame such dispatches, which the Court was compelled to forward. The Board was also invested with powers to modify or reduce the Annual Estimates for the Home Establishment of the Company, and privileged to send such dispatches as the Board might see fit so to send, through a Committee of three Members of the Court, constituted by the Act, and called the "Secret Committee." 19th Century.

The Act introduced, also, important changes in the local Government of India, which had, up to that time, been committed to three Governors at the three Presidencies invested with authority, almost co-ordinate with each other within their respective jurisdictions. By the Act of 1833, the whole Civil and Military Government of India was vested in the Governor-General, *ci-devant* "Governor-General of Fort William in Bengal," and four Councillors, three of them to be persons who had been in the Civil or Military Service of India, at any of the Presidencies for at least ten years, and the fourth a person not previously in the Service of the Company. The Council was to assemble at such place in India as the Governor-General might appoint, and to make laws (now for the first time called "Acts"), subject to the disallowance of the Court of Directors.

It was also provided that Governors and Councils

19th Century. of three should administer the Government of the Presidencies of Madras and Bombay, with powers to administer their respective Governments, but not to make laws or grant money.

All the patronage of all appointments to India, Civil and Military, from the Governor-General downwards, was by the Act vested in the Court of Directors—subject in certain cases to the sanction of the Crown, signified through the Board of Control, and the lapse of such appointments to the Crown, should any vacancy remain unfilled up for two months. By s. 86 of the Act, permission was granted to all natural-born subjects of Her Majesty to purchase and reside on lands within the territories of the East India Company. Provision was likewise made by the Act for the payment and jurisdiction of Bishops to be appointed at Madras and Bombay. The Island of St. Helena was vested in the Crown—the Governor-General was empowered to appoint a "Law Commission" to report on the system of judicial and police establishments in India,—an authority which he exercised December 27, 1833. By s. 116 of the Act, it is provided that accounts of the revenues and disbursements of the Indian Government shall be annually laid before the Imperial Parliament, the rights of which to legislate for India are, by s. 51 of the Act, expressly reserved.

Administration of Lord Auckland. In 1835, by statute 5 and 6 Wm. IV. cap. 52, the Directors of the East India Company were authorised to suspend the provisions of the last-cited Act, so far as they related to the subordinate government of Agra. And the Governor-General in Council was empowered during such suspension to appoint a Lieutenant-Governor of the north-western Provinces.

19th Century.

In the same year (1835), the hitherto protected State of Mysore was taken under direct British management. In 1838-9 Afghanistan was unsuccessfully invaded.* In 1841 Kurnool, in Madras, was annexed, and in 1843 Sinde was conquered from the Ameers. In 1845 a war with the Sikhs commenced, and ended in the cession of the Cis-Sutlej Territory and the Doab, between the latter river and the Beas, and of the sovereignty over certain other portions of the Maharajah's dominions, as defined by the Articles of the Treaty executed at Lahore, March 8, 1847. In 1848 the Territories of the Rajah of Sattara (who had been established by us thirty years before in a portion of the dominions of the then deposed Peishwah), lapsed, and were taken under the direct control of the Anglo-Indian Government.

Administration of Lord Ellenborough.

Lord Hardinge.

Lord Dalhousie.

In 1849 the Punjaub was subjected to British rule, in 1852 Pegu was conquered from the Burmese, and in 1853 Berar was annexed on the death of the Rajah.

In 1853, by statute 16 and 17 Vict. cap. 95, all the provisions of former Acts relating to the Government of India, not inconsistent with that Act, were confirmed; and the possession of their Territories in India was continued to the Company until Parliament

* The fortress of Ghuznee in Cabool was taken, and afterwards abandoned.

19th Century. should otherwise provide for the same. The Constitution of the Court of Directors was remodelled—their number being reduced from twenty-four to eighteen, ten of whom to form a quorum. Of the eighteen Directors, fifteen were, by the Act, to be in the first instance chosen out of the existing body by themselves, three to be nominated by the Crown. Provision was also made for gradually increasing the number of Crown nominees until the Court should consist of six nominated and twelve elected Directors, the whole of the former, and half of the latter section of the Court to consist of persons who should have resided for ten years at least in India.

The qualification of all Directors was by this Act fixed at 1000*l*. East India stock. Their salaries were also fixed. Those of the Chairman and Deputy-Chairman at 1000*l*., and of the other Directors 500*l* each per annum; the quorum of the General Court of Proprietors was fixed at twenty.

The Council of India was also remodelled by the Act; the fourth ordinary Member being placed on the same footing with his three colleagues, and empowered to sit and vote on all occasions. Four Legislative Councillors, entitled to sit and vote only at Meetings for making Laws and Regulations, were also added to the Council, as follows:—Two for Madras and Bombay, being Civil servants of ten years' standing, to be appointed by the Governors of those Presidencies respectively. Also the Chief Justice and one other Judge of the Supreme Court of India.

The Court of Directors was further empowered to appoint two more Members of Council to be selected by the Governor-General, being also servants of the Company of ten years' standing. 19th Century.

It was also provided by the Act, that the appointment of all the ordinary Members of the Supreme Council, and of all the Members of the subordinate Councils at all the Presidencies, should be subject to the approbation of Her Majesty.

With respect to military matters, it was provided by the Act that the Commander-in-Chief of the Queen's troops in India should be ex-officio Commander-in-Chief also of the Company's forces. The number of European troops which the Company were permitted at any time to have in pay and discipline was augmented to a maximum of 20,000 men.

With respect to legal matters, the Crown was empowered by the Act to appoint Commissioners in England to report on Law Reforms recommended by the Indian Law Commission appointed under statute 3 and 4 Wm. IV. cap. 85; such report to be presented within three years from the passing of the Act.

With respect to political matters, the Court of Directors was also by the Act empowered, subject to the sanction of the Crown, to create a new Presidency, to appoint a new Lieut.-Governor of the North-Western Provinces, and to alter the limits of existing Presidencies.

The concluding and most important provisions of the Act were those which related to the rights of patronage in respect of appointments in the Indian

19th Century. service, theretofore vested in the Court of Directors.

The primary rights of patronage or recommendation, in respect of the military and naval services, were left untouched; in respect of the civil service and the assistant-surgeons to the forces, those rights were abolished, and these last mentioned departments of the service thrown open to competition.

With respect to *all* departments of the Indian service, the Board of Control was empowered to appoint examiners and to frame regulations for the admission of candidates to the Company's civil and military colleges at Haileybury and Addiscombe respectively, and for the system to be pursued there, and for determining as to the ages and qualifications of all candidates; such regulations to be laid before Parliament.

In 1855, by statute 18 and 19 Vict. cap. 53, entitled, "An Act to relieve the East India Company from the obligation to maintain the College at Haileybury," it was provided that no students should be admitted to the College after January, 25, 1856, and that it should be finally closed on January 30, 1858, and that the Company should be empowered to sell the said College.

The system which now prevails with respect to admission to the Civil Service, will be noticed hereafter in the chapter describing the existing instruments of the Indian Government.

In 1856 took place the last event which comes under our notice in the political history of India. By proclamation of the Governor-General in Council, dated February 7, 1856, and issued at Lucknow, the territories of the Sovereign of Oude—who had previously declined to accept the terms of a proposed treaty—were annexed to the British Dominions. The circumstances which led to this event, and the proposed line of policy consequent upon it, will be found in a minute of the Marquis of Dalhousie, dated February 14, 1856.*

The British Empire in India thus briefly traced in its origin and progress, from the first charter in 1599 to the last annexation in 1856, is thus the gradual growth of nearly three centuries,—an aggregate of territorial atoms, thrown, bit by bit, under a single rule, by the bold spirit of adventure, the rough chances of war, and the subtle agencies of diplomacy. The actually-existing administration of these territories will be detailed in the succeeding chapters.

* The Treaty offered to the King of Oude, together with the Proclamation issued on his refusal to accept the same, are printed at length in Appendix B. For the minute of the Governor-General, *vide* Parliamentary Papers relating to Oude, presented by Command, 1856, p. 297.

CHAPTER II.

EXISTING GOVERNMENT OF BRITISH INDIA.

SECT. I.—HOME GOVERNMENT. SECT. II.—LOCAL GOVERNMENT.

SECT. I.—HOME GOVERNMENT.

It will appear from the preceding summary that the government of British India is administered in England by two distinct departments:—

1. By the East India Company as represented by the Court of Directors; and 2. By the Crown as represented by the Board of Control.

Constitution of East India Company—Court of Directors.

The Court of Directors, as reconstituted in 1853, consists of eighteen Members, of whom it is provided that twelve shall be elected by the votes of all Proprietors possessing the requisite qualification of 1000*l*. East India Stock, while the remaining six Directors are to be appointed by the Crown—the qualification of all Directors being fixed at 1000*l*. East India Stock. All the Directors appointed by the Crown, and six of those to be elected by the Proprietors, must have been civil servants of the Company in India of ten years' standing.

The Chairman and Deputy Chairman of the Court of Directors are elected by that body from among themselves annually by ballot, the usual practice being that the Deputy Chairman of one year is elected Chairman at the commencement of the succeeding one, and retains that office also for one year.

In the Court of Directors is vested the power to originate all measures for the government of India, and all grants of money, both at home and in India; also the patronage of all military, naval, and ecclesiastical appointments, in respect to the primary nomination of candidates, except those to the civil service, which has been, since 1853, opened to public competition under conditions hereafter to be noticed. The mode of distributing the patronage still reserved to the Court of Directors is as follows:—An estimate of the probable requirements of the service in the various departments having been framed, the appointments are distributed among the Directors in proportions arranged between themselves, the Chairman and Deputy Chairman having the largest share, and certain appointments being placed by courtesy at the disposal of the President of the Board of Control.

The patronage of certain superior appointments in India also rests with the Court of Directors. These appointments are as follows: General Officers on the Staff for the Company's Army, the Superintendent of the Indian Navy, the Master Attendant in Bengal and in Madras, and volunteers who are appointed by Directors in rotation for the pilot service, Assay-Masters for the Mint, who are generally, though, not always, members of the services in India, but appointed at home, because it is necessary that they should qualify in this country; the law-officers of the Government at each of the Presidencies, and the Members of Council, as well that of India as those of Madras and Bombay, with the exception of the fourth or legislative Member of the first-named Council, whose appointment is subject to the approbation of the Crown. With respect to appointments to vacancies among Members of Council, the ordinary course is for the Chairman and Deputy-Chairman to select three or four individuals from among the civil servants of the Company of twenty-five years' standing. The records are searched for an account of their services, of which statements are drawn up and notice is given that those documents will be laid before the Court with reference to filling up the vacancy. It is open to any Member of the Court to ask that a statement of the services of any other eligible person should be prepared. On the day of election the merits of the several parties are discussed, and the appointment is determined by ballot.

The Court of Directors possesses also the following further rights of patronage, subject to the approval of the Crown, signified through the Board of Control, that is to say, the power of appointing the Governor-General (who has, in practice, been usually selected by friendly arrangement between the Chairman of the Court and the President of the Board of Control, from the public men of the day, who supported the existing Administration); also the Governors of the subordinate Presidencies, the Commanders-in-Chief, and the fourth Member of the Supreme Council (the remaining Members being appointed by the Court absolutely).

In the event of a nomination to any of the offices subject to veto not being approved by the Crown, the Court must proceed to make another; and if this be not made before the expiration of two months, the Crown may appoint. The Court has the power of recalling or removing any of the officers or servants of the Company (except those appointed by the Crown, on default of the Court), and this power is absolute and uncontrolled.

The Court of Directors meets weekly at the East India House for the transaction of business, the ordinary details of which are discharged by three Committees, designated:—1. Finance and Home. 2. Political and Military. 3. Revenue, Judicial and Legislative. There is also a "Secret Committee," with peculiar functions altogether different from those of the three ordinary Committees. The office of the Secret Committee is purely ministerial. It receives from India all dispatches on matters with respect to which secrecy is deemed important—including those which relate to war, peace, or negociations with Native powers or States within the limits of the Charter, or other States or Princes; and forwards such dispatches to the Board of Control. The

Secret Committee.

Secret Committee also transmits to India, after signature, dispatches prepared by that Board, which it is bound to do, under oath, prescribed by statute 3 and 4 Will. IV. cap. 85, s. 35, "without disclosing the same." The Secret Committee is composed, as prescribed by Act of Parliament, of three Directors. The Court may elect whom they please, but the Chairman, Deputy-Chairman, and senior Member of the Court are almost invariably appointed.

The papers of the Secret Committee are in charge of the Examiner at the East India House, who is clerk to the Committee.

The Directors of the East India Company receive salaries (fixed in 1853 by statute 16 and 17 Vict. c. 95, s. 34), as follows:—

The Chairman and Deputy-Chairman 1000*l.*, all the other Members of the Court 500*l.* each per annum.

Court of Proprietors.

The Court of Proprietors, or "General Court," consists of all holders of a certain prescribed amount of East India stock. All holders of 500*l.* stock are entitled to attend the Court, and to speak. 1000*l.* stock is the qualification for voters, of whom there are now about 1800.

The General Court, which is held quarterly, possesses no longer its ancient powers, which were coextensive with those now exercised by the Court of Directors.

The remaining powers are as follows:—

1. Of electing twelve out of the eighteen Directors, subject to the qualifications above-mentioned.

2. Of making bye-laws not inconsistent with the laws of the land.

3. Of making money-grants, and of controlling those proposed by the Court of Directors in favour of their servants in India, exceeding 600*l.* in a round sum, or 200*l.* per annum to one person.

4. Of calling for the production of dispatches, except those in the Department of the Secret Committee.

The establishment of the East India House consists of four departments,* and is maintained at a cost of about 120,000*l.* per annum.†

The Board of Commissioners for the affairs of India, commonly called the "Board of Control," is practically a corporation sole—the duties of which devolve on a Cabinet Minister, who is designated "President" of a Board which has, for purposes of business, no real existence. **Board of Control.**

The present theoretical Constitution of the Board is defined by statute 3 and 4 Will. IV. cap. 85, by which the Crown is empowered to appoint as Commissioners for the affairs of India any number of persons, whether of the Privy Council or not; and it is enacted that the Lord President of the Council, the Lord Privy Seal, the First Lord of the Treasury, the principal Secretaries of State, and the Chancellor of the Exchequer shall, by virtue of their offices, be Members of the Board;—two to form a quorum,

* The Secretary's, the Examiners', the Military, and the Statistical.

† Exclusive of Charities, Pensioners, and Annuitants.

D 2

and the Commissioner first named in the patent to be the President.

The Commissioners never now sit as a Board, though it appears that in former times they did so, and minutes of the attendance of Mr. Dundas, Mr. Pitt, and others exist. Subsequently, when there were two paid junior Commissioners, there were occasional meetings; but since the only paid Commissioner has been the President, no Board has been held. The President is regarded as acting on his own responsibility.

The fiction of a "Board" is however still kept up, by the signature of one of the ex-officio Members, being, in conformity with the law, attached to all documents recording the decisions of the President.

The chief powers of the Board are now as follow:—

1. The supervision of all financial measures of the Courts of Directors.

2. The revision of all their correspondence.

3. The exercise of veto, in the name of the Crown, on the patronage of certain appointments above specified, and the absolute patronage of certain other appointments, as of the Indian Bishops and the Judges of the Supreme Courts.

4. The right of recalling or dismissing, in the name of the Crown, any officer or servant of the Company in India.

Two Secretaries were, by statute 3 and 4 Will. IV. cap. 85, attached to the Board; one of whom is a Member of the House of Commons, and liable to lose his office when the Administration by whom he was appointed lose theirs—the other Secretary being a permanent official.

The business coming before the Board is divided among six Departments:—

1. Revenue, embracing all matters relating to the assessment and collection of the revenues of India.

2. Finance and accounts, taking cognisance of the public expenditure, remittances, and the management of mints in India.

3. Military.

4. Marine and Ecclesiastical.

5. Political.

6. Judicial and Legislative.

These departments are all placed under the supervision of the two Secretaries, three being committed to each Secretary; and to each of the Departments are attached a senior clerk, an assistant clerk, and junior clerks. There is also a Secret Department in the Board of Control for the purpose of carrying on written and oral communications with the Secret Committee of the Court of Directors. The latter class of communications are for the most part carried on through the President personally; in the former he is assisted by a senior clerk, and occasionally by the Secretaries of the Board.

It appears that on the arrival of secret dispatches from India, the copy intended for the Board is sent to the senior clerk in the Secret Department, who prepares a précis of all the letters and enclosures, which he lays before the President, who thereupon gives him instructions, oral or written, for the preparation of an answer, or sometimes drafts one himself. It is then copied in official form and transmitted to the Secret Committee at the East India House.

The salary of the President (having been changed five times since the first constitution of the Board in 1784,) now stands at 5000*l.* per annum. The establishment consists (in addition to the two Secretaries) of about thirty clerks, and is maintained at an average annual cost of about 30,000*l.* per annum.

The present Constitution of the Court of Directors and that of the Board of Control having been thus briefly described, it remains to explain the mode by which the powers given to the latter over the proceedings of the former are exercised.

Mode of transacting business adopted by the Court of Directors and the Board of Control.

In the ordinary transaction of the business of the Home Government of India, for the purposes of that intercommunication which takes place between the Court and the Board, the former are represented ordinarily by the Chairman and Deputy Chairman, the latter by the President.

This complicated system of mutual check and intervention is nowhere more clearly described than in the evidence given by Mr. Waterfield and Sir James Melvill before the Parliamentary Committees of 1852. That evidence, as condensed in the analysis subsequently printed, is as follows :—

Each dispatch from India is laid before the Court of Directors, to which body all dispatches are addressed. They arrive in duplicate, one copy being for the Court, one for the Board. When a dispatch comes from India it is accompanied by a collection of papers bearing upon the subject, which collection contains the former correspondence relating to it, and the present proceedings of the Government upon it. The dispatch comes to the Secretary's office, and from it is immediately transferred to the department to which it relates. In that department an abstract of the contents of the dispatch is made; this is lithographed, and copies of it are sent to the Chairman and Deputy-Chairman, and the members of the Committee having the superintendence of the department to which the dispatch relates. The officer in charge of that department then communicates with the Chairman and Deputy upon the dispatch, and, in cases in which the subjects are not mere routine, receives instructions as to the tenor of the reply. A draft answer is then prepared, and submitted with the collections to the Chairman and the Deputy; they confer together, and with the officer, upon the subject; and when the draft conforms to their views, they place their initials upon it as the authority for its being sent to the President of the Board, in what is technically called "P. C.;" that is to say, previous communication. When the "previous communication" is received from the India House, it is referred, with the accompanying "collections," to the senior clerk of the department to which it may belong. It is his duty to make himself acquainted with the contents of the papers, and the "previous communication" is then, with the notes and comments of the clerk, laid before the Secretary under whom the particular department has been placed. He reads these papers, and, if not satisfied with them, he refers to the "collections." Having formed his opinion, he expresses it in writing; and the papers are, with that opinion, submitted to the President.

The President in like manner reads the "previous communication," and the notes and comments, and, if necessary, refers to the "collections." Having considered these various papers, he gives his decision; that decision may be entire approval of the "previous communication;" the cancelling of it, on the ground that it is not advisable to give any opinion on the subject; the substitution of other paragraphs in place of those proposed; or the partial alteration of them, in greater or less degree. The "previous communication" is returned to the clerk, in order that the President's decision may be carried into effect, and it is then sent back to the Chairman, together with the "collections." The "previous communication," in fact, is merely a suggestion of the way in which the Chairman and Deputy think that the dispatch or letter should be answered; so the alterations made in the "previous communication" by the President are merely suggestions back again to the Chairman and Deputy of the way in which the President thinks that the draft should stand. There is nothing authoritative till the proposed dispatch is in the form of a draft; what passes is considered on both sides merely a suggestion. If the "previous communication" be returned unaltered, the draft is immediately submitted to the Committee of the Court having superintendence of the department in which it is. If altered, the officer communicates with the Chairman and Deputy-Chairman, who either allow wholly or partially, or reject entirely, the alterations. Differences are generally settled in conference between the President and the Chairman and Deputy at the weekly meeting which takes place between them. If they do not succeed in convincing each other, or in effecting a compromise, it remains for the Chairman and Deputy to consider whether they should adhere rigidly to their opinion or not. The draft is finally arranged by them, and is then submitted to the Committee. Drafts generally lie on the table of the Committee for a week, during which time both the draft, and any papers bearing upon the case, are perused by the members of the Committee. The Committee then discuss the draft, and adopt or alter it as they think fit, after which it is submitted to the Court, who usually take a week for consideration, and then the draft comes on for discussion. Every Director has an opportunity of expressing his sentiments, and, if he differ from the majority, of recording a dissent. When the draft is approved by the Court, the Secretary sends it officially, with all the papers, including the dissents, if any, to the Board of Commissioners, and the Board return it always within two months, the period limited by law, approved or altered; and if altered, with a statement of their reasons for making the alteration. The unaltered drafts are immediately transcribed, and fair copies, signed by at least thirteen Members of the Court, are despatched to India. The altered drafts are referred to the proper Committee, upon whose report the Court decide, either that the alterations shall be adopted, in which case the draft is signed and despatched to India, or that a remonstrance shall be addressed to the Board against the alterations, in which case the draft is retained until the decision of the Board is communicated. Instances are known where, on the Board adhering to its original opinion, a second letter has been written by order of the Court, and even a rejoinder to a second reply. Ultimately the dispatch is sent out as approved by the Board; and the instances are not numerous in which the Board overrule the Court.

The Court, after remonstrance, have the power of recording a protest against a decision of the Board from which it finally dissents; and under a bye-law such protest is to be laid before the next General Court. But it is only in a case believed to be of very serious importance that the Court would have recourse to such a proceeding, and no instance of the exercise of this right has occurred since 1834.

By the 3 & 4 Will. IV. cap. 85, if the Court doubt whether any instructions of the Board be consistent with law, a case may be framed, which, when approved by the Board, is to be submitted to three judges of the Court of Queen's Bench, whose decision upon the point at issue is to be final. But neither has this right ever been exercised. Of the drafts that go to the Board in "P. C." (previous communication), more than one-half come back without any alteration at all. It appears, however, that in the Political Department (to which the statement is limited) there are not many previous communications returned without some alterations, but these are usually adopted by the Court. Of the altered drafts, a large proportion consist of alterations that are little more than verbal, and are generally acquiesced in by the Chairman and Deputy-Chairman before the draft goes to the Committee; and of the drafts that, being approved by the Committee and the Court, go to the Board officially, and are returned by it, not more than five per cent. contain any alterations.

Since the last Act came into operation, no case of irreconcilable difference between the Court and the Board has arisen. Previously there were one or two instances in which the resistance of the Court to the views of the Board was so determined, that the latter threatened to enforce their purpose by *mandamus*.

Previous communications have sometimes been returned from the Board in one or two days. Usually they are returned within three months, but oftener much sooner. In 1851 there was only one in the Political Department which remained in the office a month. There have been cases in which such communications have been detained a year or more.

The origin of the practice of making previous communications seems not distinctly traced, though a record of such papers is retained. It is thought to have arisen about the year 1793. At an early period it was restricted to questions of principle, but gradually extended itself to details. The title P. C. used to be regarded as something mysterious, until Mr. Canning made known its meaning in a speech made by him in the House of Commons, on a motion of Mr. Creevey. Some sort of communications probably took place between the President and the Chairman and Deputy before these more formal ones.

The ordinary interval between the return of the previous communication to the India House and the sending up the draft is about a month or five weeks.

Previous communication being entirely a matter of private understanding between the Court and the President, and there being no law to prevent a proposed dispatch being sent up in the first instance as a draft, this occasionally takes place. Drafts come up at once *as* drafts, sometimes because they treat of mere matters of course, sometimes because they relate to matters of a pressing nature, and a mail may be on the point of departure; but if a long dispatch were required, the previous communication would not be dispensed with.

Dispatches are addressed to the Governor-General of India in Council, to the Governor in Council of Madras, to the Governor in Council of Bombay, and the Governor of Fort William. None are addressed to the Lieutenant-Governor of the North-West Provinces, the whole of that correspondence being conducted with the Governor-General.

The Court has the initiative in the preparation of dispatches: if the Board of Control think any subject neglected it can call upon the Court to frame a dispatch in regard to it; and, in the case of the

Court's non-compliance within fourteen days, the Board has the power to frame such dispatch, and send it to the Court to be forwarded to India.

SECT. II.—LOCAL GOVERNMENT.

The Supreme Local Administration of India (which was formerly distributed between the three co-ordinate Governments of Fort William, Madras, and Bombay,) is now centred in the "Governor-General of India in Council," the seat of the Supreme Government being now at Calcutta, but removable at the will of the Governor-General.

Governor-General in Council—his powers and duties.

The Governor-General is, as has been stated, appointed by the Court of Directors, with the approbation of the Crown. The Supreme Council consists of four ordinary members, three of whom must have been civil or military servants of the Company in India of at least ten years' standing, and the fourth a person not previously in the service of the Company. The Commander-in-Chief of the forces in India is also always admitted an extraordinary member of the Council, which thus consists altogether of five members. To these were added in 1853, six Legislative Members, empowered only to sit and vote on the framing of Laws and Regulations; of these, four are civil servants of the Company of ten years' standing in Bombay, Madras, Bengal, and the North-West Provinces respectively, and the two remaining members are the Chief Justice and one other Judge of the Supreme Court of Calcutta. Two other members may be appointed by the Governor-General, under section 22 of statute 16 and 17 Vict. cap. 95.*

The Council of India may thus be said to consist, for general purposes of Executive Government, of six members, including the Governor-General and Commander-in-Chief, and for Legislative purposes of twelve members—seven to be a quorum.

The powers vested in the Governor-General are extensive. They are as follows:—

He has a veto on all legislative measures proposed in Council, and an independent prerogative of initiating and carrying out measures irrespective of the Council. He has also the patronage of nearly all appointments designated as "political" throughout India; these comprise the Residents in native States and the Commissioners in the Non-Regulation Provinces. In the Governor-General is also vested the appointment of the Lieutenant-Governor of Bengal and the North-West Provinces, also that of the Judges of the Sudder Courts and the military patronage in Bengal and the North-West Provinces.

The Governor-General in Council has also a direct control over all those districts of British India comprising the Punjab, Çis-Sutlej States, Oude, Berar, Pegu, the Tenasserim Provinces and the Straits' Set-

* It does not appear that the power given to the Court by s. 22 of statute 16 and 17 Vict. c. 95, to authorise the nomination of two additional legislative councillors, being civil servants of the Company of ten years' standing, has as yet been exercised.

tlements, which are not included within the limits of any of the four subordinate Governments. His authority extends also to the territories of all native princes with whom we have contracted subsidiary or protective relations, and to the exercise of such influence as Great Britain may possess by treaty over those independent States which have accepted of our mediation.

Official Staff of Governor General.

The official staff of the Governor-General in Council consists of four Secretaries of the four following Departments:—

1. The political or so called "Foreign" Department, to which is committed all correspondence arising out of British relations with native States.

2. The Home Department, which is charged with the judicial and revenue correspondence.

3. The Financial Department.

4. The Military Department.

There is also a Secret Department of both the Political and Finance Secretariats, to which all secret dispatches are entrusted.

Mode of transacting business.

The mode of transacting the business of the Council is as follows:—All papers involving questions for discussion or projects of law are circulated, going first to the Governor-General and then to all the Members of Council.

The Council meets at the Government House once or twice a week. At or before the Meeting, the Governor-General writes orders on the backs of the papers, in which, if the Members of Council concur, they subscribe their initials, and letters in conformity therewith are despatched from the Secretary's office. If a member of Council dissent, he writes "reserve," and the case is then brought before the Council for discussion. In other matters the Governor-General reserves the case for discussion, or minutes upon it, when the Members of Council do the same; or a Member of Council may record a minute at once, while the papers are in circulation. The mode of conducting the correspondence between the Government of India and the Court of Directors is the following: Upon questions requiring a reference to the Court's authority, and in matters of more than ordinary importance, separate letters are prepared and written; but upon the whole record it is usual that a report should be sent every quarter, which reviews the whole proceedings of the Government, and is called a quarterly general letter; that is, every letter of any importance on the record, and the substance of the reply, are abstracted and reported in paragraphs of this general letter, and these general letters are sent home now with the collections of papers referred to in each paragraph. Three copies of the Government proceedings used to be sent quarterly, the whole proceedings being completely copied out in triplicate for the purpose; but when collections were sent home, one copy was dispensed with. The letters thus transmitted are replied to by the Court with the same detail, every paragraph having its paragraph of reply. The dispatches of the Court of Directors, immediately upon their arrival in India, are circulated among the Members of the Government, as above stated, and the Secretary takes the orders upon them, paragraph by paragraph. It is then the duty of the Secretary to write the resolution upon every paragraph *seriatim*, which resolution is the foundation of orders, if such are required, to the subordinate authorities, and at the same time gives the substance of the reply, when the time comes to make the reply to the Court of Directors. The time occupied in transmitting a communication and receiving a reply varies according to the nature of the matter contained in the dispatch; sometimes orders may be required to be sent to a subordinate Board, calling for an explanation, before a full reply can be sent; those orders appear in the record as issued on the day when the Court's dispatch is read, and the reply is entered on the record on the date when it arrives, and is laid before the Council. In replying to the Court, these letters are all referred to, and the substance of the specific statements is given, but the receipt of the dispatch is always separately acknowledged. Under the present system, collections have to be made in India for every paragraph, and sent home in duplicate.

It is necessary to place everything on record; no discretion is vested in any member of the Government, or in the Secretary, of changing or withholding from the record anything which is addressed to the Government, and the exact nature of the reply to it.

In regard to the subordinate Governments, it was determined, in place of the transmission of proceedings *in extenso* (which these Governments continue to transmit to the Court of Directors), to call from each of the Presidencies below for abstracts of their proceedings, which abstracts, on coming to the different departments, it is the business of the Secretary to overlook, to put a cross upon any matter which he deems of more than ordinary importance, and then to take the orders of Council as to whether the papers shall be called for. There are other matters which the Governments themselves refer, because of the incompetency of their own powers. Their references include all questions of salary or new appointments, and all questions relating to legislation; indeed, all important subjects.

Every appointment is made by a minute of the Governor-General in Council. If the Members of Council concur, of course the appointment is made; if they do not, the dissentients record their disapproval. If a majority objected, the appointment would not be pressed, and it is said that the Governor-General would not in general propose an appointment unless he knew it would be carried in Council. If, however, it should be put and negatived, the appointment could not take place, except under the Governor-General's special power of overruling the decision of his Council. It appears to be held, without qualification, that this power may be exercised in regard to appointments, and if the Governor-General considered the appointment essential in a political point of view, it certainly would. If the Governor-General's nominee were withdrawn, another man would not be proposed by the Members of

Council, but it would be left to the Governor-General to propose another.

No new office can be established without reference to the home authorities; and the Government of India cannot expend more than 50,000 rupees upon public works without their sanction.

An increase in the military establishment being generally a matter of emergency, is, in such case, made by the Governor-General in Council at once, but when not matter of emergency, the question must be referred home.

The Governor-General ordinarily holds office for five years, and receives a salary of 25,000*l*., and each Member of his Council 10,000*l*. per annum.

The absolute authority vested in the Governor-General in Council extends, not only over those provinces which, by lapse or annexation, have fallen under his direct control, as the Punjab, Oude, Berar, the Burmese Provinces, and the Straits Settlements, but also over the four subordinate Governments of British India, and applies to all powers, legislative and executive, subject only to the limitations specified in section 43 of statute 3 and 4 Will. IV. cap. 85.*

Subordinate Governments.

The subordinate Governments are, subject to such general control, administered as follows:—

The Presidencies of Madras and Bombay are each

* The limitations to the powers of the Governor-General in Council are those which preclude any alterations of the Act of 1833, or any subsequent Imperial statute relating to India, or from promulgating laws affecting the prerogatives of the Crown, or the allegiance of British subjects.

under Governors and Councils of three Members (the Commander-in-Chief being one)—both Governors and Councillors being appointed by the Court of Directors.

Bengal and the North-West Provinces are each under Lieutenant-Governors, appointed by the Governor-General.

These Governments have no powers of legislation, nor can they create any new office, or even "grant any salary, gratuity, or allowance without the previous sanction of the Governor-General of India in Council." This provision being found to involve the necessity of a formal reference of every petty detail to the Governor-General, the rule has been established of making periodical reports of these minor matters. The Governor-General, for instance, does not require the employment of each additional menial servant in a public office to be separately reported; but every quarter, reports are made, in the form of a statement, of the additions and changes of the establishments made in the quarter, and these are so passed under the review of the Governor-General in Council. This practice, though not in strict accordance with the letter of the law, is generally adopted; everything passes under the review of the Government of India, and ultimately is sanctioned by it; while the inferior Governments are not fettered in the nomination of petty officers—as of customs or excise, by the necessity of a previous reference, but rely upon obtaining the sanction of the Government of India when they make the quarterly report. In regard to expenditure on Public Works, there is an order from the Court of Directors that no work requiring an expenditure of more than 10,000 rupees should be undertaken by any of the Governments, neither the Government of India, nor the Governments below, without their sanction first obtained; but the Court of Directors enlarged the discretion in the case of the Governor-General in Council: and now the rule is understood to be, as laid down by the Governor-General in Council to the subordinate Presidencies, that they are to refer to the Governor-General in Council all works requiring an expenditure of more than 10,000 rupees, according to the estimates. But the Home authorities often sanction expenditure for Public Works without reference to the Government of India.

Though the mode of transacting business adopted by the subordinate Governments is not uniform, it may be stated generally, that at Madras and Bombay where there are Councils, there is also a staff of Secretaries by whom the business brought weekly before the Governments is despatched in their distinct departments; and the Governors of these Presidencies exercise, with the concurrence of their respective Councils, all the ordinary local patronage which, in the case of Bengal and the North-West Provinces, is also, with the exceptions above noticed, vested in their respective Lieutenant-Governors.

The Governments of Madras and Bombay have the privilege of corresponding direct with the Court of Directors. They send their proceedings to the

Court, and furnish abstracts only to the Government of India. They have also their separate services, civil and military. A question arose very early, as to whether, in the case of a servant being suspended, or removed from office by one of the subordinate Governments, the appeal should lie to the Court of Directors or to the Government of India; and it was determined that, in consequence of the existence of separate reports to the Court from the subordinate Presidencies, and of the fact that the servants there were the Company's servants, placed under the authority of those Governments by the Court of Directors, the appeal should lie to the Court.

The power of selection for political appointments is exercised very largely in favour of military officers, who are, equally with civilians, qualified to hold those situations. Certain military appointments are considered the patronage of the Commander-in-Chief; others are the patronage of the Governor. The right of nominating to offices connected with finance, such as the Military Auditor-General, the Military Accountant, Paymasters and Commissariat Officers, is vested in the Governor. To those connected with the discipline of the army, such as the Adjutant-General and the Quartermaster-General, the Commander-in-Chief appoints, but his appointments require the confirmation of the Governor in Council.

These statements apply to the subordinate Presidencies; the rights of patronage, civil and military, vested in the Governal-General of India in Council have been already explained.

CHAPTER III.

THE INSTRUMENTS OF INDIAN GOVERNMENT.

THE SERVICES—CIVIL (COVENANTED AND UNCOVENANTED), MILITARY, NAVAL, ECCLESIASTICAL.

SECT. I.—THE CIVIL SERVICE.

THE two great functions of the Civil Service, and of all who are concerned in the Civil Government of India, are,—The collection of the Revenue, and the Administration of Justice.

It is either in a fiscal or a judicial capacity, or in a combination of both, that all Civil Officials, from the highest to the lowest, are employed.

The Civil Service in India consists of two classes:—

1. Those who, having passed an examination in England, and subjected themselves to a certain degree of training in India, have entered into the covenant prescribed by ancient custom, "That they "shall obey all orders; that they shall discharge all "debts; and that they shall treat the natives of India "well." This select body, consisting of Europeans only, by whom the higher class of Government duties are performed, are termed the "Covenanted Service."

2. Those Europeans, Natives, and half-castes, to

whom subordinate duties, fiscal and judicial, are committed, and who are not subjected to any preliminary training, and do not enter into covenant with the Company, and are consequently designated as the "Uncovenanted Service."

Covenanted Civil Service.

The Covenanted Civil Service in India, which none could formerly enter but those who, at the nomination of Directors, had been admitted to a preliminary two years' training at the Company's College at Haileybury, is now open, by a prescribed system of examination, to public competition.

By s. 36 of statute 16 and 17 Vict. cap. 95 (which applied not only to the Civil Service proper, but to all candidates for employment as Assistant-Surgeons to the Company's forces in India), the Directors' rights of patronage to primary appointments were extinguished. And by statute 18 and 19 Vict. cap. 53, Haileybury College was prospectively abolished. The Board of Control was also, by the first-mentioned Act, empowered to appoint Examiners, and to frame Regulations for conducting Examinations to be laid before Parliament. Doubts having arisen as to the mode in which the powers conferred by the Act should be exercised, the question was referred by the Board of Control to a Committee, who were requested to take the subject into consideration, and who subsequently reported thereupon.*

* The Committee consisted of Lord Ashburton, Mr. J. G. Shaw Lefevre, the Rev. H. Melvill, the Rev. B. Jowett, and the present Lord Macaulay. For their Report, *vide* Parliamentary Paper 34, 1855.

Regulations * prescribing the mode and subjects for the examination of candidates for the Civil Service were promulgated by the Board of Control, in January, 1855, by which it was provided that two examinations of all such candidates should take place: the first in ancient and modern languages, mathematics, Arabic, and Sanscrit; the second, which was to be held at an interval of a year after the first, in law, Indian history, and political economy. The second examination, which, on the special ground of an immediate demand for recruits for the Civil Service in Sinde was waived in 1856, has never in fact taken place.†

The present practice is, to send out all youths who shall have passed the single examination now required, to those parts of India where they may be wanted. Those intended for the Civil Service in Bengal, the N. W. Provinces, and those districts which are directly under the Supreme Government, are sent to Calcutta, where they are subjected to a further course of study, concluded by an examination in the native languages at the College, Fort William. At Bombay and Madras there are no establishments for preparing young Civil servants (or writers, as they were formerly called) for their duties, by the study of the native languages. It is pursued under certain teachers appointed for the purpose. It may be stated, as a general rule, that every member of

* The first Regulations issued by the Board of Control, under the Statute of 1853, are printed at length in Appendix C.

† *Vide* Parliamentary Paper 317. 1856.

the Civil Service is entitled to *some* office, though not at once nominated to any particular office. During the probationary period, from the time of their arrival in India, all receive a certain rate of pay, called the "out of employ allowance."

In Bengal, after passing the necessary examination, they are sent into the Mofussil (the country, as distinct from the Presidency), and become assistants to collectors and magistrates. Assistants are subjected to two examinations, before they can rise to superior grades in the service: the first, chiefly to test their familiarity with the vernacular languages; the second, to ascertain their further proficiency therein, and also their knowledge of criminal and fiscal law and practice. These examinations are conducted by Divisional Committees at certain large stations, under a Central Committee at the Presidency. The Divisional Committees consist of the Commissioners of the division, the Judge of the district, and others. These report to the Central Committee, who report to the Government.

On first entering the Public Service, the civilian is occupied with magisterial and fiscal duties simultaneously. In his magisterial capacity he takes the depositions of witnesses, and prepares cases for the decision of his superior, or he hears and determines, subject to revision, cases specially made over to him by the Magistrate. His power of punishment extends to two months' imprisonment, a period which, when he is entrusted with special powers by the Government, is enlarged to twelve months. As assistant in the revenue department, he decides petty claims relating to arrears or exactions of rent.

After an apprenticeship of several years, the assistant is regarded as a candidate for promotion. He is then subjected to a further examination, with the view of testing his knowledge of the languages and laws of the country; and his promotion depends on the success with which he passes the test. A successful candidate is then deemed qualified for the office of Collector or Magistrate. As Magistrate he directs the police operations of his District, and takes cognisance of all criminal matters. The law provides for his dealing with certain classes of offences, but limits his power of punishment to three years' imprisonment. Appeals from his sentences, or from those of his assistant, when vested with special powers, lie to the Sessions Judge.

As Collector he has charge of the district treasury. He superintends the collection of the Government rental; puts in execution coercive measures against defaulters; sells estates for arrears of revenue; and manages those escheated or bought by Government. He superintends the partition of estates, and regulates the distribution of the Government Assessment among the several sub-divisions. He also exercises judicial powers in settling, by summary process, disputes among the agricultural community regarding rents.

The gradations of the Service differ in some respects in the different Presidencies.

In Bengal, the offices of Judge, Magistrate and Collector are held by three distinct persons. In Madras, Bombay, and the North-West Provinces, the functions of Magistrate and Collector are discharged by one individual, the office of Judge by another. In the Non-Regulation Provinces, which are under the direct control of the supreme Government, all the three offices are united in the person of a single representative of the local Executive Government.

To a certain extent, advancement in the Civil Service is regulated by law, but there is also opportunity for selection. The mode of proceeding under the supreme Government (and the same general rule is acted upon throughout British India) is as follows:—When an appointment is vacant, it is the business of the Secretary to lay before the Governor-General a statement of all those who can be considered to have any claim, with his own opinion as to their relative fitness, and also his opinion whether the office requires peculiar fitness. The Governor-General thereupon makes his selection. He is not bound to regard seniority, and if it be an important office, he will choose the most competent. Seniority, however, has large influence in advancement. The Covenanted Service is by law a seniority service, every member of which, in consideration of his having been specially, and expensively, trained up for the service, is supposed to possess certain prescriptive rights, which can only be forfeited by misconduct or gross incapacity, and cannot be witheld *quamdiu se bene gesserit*: here, with some exceptions, the office of the local Government is merely to distribute. In practice, however, the superior appointments, such as Secretaries to Government, Judges of the Sudder Adawlut, Revenue Commissioners, and a few others, are filled by selection.

Military men are employed to a considerable extent in Civil duties, chiefly in the Political Department, or in the Civil Administration of districts not brought regularly under the existing laws of British India. They are especially selected for particular duties, and the practice has prevailed since the time of Lord Cornwallis. Instances have occurred, under the Presidency of Bombay, of their being appointed Collectors in the Regulation Provinces; but such instances are few, and it is believed that a deficiency of Civil servants led to the appointments being made. The officers selected are generally appointed young, and with especial reference to their knowledge of the native languages, without which important qualifications no officer can be removed from his regiment to Civil duty. The proportion of military employed in diplomatic duties is conjectured to be one-third of the whole, but this estimate is restricted to high appointments: if inferior situations be admitted, the number of military men employed, as already described, has a great preponderance; and if Sinde be included, the proportion to Civilians is stated to be as twelve to seven.

The Members of the Covenanted Civil Service receive salaries graduated according to the nature and duties of their respective offices, from that of the lowest Assistant Collectors to the Members of the Supreme Council, and ranging in amount between £500 and £10,000 per annum, payable in rupees per mensem.

Uncovenanted Civil Service.

The Uncovenanted Civil Service comprises that large class of Indian officials who are appointed by the local Governments, and who do not, as their designation implies, enter into covenants with the Company, and who, though subjected to certain prescribed examinations on promotion, are not placed under any preliminary training.

There is no precise line drawn as to the offices which Covenanted Servants alone may fill, and those which are open to Uncovenanted Servants also. The distinction exists with regard to the Services only; the appointments to the Covenanted Service which are made at home, forming one class, and those left in the hands of the local Government the other—the former being entitled on vacancies to promotion, the latter not. The Covenant is in fact an old form, having its origin at a time when the East India Company was a Commercial body, but it now indicates a separate and exclusive Service.

Of the Uncovenanted Civil Servants, some are Europeans—some of mixed origin, European and native—some—and by far the largest proportion—pure natives.

The European Uncovenanted Servants consist chiefly of persons who have gone out to India in some other calling, and of sons of commissioned officers who have obtained Government employ. Though they do not ordinarily attain the higher offices, and are not entitled to furlough, exceptions to this rule have arisen. Pensions also have been granted to them on retirement.

The total number of Europeans, and of persons belonging to the half-caste population in the Uncovenanted Service in India, appears to have amounted in 1853 to between two and three thousand individuals.

The employment of native agency in the Uncovenanted Service, which may be said to have commenced about thirty years ago, under Lord William Bentinck, and was promoted in 1834 by s. 85 of statute 3 & 4 William IV. cap. 85, removing all disqualifications for office on account of descent, creed or colour, has been since so largely extended, that at this time almost the whole of the Judicial Administration of the lower Courts is in the hands of natives. Not only the Vakeels or Pleaders, but the three grades of Judges called Principal Sudder Aumeens, Sudder Aumeens, and Moonsiffs, numbering altogether about 700 in all India, are now natives. The subordinate Revenue Collectors in the Salt, Opium and Customs Departments, with the Land Revenue Officers, called Tehseldars, in which various duties about 1200 functionaries are employed, are also natives. There is also a class of Medical Officers, called Sub-assistant Surgeons, which consists entirely of natives; and every regiment has a native Doctor to assist the Surgeon. Added to these, there is a large number of natives employed in subordinate police and revenue duties, and drawing less than twenty rupees per month, amounting in Bengal alone to upwards of 40,000 in number, exclusive of the village watchmen, of whom there were said to be, in 1853, more than 170,000 in the lower Provinces. Natives are admitted to all offices in the Uncovenanted branch, for which they are deemed qualified in point of trustworthiness, and the principle now in progress throughout the Civil administration of India, is native agency and European superintendence.

The salaries received by the higher officials employed in the Uncovenanted Civil Service range from £100 to £900 per annum. It appears that a native who recently held the office of Judge of the small Cause Court, at Calcutta, received no less than £1560 per annum. The Judicial appointments are held chiefly by Mohammedans, but many Hindoos are employed, and at the head of the factory at Bombay a Parsee presides, who has Europeans placed under his authority.

SECT. II.—THE MILITARY SERVICE.

The army ordinarily used for the defence of British India is (or rather was before the recent revolt) composed of four elements:—

1. The East India Company's native Forces officered by Europeans.

2. The East India Company's European Forces.

3. The Queen's Forces, which at the request of the Court of Directors are furnished for the Indian service, the cost of their conveyance and extra pay being provided by the East India Company.

4. The contingent Forces, which are at the command of the British Government under Treaties with native Princes.

The total number of the East India Company's native Forces of all arms, including commissioned and non-commissioned native officers and men, up to the latest period received before the recent revolt, was as follows:—

	Regiments.	Officers and Men.
Engineers.—Native Commissioned and Non-Commissioned, Rank and File		3,158
Artillery.—Horse	Brigades 5	1,073
Foot	Batts. 18	7,676
Cavalry.—Regular and Irregular * .	Regts. 50	26,129
Infantry.—Regular and Irregular * .	Regts. 196	189,008
Veterans.—Native Officers and Men .		3,374
Native Medical Establishment . .		858
	Total, 269	231,276

Giving a total number of 269 native regiments of all arms, and of 231,276 native officers and men. A large portion of this force, comprising about one-half

* The Irregular Forces have four Officers to each Regiment.

of the whole, has by mutiny and disarmament ceased to exist, leaving a total number of native Forces of all arms practically available of about 120,000 men.

The total number of the East India Company's European Forces now in India (not deducting losses arising out of the recent revolt, of which no complete authentic return has been received), is as follows, and presents a total of 22,047 European officers and men:—

Engineers.—European Officers and Men . .	434
Artillery.—Horse and Foot, do. . .	6,585
(of which there are 12 Battalions of European Foot.)	
*Cavalry.**—European Officers and Men . .	509
Infantry.—Do. do. . .	13,032
Veterans.—Do. do. . .	436
Medical Establishment.—Europeans, including European Warrant Officers . .	1,051
Total . . .	22,047

The total number of Queen's troops now in and on their voyage to India amounts to about 63,500 men.

The contingent Troops of the native States commanded by British officers, and bound under Treaties to serve the British Government, amounted, before the mutiny of 1857, to about 32,000, viz.:—

Hyderabad (Nizam's) Auxiliary Force . .	8,094
† Gwalior (Scindiah's) Contingent . .	8,401
† Kotah Contingent	1,148
Mysore Horse (officered by Natives) . .	4,000
Guzerat (Guicowar's) Contingent . . .	3,756

* Four additional Cavalry Regiments are now in course of formation.

† The Contingents which have mutinied are marked with an obelisk.

† Bhopal Contingent	829
† Malwa United Contingent	1,617
Malwa Bheel Corps	648
† Joudpore Legion	1,246
Meywar Bheel Corps	1,054
Colapore Local Horse	907
Sawunt Warree Local Corps	611
	32,311

Holkar is bound by Treaty to furnish a contingent of 1000 horse; but these troops are not commanded by British officers.

The Commander-in-Chief of Her Majesty's Forces in India is *ex-officio* Commander-in-Chief of all the Company's Forces there; and any officer who may be appointed by Her Majesty to be Commander-in-Chief of Her Forces in any Presidency in India is, by virtue of such appointment, also Commander-in-Chief of the Company's Forces in such Presidency.

Rules for admission to the Military Service, Addiscombe.

The officers of the East India Company's Forces are primarily nominated to the service by the Directors, and those who receive "direct appointments" are examined (see Appendix B) and sent out at once—the rest are trained for two years at Addiscombe.

The seminary at Addiscombe is for the preparation of youths for those branches of the Military service where scientific attainments are indispensable,—the Engineers and the Artillery; but as the establishment will accommodate a larger number than is required for those branches, others are admitted. There is a preliminary examination. At the final examination the most distinguished obtain appointments in the Engineers,* and those next in merit in the Artillery.

* The Engineers are afterwards trained for a year at Chatham.

These are the prizes of the institution. The Cadets who fail to obtain them go into the infantry. Those receiving cavalry appointments in no case pass through Addiscombe, but proceed direct to India, as do a large portion of Infantry Cadets. These, however, are subjected to an examination, and are eligible up to twenty-two years of age. The number of Cadets at Addiscombe is 150. There are four terms, which extend over a period of two years; and the age of admission is from fourteen to eighteen. The payment to the Company is 100*l.* a year; the total expenses of a Cadet may be stated at 120*l.* or 130*l.* a year. The Company's charge was formerly much lower. It is the same to all. The only Oriental language taught is Hindostanee.

SECT. III.—THE NAVAL SERVICE.

The East India Company maintain an independent Marine, under the orders of the Government of India.

The chief branch of that service is the Bombay Marine, the officers of which are primarily appointed by the Directors (the patronage being allotted between the members of the Court), and sent out from England. From 15 to 18 is the age for Naval Cadets.

The duties of the Bombay Marine consist of Surveys on the coast of Arabia and the Red Sea, and the coast of Sinde. The Force is also used for the prevention of piracy in the Persian Gulf.

The total present strength in vessels and men of the Bombay Marine, consists of 53 steam and sailing vessels, and 4286 European and Native men,—according to the latest returns.

The general correspondence relating to this force is carried on with the Home authorities, and not with the Government of India. In regard to the expenditure, it is partly managed from home and partly by the Government of India. The Indian Navy is connected with the overland communication; and therefore, on many points, such as the building of ships, steam-factories, and docks, instructions are received from England. But as regards the repair of ships and the establishments in those ships, any increase is referred to the Government of India, like any other increase. As an example of the control exercised by the Government of India, if repair of a vessel be wanted, and the expense is estimated to exceed Rs. 10,000, it must be referred for the sanction of that Government.

There is a small Marine force under the Bengal Government. Those acting as officers have no commissions, and the force is not subject to the Articles of War or the Mutiny Act. They have been employed in the China war, and are constantly employed in the Eastern Archipelago.

SECT. IV.—THE ECCLESIASTICAL SERVICE.

The Ecclesiastical establishment is maintained at the charge of the Indian revenue for the exclusive benefit of the servants of the Company, and without reference to the population of India generally, with whose religion the Government profess not to interfere. The present establishment consists of three Bishops—of Calcutta, Madras, and Bombay, respectively; and 135 Chaplains, English and Scotch, who are covenanted servants of the Company, and are placed on the same footing, as to furlough and other privileges, with other classes of European servants.*

There are also three Roman Catholic Bishops, and 78 Roman Catholic Priests, who participate in an annual grant from the Indian Government of about 5000*l.* per annum.

The three Anglican Bishops receive salaries from the Indian revenues as follows:—The Bishop of Calcutta, 5000*l.* per annum; the Bishops of Madras and Bombay, 2560*l.* each per annum. The jurisdiction of the Bishops extends, not only over the Chaplains, but over all the clergy of the Church of England within the limits of their respective dioceses. The present metropolitan jurisdiction of the Bishop of Calcutta extends over all the British territories, from the Punjab to Singapore. In addition to his salary he has, while on his tour, an allowance of 1000 rupees per month for his expenses, besides which the means of travelling, either vessels or carriages, are provided for him by the Government.

The total aggregate amount charged on the territorial revenues of India for ecclesiastical salaries, exclusive of travelling allowances, is 111,030*l.* per annum.

* Candidates for the Office of Chaplain must have been two years in Orders, under forty years of age, and approved by the Archbishop of Canterbury and the Bishop of London.

CHAPTER IV.

ADMINISTRATION OF JUSTICE IN BRITISH INDIA.

SECT. I.—LAWS IN FORCE IN BRITISH INDIA GENERALLY. SECT. II.—LAWS AND JUDICIAL PROCEDURE APPLICABLE TO BRITISH-BORN SUBJECTS—THE SUPREME COURTS. SECT. III.—LAWS AND JUDICIAL PROCEDURE APPLICABLE TO THE NATIVE POPULATION OF INDIA—CIVIL COURTS—CRIMINAL COURTS AND POLICE. SECT. IV.—THE INDIAN LAW COMMISSION.

SECT. I.—LAWS IN FORCE IN BRITISH INDIA GENERALLY.

IN the legal and judicial Administration of India, the uniform principle of British policy in respect of Territories acquired by conquest or cession, has been adopted.

The laws and system of jurisprudence, Mahomedan or Hindoo, to which we have succeeded, have, in every case, been recognised as valid, until superseded by the supreme authority of the British Government. The circumstance that this authority has, in the case of British India, been in some degree delegated to a chartered Company, has occasioned no difference in the practical application of the rule.

In the territories of the East India Company, as in all British dependencies similarly acquired, and not possessing Representative Institutions, the dominant country has exercised its legislative powers, either by Order in Council, or by Act of Parliament.

At the present time, both the Imperial Parliament and the Governor-General in Council have the power of legislating for India; but there are certain exceptions to the power of the latter authority, by one of which it is restrained from interfering with any Act of Parliament passed subsequently to 3 & 4 Will. IV. cap. 85, and applying to India. Acts not so made applicable by the British Parliament are sometimes made so by the local Legislature.

All laws passed by the Governor-General in Council extend, unless specially limited in their application by the Acts themselves, to all inhabitants, whether British or Native, of all territories within the Company's Charter.

Drafts of all laws, previously to being enacted, are published in the newspapers at all the Presidencies, in order that any parties thinking themselves likely to be affected by them, may apply to the Government. The publication does not take place at any fixed time before the enactment is passed; but it is usually from six weeks to two or three months. This practice of preliminary publication originated with the Court of Directors, and was adopted with the view of preventing precipitate legislation, by interposing a delay between the proposing and passing of a legislative Act.

The laws themselves, when they become such, are published in English—in Oordoo, a higher dialect of

Hindustanee—and in other Native languages, according to the part of India to which they may apply.

Power is reserved to the Imperial Parliament (before which all such laws are to be laid) to alter or repeal them.

SECT. II.—LAWS AND JUDICIAL PROCEDURE APPLICABLE TO BRITISH-BORN SUBJECTS IN INDIA—THE SUPREME COURTS.

British-born subjects and their descendants, resident in India, whether in the service of the Company or otherwise, are, with certain exceptions,* amenable only to British law, as administered by the Courts called the Supreme Courts, now existing at Calcutta, Madras, and Bombay. The history of this exemption, from the ordinary tribunals of the country, is described in the appendix to the first report of the Indian Law Commissioners, wherein also the present constitution and jurisdiction of the three Supreme Courts is minutely described.

The first Charter of the East India Company which contained any provision for the administration of justice was that of the 13th Charles II., which empowered the Company to appoint Governors and other Officers to govern their plantations, forts, fortifications, factories, or colonies, and authorised the

* The exceptions are cases of oppression of the natives, or judicial malversation, cognizable by the ordinary tribunals, which also try civil suits between natives and British subjects.

Governor and Council so appointed to "judge all persons belonging to the said Governor and Company, or that should live under them, in all cases, whether civil or criminal, according to the laws of the kingdom, and to execute judgment accordingly."

By the 35th Charles II. the Company were empowered to erect Courts of judicature, "consisting of a person learned in the civil laws, and two merchants, who were to decide according to equity and good conscience, and according to the laws and customs of merchants." And similar provisions were contained in the subsequent Charters down to the period of the union of the old and new Companies.

By the first Charter granted to the United Company, which was that of the 13th George I. in 1726, a Mayor's Court was established at each of the settlements "to be a Court of Record, to try, hear, and determine all civil suits between party and party that should arise within the towns of Madras, Bombay, and Calcutta, or within any of the factories subject thereto, between all persons there residing, or who, at the time of action accrued, did reside or be within the said towns, or the precincts, districts or territories thereof, and to determine according to justice and right."

From the decisions of this Court an Appeal was given to the Governor and Council, whose decision was declared to be final in all suits under 1000 pagodas; * but if the suit exceeded that amount a further appeal was given to the King in Council.

* A pagoda is about eight shillings.

The criminal jurisdiction was given to the Governor and Council, who were appointed Justices of the Peace, with power to hold Courts of Quarter Sessions, and Oyer and Terminer and Gaol Delivery, for the trial of all offences except treason, committed within the said towns, or within any of the factories subordinate, or within ten miles of the same. They were also empowered to grant probates of wills.

By the Charter of the 26th George II. upon the surrender of the previous Charter, the Mayor's Court and the Court of Oyer and Terminer and Gaol Delivery were again established at the three settlements, and similar provisions made—with this difference, that the native inhabitants of the respective towns were excepted from the civil jurisdiction of the Mayor's Court, unless with their own consent; and the criminal jurisdiction of the Court of Oyer and Terminer was limited to the trial of offences committed within the said towns, or within any of the factories or. places subordinate thereto, the words "or within ten miles of the same" being left out.

A Court of Requests was also established, to which natives were liable for suits under five pagodas.

By the Act 13th George III. c. 63, so much of the said charter as related to the establishment of the Mayor's Court at Calcutta was cancelled, and His Majesty was empowered to grant a Charter or Letters Patent for the erection of a Supreme Court of Judicature at Fort William in Bengal, to consist of a Chief Justice and three other Judges, being barristers of England or Ireland, of not less than five years' standing. And the Supreme Court was accordingly constituted by Royal Charter, dated the 6th March, 1774. By the 37th George III. c. 142, s. 1, the number of Judges was reduced to a Chief Justice and two other Judges, and the Court now consists of that number, the qualification of the Judges being the same.

The Court exercises civil and criminal jurisdiction, the former under the different heads of Common Law, Equity, Ecclesiastical, and Admiralty, and the latter as a Court of Oyer and Terminer. The Judges are also Commissioners of the Court for Relief of Insolvent Debtors, established by the Act 9th George IV. c. 73.

The Supreme Court appoints its own ministerial officers; and the same persons may hold offices on different sides of the Court at the same time. The officers are paid by salaries. The whole annual expense of the Court is 471,248 rupees, of which 208,367 rupees are for the salaries of the Judges, and 262,880 for the salaries of the officers and other expenses attending their establishments. This is exclusive of the emoluments of the Registrar, who is paid by a commission on the estates of persons dying intestate.

The Court is also authorised by its Charter to admit and enrol such and so many advocates and attornies as shall seem meet; and no other persons but such advocates and attornies are allowed to plead or act for the parties.

The general qualification for an advocate of the Supreme Court is, that he shall produce a certificate of having been called to the bar in England or Ireland, or of being entitled to practise as an advocate in the principal courts of Scotland, except the Judges shall see fit to dispense with the same.

The qualification for admission as an attorney is, that the applicant has been admitted an attorney of one of Her Majesty's Principal Courts of Record in England or Ireland, or a writer to the Signet in Scotland, or a member of the Society of Solicitors practising before the Court of Session there, or that he has served a regular clerkship of five years, under a contract in writing to some attorney practising in the Court, or that he is or has been a principal clerk to one of the Judges.

The advocates and attornies practise on all sides of the Court, under the same professional designations as in England.

The local jurisdiction of the Supreme Court is limited to the town of Calcutta, which for this purpose is bounded on the west side by the river Hooghly, and on the other sides by what is called the Mahratta Ditch. Within these limits the Court exercises all its jurisdictions, civil and criminal, over all persons residing within them, with the exception of its ecclesiastical jurisdiction, which has not been applied to Hindoos and Mahomedans beyond the granting of probates of wills.

The persons residing within these limits, and therefore subject to the local jurisdiction of the Supreme Court, are computed, according to the latest information, at about 400,000.

Secondly. In like manner the Court exercises all its jurisdictions over all British-born subjects, that is, persons who have been born within the British islands, and their descendants, who are resident in any of the provinces which are comprehended within the Presidency of Bengal, or the North-Western Provinces. The number of persons so subject to the jurisdiction of the Court, including the members of the Covenanted Services, civil and military, but exclusive of the Queen's troops and their families, was, on the 30th March, 1851, according to the Parliamentary census returns, 22,387, and is now probably larger.

Thirdly. All persons resident at any places within the said provinces, who have a dwelling-house and servants in Calcutta, or a place of business there where they carry on any trade, through their agents or servants, are held to be constructively inhabitants of Calcutta for the purpose of liability to the common law and equity jurisdictions of the Court.

Fourthly. Natives of India, within the said provinces, who have bound themselves upon any contract or agreement in writing with any British subject, where the cause of action exceeds the sum of 500 rupees, to submit to the jurisdiction of the said Court, are subject to its jurisdiction in disputes relating to the said contract.

Fifthly. In like manner, persons who avail themselves of the Court's jurisdiction for any purpose, are held liable to its jurisdiction in the same matter, even on other sides of the Court than that of which they have availed themselves; as, for instance, persons who have applied for and obtained probates of wills, are held liable to the Court's equity jurisdiction for the due administration of the estate.

Sixthly. All persons who, at the time of action brought or cause of action accrued, are or have been employed by, or directly or indirectly in the service of, the East India Company, or any British subject, are liable to the civil jurisdiction of the Court in actions for wrongs or trespasses, and also in any civil suit by agreement of parties in writing to submit to the jurisdiction of the said Court: and all persons who, at the time of committing any crime, misdemeanor, or oppression, are or have been employed, or directly or indirectly in service as aforesaid, are liable to the criminal jurisdiction of the Court.

Seventhly. The Admiralty jurisdiction of the Court extends over the provinces of Bengal, Behar, and Orissa, and all other territories and islands adjacent thereto, which at the date of the charter were or ought to be dependent thereon, and comprehends all causes, civil and maritime, and all matters and contracts relating to freights, or to extortions, trespasses, injuries and demands whatsoever between merchants or owners of ships and vessels employed or used within the jurisdiction aforesaid, or other persons, contracted, done, and commenced in or by the sea, public rivers, or creeks, or within the ebbing and flowing of the sea about and throughout the said three provinces and territories. The criminal jurisdiction extends to all crimes committed on the high seas by any person or persons whatsoever in as full and ample a manner as the jurisdiction of any other Court of Admiralty in any colony or settlement belonging to the Crown.

Lastly. The Supreme Courts at Calcutta, Madras, and Bombay have criminal jurisdiction over all British subjects for crimes committed at any place within the limits of the Company's Charter, that is, any part of Asia, Africa, or America, beyond the Cape of Good Hope to the Straits of Magellan, or for crimes committed in any of the lands or territories of any Native Prince or State, in the same way as if the same had been committed within the territories subject to the British Government in India.

The law administered in all cases, except as hereinafter mentioned, is as follows:—

First. The Common Law as it prevailed in England in the year 1726, and which has not subsequently been altered by Statutes especially extending to India, or by Acts of the Legislative Council of India.

Secondly. The Statute Law which prevailed in England in 1726, and which has not subsequently been altered by Statute especially extending to India, or by the Acts of the Legislative Council of India.

Thirdly. The Statute Law expressly extending to India, which has been enacted since 1726, and has not been since repealed, and the Statutes which have been extended to India by the Acts of the Legislative Council of India.

Fourthly. The Civil Law as it obtains in the ecclesiastical and Admiralty Courts.

Fifthly. Regulations made by the Governor-

General in Council, previously to the 3rd and 4th Will. IV. c. 85, and registered in the Supreme Court, and the Acts of the Legislative Council of India made under the 3rd and 4th Will. IV. cap. 85.

The exceptions are Hindoos and Mahommedans in the following cases:—

First. Actions regarding inheritance and succession to lands, rents, and goods, and all matters of contract and dealing between party and party in which both parties are Hindoos. Such cases are to be determined by the laws and usages of Hindoos.

Secondly. Actions of the same kind where both parties are Mahommedans, and in these the case is to be determined by the laws and usages of Mahommedans.

Thirdly. Actions of the same kind where only one of the parties is a Mahommedan or Hindoo; and these are to be determined by the laws and usages of the defendant.

The procedure on the different sides of the Court is similar to the procedure of the corresponding Courts in England, with this difference, that, as directed by the Charter, the *vivâ voce* examinations of witnesses are taken down in writing, and the depositions are signed by the witnesses. The new rules in law and equity passed from time to time in this country are quickly adopted by the Judges in India, as far as circumstances will admit, and applied with the requisite modifications to their own practice.

The suits are generally of the same description as in England; those on the common law side being very similar to the cases at *nisi prius*. They are tried, however, without a jury, the Judges determining both fact and law; though the latter, when points are raised, is commonly reserved, as in England, for further argument. Calcutta is a commercial town, almost all the European inhabitants, with the exception of the Company's servants and professional persons, being engaged in commerce. The common law suits are therefore much of the mercantile character, the equity suits are most commonly between natives, and then generally relate to wills, or the succession to intestate estate, or the partition of joint property, and frequently involve questions of Hindoo law, and matters of account.

In all suits, where the property in dispute is of the value of 10,000 rupees, there is an appeal to Her Majesty in Council. When a suit is appealed, it is the practice for the appellant to take two examined copies of the whole proceedings, including the depositions of the witnesses, which are committed to some trustworthy person, usually the master of a ship, to be delivered to the proper officer in this country.

So much of the Charter of 1726 as related to the Mayor's Court at Madras, or to the President and Council, as a Court of Appeal therefrom, or of Oyer and Terminer and Gaol Delivery, was cancelled by the Act 37 Geo III. c. 142; and by virtue of letters patent, issued in pursuance of the Act, a Court of Record was established within the settlement of Madras, called the Court of the Recorder of Madras, with such civil, criminal, and ecclesiastical jurisdiction, and with such powers and authorities, as in the said letters patent mentioned.

The Recorder's Court at Madras was abolished by the Act 40 Geo. III. c. 79; and by letters patent, dated the 26th December 1800, and issued in pursuance of the Act, the Supreme Court of Judicature at Madras was established, to be a Court of Record, and consist of a Chief Justice, and two other Judges, who should be Barristers in England or Ireland of not less than five years' standing.

The Court has generally the same powers, and its jurisdictions are generally the same, within the settlement of Madras, as those of the Supreme Court of Judicature at Fort William within the territories attached to the Presidency of Bengal and the North-West Provinces.

The local jurisdiction of the Court is confined to the town of Madras, which for this purpose is held to be bounded by the sea on the east, the Saint Thomé river on the south, the banks of the Long Tank and the Nungumbaukum Tank, with the villages of Kilpaukum and Peramboor on the west, and a line from the latter village to the sea on the north, and to comprise all the lands included in the villages of Chettapet, Kilpaukum, Peramboor, and Tandear. The inhabitants of Madras within these limits are computed at about 720,000.

The British subjects residing within the provinces attached to Madras, and subject to the jurisdiction of the Supreme Court, were, on the 30th March

1851, according to the Parliamentary Census Returns, 15,133, including the civil and military members of the Covenanted Services, but exclusive of the Queen's troops. The Court's civil jurisdiction extends to British subjects within any of the dominions of the native Princes of India in alliance with the Government of Madras.

So much of the Charter of 1726 as related to the Mayor's Court at Bombay, or to the President and Council as a Court of Appeal, or of Oyer and Terminer and Gaol Delivery for the town and island of Bombay and the limits thereof, was cancelled by the Act 37 Geo. III. c. 142; and by virtue of letters patent issued in pursuance of the Act, a Court of Record was established within the settlement of Bombay, called the Court of the Recorder of Bombay, with the civil and criminal jurisdiction in the letters patent mentioned.

The Recorder's Court at Bombay continued till the 4th Geo. IV. c. 71, when it was superseded by letters patent, bearing date the 8th of December 1823, and issued in pursuance of the Act, constituting the Supreme Court of Judicature at Bombay to be a Court of Record, and consist of a Chief Justice and two other Judges, who should be Barristers of England or Ireland of not less than five years' standing.

The local jurisdiction of the Court is confined to the Island of Bombay, the inhabitants of which are computed at 566,119.

The British-born subjects who reside within the

provinces comprised in the Presidency of Bombay, including the Covenanted Servants of the Company, were, on the 30th March 1851, according to the Parliamentary Census Return, 10,704, exclusive of the Queen's troops.

The Supreme Courts at Madras and Bombay have generally the same powers, and their jurisdictions are generally the same within the settlements of Madras and Bombay, as those of the Supreme Court of Judicature at Fort William within the territories attached to the Presidency of Bengal and the North-West Provinces.

SECT. III.—LAWS AND JUDICIAL PROCEDURE APPLICABLE TO THE NATIVE POPULATION OF INDIA—CIVIL COURTS—CRIMINAL COURTS AND POLICE.

The native population of India is now under a system of judicial administration, Civil and Criminal, which has been organized by the Anglo-Indian Government, founded on pre-existing native systems of jurisprudence. On the Hindoo and Mahommedan stock have been grafted, from time to time, modifications resulting from legal precedents and constructions, which have been, in the Regulation Provinces of India, embodied into a system by successive enactments, though at present no uniformity exists. "The Courts profess to administer to every man the law of his own religion, country, or tribe, and, where the plaintiff and defendant are of different tribes, to decide according to the custom of the country, or the law of the defendant."*

An exception must here be noted in respect to the Presidency of Bombay, which has a special code of its own, compiled during Mr. Elphinstone's Government, and called after his name. It affects natives only, and is both Civil and Criminal. Its chief operation is in regulating Civil procedures. The Mahommedan law may be said to be unknown in the Bombay Presidency, except as to inheritance and similar matters among Mahommedans.

Civil Courts.

The Constitution and Procedure of the East India Company's Courts of Civil Judicature are in their main features alike throughout India, though in the practice of the Courts and titles of the functionaries differences are observable in the judicial machinery now existing in the different Presidencies.

The inferior Civil Courts of Justice are, as has been stated, almost entirely in the hands of Native Judges. The lowest and most numerous class of these is that of Moonsiffs,† to each of whom a small district is allotted, and who have power to try all causes affecting real or personal estate in which the amount in dispute does not exceed 30*l*.‡ Candidates for Moonsiffships are annually examined, and those qualified receive diplomas, which render them eligible

* *Vide* Campbell's "India as it is," p. 535.

† Arabic, judge, from *insaf*, justice; literally, dividing in half.

‡ In Madras and Bombay the Moonsiffs have larger jurisdiction, extending to 100*l*. in the former, and 500*l*. in the latter Presidency.

for appointments. These diplomas are generally obtained by the pleaders practising in the Courts, called Vakeels.*

There are two grades of Moonsiff: 10*l.* per month is the usual allowance for the lower, and 15*l.* per month for the superior grade, to which they are promoted according to merit.

The next rank of Civil Judges above Moonsiffs is that of Sudder Aumeens,† also Natives, who have power to try all causes between 30*l.* and 100*l.* in amount, and who receive salaries of 25*l.* per month each.

Immediately above the Sudder Aumeens comes the third and highest grade of Native Judges, called the Principal Sudder Aumeens, who try suits from 100*l.* and upwards to any amount. Of these Judges there are two grades; 40*l.* per month is the usual allowance of the lower, 60*l.* of the superior grade, which is the reward of merit.

The next Court of Civil Justice above that of the Principal Sudder Aumeen, is that of the Zillah‡ Judge, who is a European functionary belonging to the Covenanted Service (and who is invested, besides his powers as Civil Judge, with criminal jurisdiction hereafter to be noticed). To the Zillah Judge an appeal lies from the decisions in original suits of the Moonsiffs and Sudder Aumeens, also from the decisions of the Principal Sudder Aumeens up to 500*l.*;

* Arabic, general word for agent or attorney.

† Arabic, literally "chief trustees."

‡ A Zillah is a large division of country.

but the Zillah Judge has power to refer to the Principal Sudder Aumeens appeals from the Moonsiffs and Sudder Aumeens, and of this power he makes large use. The Zillah Judge tries all original suits above 500*l.*, if he has not referred them to his Principal Sudder Aumeen, which he may do.

In the trial of civil suits, original or appeal, it is competent to the European Zillah Judge to avail himself of the assistance of Natives in one of the three following modes:—

1. By a Punchayet,* or Court of Arbitrators (generally five) chosen by the parties, who conduct their inquiries on points submitted to them apart from the Court, and make their report to the Judge.

2. By Native Assessors who sit with the Judge, make observations, examine witnesses, and offer opinions and suggestions.

3. By a Jury who attend during the trial, and, after consultation, deliver in their verdict.

Under all these modes of procedure, the decision is, however, vested solely and exclusively in the Judge.

It may here be remarked that the mode of procedure adopted in all the Courts above-mentioned is generally the same. All pleadings are in writing. The plaint must be lodged on a stamp of a value proportioned to the sum claimed. Attached to the "declaration" is a power of attorney naming a licensed pleader. A formal notice is served on the defendant, or stuck up in the village where he is supposed to reside, and he is required to file an answer

* From *punj* or *panch*, the Persian or Hindoo word for five.

and defend the cause within a certain number of days. The pleadings, all of which are on stamped paper, then go on till all the points of law and fact being raised for decision, issue is joined. The witnesses who may be called on either side are not subject to cross-examination. In carrying out the process of the Courts, execution is enforced either by distress of personal property, or sale of landed rights, which latter are at once sold to the highest bidder in satisfaction of the decree.

From the decisions of the Zillah Judge, by whichever of the processes above indicated they may be arrived at, an appeal lies to the High Court of Civil Justice, called the Sudder Dewanny Adawlut.* There are four of these High Courts of Civil Justice in India, possessing co-ordinate jurisdiction within their respective limits. At Calcutta for Bengal, at Madras and Bombay for those Presidencies respectively, and at Agra for the North-West Provinces. In the Calcutta Court there are five Judges, in that at Bombay four, at Madras three, a member of council being added as President of the Court at the two last-named Presidencies. In the Court at Agra there are three Judges. In all the Courts the Judges are selected from members of the Covenanted Civil Service of considerable standing in the judicial department.

The Sudder Dewanny Adawlut exercises no origi-

* The words are Arabic. *Sudder* means chief or first of anything; *Dewan*, a seat, or tribunal; and *Adawlut*, justice. *Dewanny* is generally used in India to signify the civil government.

nal jurisdiction. It is the Court of final appeal in each Presidency, and controls all the subordinate civil tribunals. Besides regular appeals from the original decisions of the European Zillah Judge, and in certain cases from those of the Principal Sudder Aumeen, the Court is competent to admit second or special appeals from decisions of the Courts below. The grounds for special appeal are, when the judgments shall appear inconsistent with law or the practice and usage of the Courts. The power thus given to the Sudder, or High Civil Courts of hearing special appeals, extends their means of supervision, and brings judicially before them the proceedings and decisions of all classes of judicial offenders, and affords opportunity for correcting errors, it being one of their duties to regulate the practice and proceedings of the lower Courts, each judicial officer of which is required by law to record his decisions and the reasons for them in his own vernacular tongue. This process is supposed to afford the Sudder Court means of judging correctly of the individual qualifications of their subordinates. In the trial of appeals, the proceedings of the lower tribunals are read before one or more Judges. A single Judge is competent to confirm a decree. Two or three sitting together must concur for its reversal, whether the appeal be regular or special. The Sudder Courts sit daily, except during the Dusserah * and the Mohurrum,* when all civil proceedings are suspended. The salaries of the

* The great Hindoo and Mahommedan anniversaries.

Judges of the Sudder Courts are not uniform, but none receive less than 4200*l*. per annum.

From the decisions of the Sudder Courts an appeal lies to the Queen in Council in cases where the amount in litigation is not less than 1000*l*. The petition for an appeal must be presented to the Sudder Court within six months from the decree, and accompanied with security for the respondent's costs, now fixed at 500*l*., which may be either money, or Government securities, commonly called 'Company's paper' or a *Mal Zaminy* or land mortgage.

Pending the appeal the Sudder Court may either cause their judgment to be executed provisionally, or suspend it, according to their discretion.

The administration of the Criminal Law in India differs materially in the different Presidencies. But it may be said generally, that its basis is the Mahommedan Law, modified by the Acts and Regulations of the British Government. Criminal Courts.

Before noticing the higher departments of Criminal Administration in India, it may be observed that the powers of Magistrates appointed by the Government in the Presidency Towns, have been defined from time to time at Calcutta, Madras, and Bombay, by the provisions of Imperial Statutes and local Acts and Regulations.

The gradations in the authority of the Magistrates and Criminal Courts are for the most part alike in all the Presidencies. In the Mofussil, or Country Districts of Bengal, the system of Criminal Administration is as follows:—"Each district is committed to a

Magistrate, and contains fifteen or twenty subdivisions or "Thanahs," each of which is placed under a subordinate officer, called a Thanadar or Darogah. Each of these last-named functionaries has under him the following establishment:—a Clerk or writer, a "Jemadar" or sergeant, and twenty or thirty policemen. The Darogahs are generally Mahommedans or Hindoos. Besides this machinery for the apprehension of criminals, there are also a large number of village police or watchmen, appointed by the village Committees, or by the Zemindars. These functionaries, who are not generally supposed to be very efficient, amount, in Bengal Proper, to the large number of 170,000. The Darogahs, or Inspectors of Police, are invested with a certain measure of summary authority in cases of affrays, disturbances of the peace, &c., but are bound to bring all other matters under the previous cognizance of the Magistrate, who has the power of punishment to the extent of imprisonment for two years in certain cases, in some others for three years; but ordinarily his power extends to imprisonment for six months, and a fine of 200 rupees, and if the fine be not paid, to a further imprisonment of six months. Corporal punishment was abolished by Lord William Bentinck, but has since been revived in case of theft, where the property stolen does not exceed fifty rupees in value, and for juvenile offenders, as well as in certain crimes committed by convicts.

The Sessions Judge is the officer next in the ascending scale of rank, and appeal lies to him in certain cases from the Magistrate. He is the same individual who acts in a Civil capacity, as before mentioned, as "Zillah" Judge. In Bengal his original jurisdiction is limited to offenders committed by the Magistrate to take their trial at the Sessions.

In Madras, the Sessions Judge is aided by a subordinate Judge, who acts as Committing officer instead of the Magistrate. In Bombay, the Sessions Judge is aided by an officer called the "Assistant Sessions Judge."

The Sessions Judge has the power of punishment to the extent of nine years' imprisonment, and, in certain aggravated cases, of sixteen years. All cases involving punishments above those limits are referred to the Sudder Court, which is composed of the same Judges as the Supreme Court of Civil Appeal, and is called the Sudder Nizamut* Adawlut, in Bengal, the Foujdary† Adawlut, in Madras and Bombay. This Court decides on the record and report of the Sessions Judge. It never hears oral evidence; but if the case requires more elucidation, sends it back to the Sessions Judge, with orders to take further evidence on particular points; and its ultimate decision is final.

If the Judges of the Nizamut concur in the verdict of the Lower Court, and the prisoner be considered deserving of a higher degree of punishment than could be awarded by the Sessions Judge, he may be

* *Nizamut* is an Arabic word, which means "arrangement, or reducing to order," and governors of provinces under the Mahommedan Government were sometimes designated by names derived from the same root, as the *Nazim* and the *Nizam*.

† From *Foujdar*, the General, or holder of a *fouj* or army.

sentenced to suffer death, or to undergo imprisonment for twenty-one years; but if sentenced to imprisonment for life, then transportation for life, either to the penal settlements of Singapore, Penang, or Malacca, the Tenasserim Provinces, Arracan, or Aden, would be substituted; but no native of India can be transported beyond the Company's territories. If the case be not capital, it is decided by the sentence of a single Judge. Sentences of death require the concurrence of two Judges. The Government has the power of pardon or mitigation, but it is seldom exercised.

There are in Bengal two modes of trial, in one of which a Mahommedan law officer, or Assessor, expounds the law; but if the prisoner is not a Mahommedan, he may refuse to be so tried, and for such cases there is a system of Juries, or Assessors, or Punchayet. The Sessions Judge may reject the opinion of the Mahommedan law officer, on points expressly provided for by the Regulations, and that opinion may be overridden altogether by the Sudder Court. When the case is tried with a Jury, or Punchayet, the decision may be overruled, and sentence awarded to the extent of the Judge's competence. Cases tried by the Magistrate are generally prosecuted by the party injured.

With respect to Madras and other parts of British India, except Bombay, it may be stated generally that the system of criminal administration, though differing in some particulars, is based on the same general principles as that existing in Bengal. The

Police, who are, in Bengal and Bombay, placed under the command in chief of a superintendent, specially charged with that duty, are, in Madras, placed under the Governor in Council, and in the North-West Provinces under the Commissioners of Revenue. In the Punjaub there is a military preventive Police of foot and horse, who furnish guards for jails, treasuries, frontier-posts, and escorts of treasure.

It may also be noticed that, with respect to the professional criminals peculiar to India, and called Thugs and Dacoits, a special Police invested with summary powers, is organized under one superintendent for all India.

SECT. IV.—THE INDIAN LAW COMMISSION.

Reforms in the Laws, Judicial Establishments, and procedure of British India, have been now under the consideration of the Imperial Parliament and of the Indian Government for a quarter of a century. Though no practical result has been yet attained, a brief notice of the origin, progress, and present stage of these investigations seems an essential appendix to any sketch of the existing system of Judicial Administration in British India.

In 1833, by s. 53 of statute 3 and 4 William IV. cap. 85, the Governor-General of India in Council was empowered to appoint a Commission, not exceeding five members, to inquire into and report upon the

Jurisdiction of the existing Courts of Justice, and the operation of the Laws in India, with a view to their consolidation and amendment. The sections of the statute relating to the appointment of this Commission are as follows :—

S. LIII. Whereas it is expedient that, subject to such special Arrangements as local Circumstances may require, a general System of Judicial Establishments and Police, to which all Persons whatsoever, as well *Europeans* as Natives, may be subject, should be established in the said Territories at an early Period, and that such Laws as may be applicable in common to all Classes of the Inhabitants of the said Territories, due Regard being had to the Rights, Feelings, and peculiar Usages of the People, should be enacted, and that all Laws and Customs having the Force of Law within the same Territories should be ascertained and consolidated, and as occasion may require amended: be it therefore enacted, that the Governor-General of *India* in Council shall, as soon as conveniently may be after the passing of this Act, issue a Commission, and from time to time Commissions, to such persons as the said Court of Directors, with the approbation of the said Board of Commissioners, shall recommend for that purpose, and to such other persons, if necessary, as the said Governor-General in Council shall think fit, all such persons, not exceeding in the whole at any one time five in number, and to be styled "The *Indian* Law Commissioners," with all such powers as shall be necessary for the purposes hereinafter mentioned; and the said Commissioners shall fully inquire into the Jurisdiction, Powers, and Rules of the existing Courts of Justice and Police Establishments in the said territories, and all existing forms of judicial procedure, and into the nature and operation of all laws, whether civil or criminal, written or customary, prevailing and in force in any part of the said territories, and whereto any inhabitants of the said territories, whether *Europeans* or others, are now subject; and the said Commissioners shall from time to time make Reports, in which they shall fully set forth the result of their said inquiries, and shall from time to time suggest such alterations as may in their opinion be beneficially made in the said Courts of Justice and Police Establishments, forms of judicial procedure and laws, due regard being had to the distinction of castes, differences of religion, and the manners and opinions prevailing among different races and in different parts of the said territories.

LIV. And be it enacted, that the said Commissioners shall follow such instructions with regard to the researches and inquiries to be made and the places to be visited by them, and all their transactions with reference to the objects of their Commission, as they shall from time to time receive from the said Governor-General of *India* in Council; and they are hereby required to make to the said Governor-General in Council such special Reports upon any matters as by such instructions may from time to time be required; and the said Governor-General in Council shall take into consideration the Reports from time to time to be made by the said *Indian* Law Commissioners, and shall transmit the same, together with the opinions or resolutions of the said Governor-General in Council thereon, to the said Court of Directors; and which said Reports, together with the said opinions or resolutions, shall be laid before both Houses of Parliament in the same manner as is now by law provided concerning the rules and regulations made by the several Governments in *India*.

LV. And be it enacted, that it shall and may be lawful for the Governor-General of *India* in Council to grant salaries to the said *Indian* Law Commissioners and their necessary officers and attendants, and to defray such other expenses as may be incident to the said Commission, and that the salaries of the said Commissioners shall be according to the highest scale of remuneration given to any of the officers or servants of the *India* Company below the rank of Members of Council.

In pursuance of the powers thus conferred, an Indian Law Commission was, in the year 1834, appointed. It consisted of five Members—the Legislative Councillor appointed under the Act of 1833 (Mr. Macaulay), another English barrister, and three Civil Servants from each of the three Presidencies.

The question with what part of the Law the Commissioners should begin, was determined by the Government. Their first work (which occupied about two years) was to prepare a single penal Code for all British India. By this Code (known as Macaulay's Code) the Mahommedan Criminal Law was to be swept away, and that substituted was to apply to all classes of persons without exception; but the penalties were to be varied according to the diversities of birth, class, and circumstances. This Code was afterwards recast under the auspices of Mr. Bethune, who subsequently held the office of Legislative Councillor, but, in consequence of differences of opinion at home and in India, has never received authoritative sanction.

Other suggestions relating to the Administration of Civil Justice were made by the Law Commission, as for a Model Civil Court and a plan of civil procedure, under which the administration of law and equity was to be united, and the whole case brought under the cognizance of one Judge, while small-cause judicature was not to be committed to inferior Judges, but all causes, whatever their amount, were to be cognizable in the same Courts. In regard to Appeals, the scheme of the Law Commission was, to have a General Court of Appeal in each Presidency, consisting of the Judges of the Supreme Courts and the Judges of the Sudder Courts, which should receive appeals both in civil and criminal cases, and from all the Courts in the country. The Mahommedan law was to be codified; the Hindoo law was to be codified, and a third civil code, the *lex loci*, was to be applicable to all but Mahommedans or Hindoos.*

The conflict of opinion both in England and in India as to the various suggestions offered by the Law Commission having rendered its inquiries practically inoperative, the vacancies arising in it from time to time by death or resignation were not filled up, and it was thus permitted to become gradually extinct.

In 1853, by s. 28 of statute 16 and 17 Vict. cap. 95, Her Majesty was empowered to appoint Commissioners in England to consider and report upon the Reforms proposed by the Indian Law Commissioners, appointed under the provisions of statute 3 and 4 Will. IV. cap. 85.

The section of the Act of 1853, relating to the appointment of this second Commission, is as follows:—

XXVIII. Whereas by the Act of the third and fourth years of King *William* the Fourth it was provided, that Commissioners to be appointed thereunder, and to be styled the *Indian* Law Commissioners, should inquire into the jurisdiction, powers, and rules of the existing Courts of Justice and Police Establishments in the said Territories, and all existing Forms of Judicial Procedure, and into the nature and operation of all Laws, whether civil or criminal, written or customary, prevailing and in force in any part of the said Territories, and should from time to time make reports, in which

* Certain parts of the *lex loci* Code, which protect converts from Mahommedanism and Hindooism from loss of ancestral or other property, which they previously incurred, have since become law.

they should fully set forth the result of their inquiries, and should from time to time suggest such alterations as might in their opinion be beneficially made in the said Courts of Justice and Police Establishments, Forms of Judicial Procedure, and Laws, due regard being had to the distinction of castes, difference of religion, and the manners and opinions prevailing among different races and in different parts of the said territories. And whereas the *Indian* Law Commissioners from time to time appointed under the said Act have, in a series of Reports, recommended extensive alterations in the Judicial Establishments, Judicial Procedure, and Laws established and in force in *India*, and have set forth in detail the provisions which they have proposed to be established by Law for giving effect to certain of their recommendations, and such Reports have been transmitted from time to time to the said Court of Directors; but on the greater part of such reports and recommendations no final decision has been had:

It shall be lawful for Her Majesty, at any time after the passing of this Act, by Commission under the Royal Sign Manual, to appoint such and so many persons in *England* as to Her Majesty may seem fit to examine and consider the recommendations of the said *Indian* Law Commissioners, and the enactments proposed by them for the reform of the Judicial Establishments, Judicial Procedure, and Laws of *India*, and such other matters in relation to the reform of the said Judicial Establishments, Judicial Procedure, and Laws, as may, by or with the sanction of the Commissioners for the affairs of *India*, be referred to them for their consideration, and to authorise and direct the persons so appointed, or such number as may be limited by their commission in this behalf, to report their opinion to Her Majesty on the matters aforesaid, and especially to report from time to time what Laws or Regulations should be made or enacted in relation to the matters aforesaid, but so that every such report be made within three years after the passing of this Act; and for the purposes of such examination it shall be lawful for Her Majesty to authorise the persons so appointed, or the number limited by the Commission in this behalf, to call before them and examine in *England* such persons in the service of the Crown and the said Company respectively, and to require the production of such official documents in the possession of the Board of Commissioners for the affairs of *India*, or of the said Company, as they may think fit.

In pursuance of the powers thus reserved to Her Majesty, a Commission was issued under the Royal Sign Manual, dated November 29, 1853, appointing Sir John Romilly, Sir John Jervis, Sir Edward Ryan, C. H. Cameron, J. M. Macleod, J. A. F. Hawkins,* T. F. Ellis, and R. Lowe, Esquires, to be members of the said Commission, and authorising them, or any three or more of them, to make a diligent and full inquiry into and to examine and consider the recommendations of the Indian Law Commissioners, and the enactments proposed by them for the reform of the Judicial Establishments, Judicial Procedure, and Laws of India, and such other matters in relation to the reform of the said Judicial Establishments, Judicial Procedure, and Laws, as might, by or with the sanction of the Commissioners for the affairs of India, be referred to them for their consideration. And full power and authority was granted to the said Commissioners to call before them, or any three or more of them, such persons in the service of the Crown or of the East India Company, and all such other persons as they should judge necessary.

Also to cause all or any of the officers and clerks in the service of the Crown or of the East India Company to bring and produce before them all records,

* By a subsequent Commission, dated March 17, 1854, the name of F. Millet, Esq., was substituted for that of Mr. Hawkins, who became Secretary to the Commission.

orders, books, papers, and other writings in the possession of the Board of Commissioners for the affairs of India or the East India Company. And within three years after the twentieth day of August, one thousand eight hundred and fifty-three, or as soon as the same could conveniently be done, to certify under their hands and seals, what they should have done in the premises.

In fulfilment of the duties thus devolved on them, the Commissioners have since presented four Reports, the last of which bears date May 20, 1856.

These Reports recommend an amalgamation of the Supreme and Sudder Courts now existing at Calcutta, Madras, and Bombay, respectively, into one Court at each of those Cities, to be designated the "High Court." They also recommend the establishment at Agra, where no Supreme Court now exists, of a "High Court" for the North-West Provinces, similar to those proposed for the three Presidencies.

They also propound uniform Codes of civil and criminal procedure, applicable both to the High Courts so to be formed, and to all inferior Courts within the limits of their respective jurisdictions.

They further recommend that the High Court at Calcutta shall consist of not less than eight Judges—those at Madras and Bombay respectively of not less than five, and that at Agra of not less than four Judges. A proportion of the Judges in each Court to be appointed by the Crown, the others by the Governor-General in Council at Calcutta and Agra; and by the Governors of Madras and Bombay at those Presidencies respectively. The Judges to be appointed by the Crown, to be selected from Barristers of England and Ireland, and members of the Faculty of Advocates in Scotland, of not less than five years' standing. The Judges to be appointed by the Governor-General or other Governors, to be members of the Covenanted Civil Service, of not less than ten years' standing. All the Judges to hold their offices at the pleasure of the Crown.

Further detailed suggestions were also offered as to the civil and criminal jurisdiction, both original and appellate of the High Courts, and as to the area to which the proposed Codes of civil or criminal procedure should extend.

The Commissioners also advised that in order to harmonize the system of Civil Law at the capitals and in the Provinces of India, a body of substantive Civil Law should be constructed on the basis of the law of England to be the Law of India on all the subjects it embraced.*

No Legislative Measure has been founded on these Reports, all of which have been sent out to India. The first on December 12, 1855, the second on February 20, 1856, the third and fourth on June 25, 1856, and are reported to be now under the consideration of the Legislative Council at Calcutta.

* The Commissioners were not unanimous in their recommendations, Mr. Lowe and Chief Justice Jervis dissenting from the 3rd Report, and the latter having refused to sign both the 3rd and 4th Reports, and after their presentation having formally retired from the Commission.

CHAPTER V.

EXISTING REVENUE SYSTEM OF BRITISH INDIA.

SOURCES OF REVENUE.—LAND—SALT—OPIUM—CUSTOMS—MISCELLANEOUS.

THE territories comprised in the East India Company's Charters form the only portion of the British Dependencies which have hitherto borne the entire cost of their own Civil and Military Administration.

This result has been attained under a Revenue System, inherited from our Mahommedan predecessors, engrafted by them on ancient Hindoo customs, and modified from time to time, under British rule, by a series of Regulations, by which the system, as it now exists, has been constructed.

The estimate of the total revenues of British India, for the year ending April 30, 1857 (without deduction for costs of collection, allowances, and drawbacks), is as follows:—

Land Revenue	£16,682,908
Opium	4,487,269
Salt	2,362,308
Customs	2,029,270
All other Sources of Revenue (comprising Stamps, Post-Office, Sayer, Abkarry, Mint, Marine, Pilotage, Judicial, Electric Telegraph Receipts, Subsidies from Native States, and other Miscellaneous Revenues	3,605,702
Total Revenues	£29,167,457

The collection of these revenues forms, as has been already stated, one of the most important duties of the Civil Service in India. These duties are discharged under the general superintendence of Boards of Revenue, of which there are three in India: namely, for Bengal, the North-West Provinces, and Madras. The Bengal Board consists of three members, that at Agra, for the North-West Provinces, of two, that at Madras of one Member of Council as President, and three ordinary members.

In Bombay there is no Board of Revenue, but two Revenue Commissioners divide the whole territory, and are immediately under the Government. Subordinate to these Boards of Revenue, there are also throughout India in all the Revenue "Divisions," officers charged with all details and petty appeals, who were first appointed by Lord William Bentinck, and who are, in some cases, exclusively revenue functionaries; in others entrusted also with magisterial and other duties.

SECT. I.—LAND REVENUE.

The chief source of revenue in India is the land. This revenue (which as now levied under various systems in the Presidencies of Bengal, Madras, and Bombay, in the North-West Provinces, and in the Panjaub, yielded by the latest returns, previous to the recent disturbances, more than sixteen millions sterling) is sometimes designated as a tax, sometimes as a land-rent, but is practically an annual payment, levied by the Anglo-Indian Government, and payable (subject to certain exceptions hereafter to be noticed) by all who hold land within the territories of the East India Company.

To trace the origin of this tax, or to discuss the various theories relating to it, is beyond the province of these pages; but in order to a correct apprehension of the existing system, it will be necessary to take a brief review of the modifications to which it has been subjected.

The various systems of Administration in respect to the Land Revenue of India, which have from time to time been adopted, and of which distinct and varying samples are now to be found throughout the different Presidencies, have all their foundation in a state of things which existed anterior to the British or even the Mahommedan Conquest.

The ancient village* communities which almost everywhere existed in form, more or less perfect—sometimes managed by a single head-man—sometimes by a committee of their own number—sometimes by Zemindars,† hereditary Hindoo Chieftains, or Bailiffs of Mogul Emperors, were, wherever those

* A "village" is not a collection of houses, but a tract of land, bounded and named, and occupied by hereditary cultivators.

† *Zemindar.*—A Persian Word, signifying "landholder," originally applied to hereditary Hindoo Chiefs, afterwards to functionaries appointed by the Mogul Emperors to collect revenue, receiving a percentage.

communities existed, the foundation of the Revenue System of India. Where they did not exist, attempts were made to construct imitations of them, in order to provide a convenient machinery for levying that share of the produce of the land which the successive sovereigns of India have claimed; and which, under our present system of commutation, is said to amount to nearly one-fourth of the gross produce,* or, taking an average of the cultivated lands throughout India, about 3*s.* 6*d.* per acre in English money.

It was not until a century and a half after the establishment of our first factories in India, that any territorial rights devolved on the East India Company.

In 1765, with the grant of Bengal, Bahar, and Orissa, to the Company, by the Mogul, the necessity of providing some Revenue System arose. For four years the system was carried on by the Native Officers who had been employed in the same service by the Nawab of Bengal. The Zemindars, aided by District-Registrars called Canongoes, contracted with the Government on behalf of the villagers—the revenues being dependent on the produce, and, in some cases, subdivisions of the villages, called

* "It is desirable that the Government should not demand more than two-thirds, of what may be expected to be the net produce to the proprietor during the period of settlement, leaving to the proprietor one-third as his profits and to cover the costs of collection. By net produce is meant the surplus which the estate may yield, after deducting expenses of Cultivation."—*Directions to Revenue Settlement Officers, North-West Provinces*, Section 52.

"*Pattees,*" being chief tenants in a corporate capacity, gave the name to an intermediate tenure called "Patteedaree."

In 1769, Supervisors, being covenanted servants of the Company, were appointed in each district to report on the existing Revenue System, with a view to its amendment.

In 1772, by Proclamation, dated May 11, the Company asserted their authority under the Mogul's grant to the "Dewannee," or Civil Government, and by Regulations dated May 14, a system of lease for five years to the highest bidder was inaugurated.

In 1776, instructions were issued by the Directors, authorising the sale of lands, in default of payment on the part of the Zemindars, or landholders, with whom the Government contracts were made.

In 1781, Regulations were framed and passed by the Governor in Council, establishing a plan of annual leases; preference to be given, in all cases, to the Zemindars.

In 1789, by a Minute of the Governor-General (Lord Cornwallis), a Settlement, involving a fixed payment of Revenue for ten years, was announced.

In 1793, by Proclamation, dated March 22, the decennial settlement was declared to be permanent and irrevocable for ever, and regulations were framed for carrying it out.

In 1799, an Act was passed relaxing the stringent power of sale given theretofore to the Government over the estates of defaulting Zemindars.

In 1802, the permanent Revenue System of Bengal was extended to a portion of the Madras Presidency, in which, under the auspices of Munro, a system had been established of direct dealing with individual cultivators, on yearly agreements, with allowances for irrigation or other improvements, and providing also for the liability of villages for individual defaults.

In 1803–4–5, the district called the Barahmal, in Madras, was mapped out into Zemindarries, and disposed of on fixed permanent terms.* After many changes and modifications of system, we find—

In 1817, three different systems existing in different parts of Madras. 1. The Cornwallis or Zemindarry System. 2. The Ryotwar or Munro System, above described; and 3, the Village System of leases for years of all the lands comprised in the village, together with all the profits; the liability for rent, and the duty of internal management being committed to the leaseholders collectively.†

In 1820, the Ryotwar System was made general through all parts of the Madras Presidency not already permanently assessed.

In 1821, a Commission was appointed to investi-

* A full account of the Land Revenue System, as it existed in 1812, will be found in the Fifth Report of the House of Commons of that year.

† The first of these systems, the Zemindarry, prevailed in Ganjam, Vizagapatam, Rajahmundry, Masulipatam, Guntoor, Salem, Chingleput, Cuddalore, and the Pollams.

The second or Ryotwar—in Malabar, Canara, Coimbatoor, Madura, and Dindigul.

The third or Village System—in the Ceded Districts—Nellore, Arcot, Palnaud, Trichinopoly, Tinnevelly, and Tanjore.

gate and report upon alleged abuses in the Revenue System of the North-West Provinces, and in 1822, by Regulation VII., a system, of which Mr. Holt Mackenzie was the author, was promulgated, the leading object of which was to combine the advantages of the Ryotwar System with that of village leases.

In 1827, by the Bombay Code of Regulations, the work of Mr. Mountstuart Elphinstone, a system was established, which, with subsequent modifications hereafter to be noticed, still exists.

In 1833, by Regulation IX. (under Lord William Bentinck) the Settlement of the North-West Provinces was further carried out, and in 1842 it was completed. In the working of this system native functionaries were largely employed. In the North-West Provinces, Madras, and Bombay, the offices of Collector and Magistrate were at this time united in the same person. In Bengal they were kept distinct.

In 1844, Sinde (in which territory a plan of collecting Land Revenue under military superintendence had been attempted by Sir C. Napier) was annexed to Bombay, and partly subjected to the same system with that Presidency.

In 1847, a system of thirty years' leases of "Fields" (the name given to so much land as one man and a pair of bullocks could cultivate) was established in part of the Bombay Presidency—the boundaries of the fields to be marked by stones—portions of the territory being also annually let for grazing grounds. Under this system the dealings of the Government were (on the Ryotwar plan) with the individual cultivators, and the fields were to be sold in default of payment.

In 1849, the Punjaub system of decennial contracts with the village communities for the Land Revenue was established by Lord Dalhousie.

In attempting to reduce into chronological order the various changes which have taken place in the Land Revenue System of India, the transitions from one district to another are necessarily so frequent and so rapid, that it is difficult to present the net result of these changes, and the system as it now stands, in an intelligible form. It will, nevertheless, be seen, that (notwithstanding the sub-divisional rights and titles brought under our notice in any historical survey of Indian territories, partly by the introduction of Middlemen,* or collectors of revenue for the Government, partly by the various nomenclatures adopted in different districts for the proprietary body)† the land tenures of India fall, in fact, under two great classes.

1. The Zemindary, where the ground is cultivated by tenants under a landlord standing between themselves and the Government—that landlord being

* These Middlemen of India are found under various designations as the Polygars and Mootadars of Madras; the Dessayes and Mozumdars of Guzerat; the Deshmooks of the Deccan and Bombay; the Talookdars of the Moguls, &c.

† Proprietors and Headmen are variously called Zemindars in Bengal and the North-West Provinces; Bhumyas in Rajpootana; Potails in Malwa, Guzerat, and the Deccan; Merrassidars in the Carnatic; Vellalers in the Southern Peninsula, and Patteedars in the Punjaub.

sometimes an hereditary chief, sometimes a mere district officer, sometimes a village corporation.

2. The Ryotwar, where, under all its various modifications, the cultivator and the proprietor are identical, and are brought into immediate tenant-relations to the Government.

The actually existing Land Revenue Systems in Bengal, the North-West Provinces, Madras, Bombay, and the Punjaub, are thus described in a Return recently made in pursuance of an order of the House of Commons :—*

Existing system in Bengal.

In the Lower Provinces of the Bengal Presidency, the land is held by Zemindars, on payment of an annual sum fixed in perpetuity in 1793 by Lord Cornwallis, the estates being liable to be sold in default of payment, under the provisions of Act 1 of 1845. The only land at the disposal of Government consists of estates which have been thus sold, and purchased on the public account. The rate of land tax is believed to amount, on the average, to about half the rental. Between the actual contractors of the soil in Bengal, and the Zemindar who pays the

* *Vide* Return, "Showing under what Tenures, and subject to what Land Tax, Lands are held in the several Presidencies of India."—*Parliamentary Paper*, 1857. 112.

Also, "A Selection of Papers illustrative of the Character and Results of the Revenue Surveys and Assessments, which have been introduced into the North-West Provinces and Bombay, since the Year 1833.—*Parliamentary Paper*, 1853. 999.

Also, "Papers relating to the Revised Survey and Assessment of the Madras Presidency."—1857. 51.

revenues to the Government there are several (sometimes three or four) intermediate renters or farmers.

Existing System in the North-West Provinces.

The system pursued in the North-West Provinces is briefly described in the following extract from the "Directions for Revenue Officers," promulgated under the authority of the late Lieutenant-Governor, Mr. Thomason.

First. All the inhabited part of the country is divided into portions with fixed boundaries, called Mehals or estates; on each Mehal a sum is assessed for the term of twenty or thirty years, calculated so as to leave a fair surplus profit over and above the net produce of the land; and for the punctual payment of that sum the land is held to be perpetually hypothecated to the Government.

Secondly. It is determined who are the person or persons entitled to receive this surplus profit. The right thus determined is declared to be heritable and transferable, and the persons entitled to it are considered the proprietors of the land, from whom the engagements for the annual payment of the sum assessed by the Government on the Mehal are taken.

Thirdly. All the proprietors of a Mehal are, severally and jointly, responsible in their persons and property for the payment of the sum assessed by the Government on the Mehal. When there are more proprietors than one, it is determined according to what rule they shall share the profits, or make good the losses on the estate. If the proprietors are numerous, engagements are only taken from a few of the body, who on their own parts, and as representatives of the rest, undertake to manage the Mehal, and to pay the sum assessed upon it.

The rate of assessment was in the first instance limited to two-thirds of the net produce* of each Mehal or estate, but, on the revision which is about to take place on the expiration of the thirty years which formed the first term of settlement, it has been determined to restrict the demand of the State to one-half of the average net assets.

In some districts, such as Goruckpore, the Deyrah Dhoon, and Kumaon, there are large tracts of land in which no private rights exist, and which are consequently at the abolute disposal of the Government. These are granted to applicants on favourable terms, such as those mentioned in the following Notification, which was issued in September, 1855:—

1. Grants of land for the tea cultivation in the Kumaon and Ghurwal districts of the Kumaon province, will be made on the following conditions, on application to the Senior Assistant Commissioner of the district.

2. Each grant will be of not less than 200 or more than 2000 acres; more than one grant may be taken by one person or company, on the applicants satisfying the local authorities, acting under the usual control in the Revenue department, of their possessing sufficient means and capital to undertake an extended cultivation and manufacture of tea.

3. One-fourth of the land in the grant will be given free from assessment in perpetuity, on fulfilment of the conditions below stated.

4. The term of first lease will be for twenty years; for the first four years the grant will be rent free; in the fifth year, one

* By net produce is meant the surplus which the estate may yield after deducting the expenses of cultivation, including the profits of stock and wages of labour.

anna per acre will be charged on three-fourths or the assessable portion of the grant; two annas per acre in the sixth year; three annas in the seventh year, and so on, one more anna being added in each year, till, in the last year, the maximum rate is reached of one rupee per acre. The full assessment on a grant of 2000 acres will thus not exceed 1500 rupees per annum.

5. The following are the prescribed conditions of clearance: At the close of the fifth year from the date of grant, a twentieth part of the assessable area; at the close of the fifteenth year, half of the assessable area; and at the close of the last year three-fourths of the assessable area is to be cleared and well stocked with tea plants.

6. In the twenty-first year, on the fulfilment of the above conditions, the proprietary right in the grant and the right of engagement with Government shall vest in the grantee, his heirs, executors or assignees, under the conditions generally applicable to the owners of estates in Kumaon; and the rate of assessment on the lands in the grant, in whatever manner cultivated, shall never exceed the average rate on grain crop lands in the same locality.

7. On failure of payment of the prescribed assessment in any year, or of any of the above conditions (the fact of which failure shall, after local inquiry, conducted by the Senior Assistant Commissioner, be finally determined by the Sudder Board of Revenue), the entire grant shall be liable to resumption at the discretion of the Government, with exception of the portion of the assessable area which may be *bonâ fide* under tea cultivation, and of a further portion of land which shall be allowed in perpetuity free of assessment to the extent of one-fourth of such cultivated area. The portions so exempted will remain in the possession of the grantee, subject to the usual rates and rules of assessment in the district.

8. Grantees shall be bound to erect boundary pillars at convenient points round the circuit of a grant within six months from its date; failing which, such pillars will be put up by the Government officers, and the cost thereof shall be recoverable from the grantee in the same manner as the regulated rate of assessment.

9. No claim to the right and interest in the grant on any

transfer by the original grantee, will be recognised as valid unless on registry of the name of the transferee in the office of the Senior Assistant Commissioner.

10. So long as Government establishments for the experimental growth and manufacture of tea shall be maintained in the Provinces, supplies of seeds and plants will be given gratis to grantees, on application to the Superintendent Botanical Gardens, North-Western Provinces, as far as may be in his power.

Existing System in Madras.

The tenures of land under the Madras Presidency are thus described in a Report recently received from that Government.

The Revenue Systems in force in the Madras Presidency are the Zemindary, Village joint rents, Ryotwar, Oolungoo.

The Zemindary System is also termed the Mootahdary,* the former designation being usually applied to old ancestral estates, and the latter to those created under the Regulations of 1802.

Under this system estates, of greater or less extent according to circumstances, are held by the proprietors direct from the Government, on payment of a fixed annual sum, or "peishcush." This payment was fixed on the creation of the estate by a calculation of its actual proceeds at the time, and for some years previously, a deduction, generally of from 33 to 15 per cent., being made therefrom to cover the expenses of management, and to constitute (with the future revenue of the whole of the culturable lands then waste), the emoluments of the Zemindar or proprietor.

* From *Mootah*, the name given to the subdivision of a district in the Northern Circars.

The Zemindary tenure prevails chiefly in the Northern Circars, though there are large proprietary estates in other districts, as Madura, Nellore, North Arcot, &c.

In the Village-renting System the villagers stand in the Zemindar's position, and jointly hold from the Government. The village is rented to the whole body, or a section of them, for a term of years, and they make their payments direct to Government, managing their affairs independently, and allotting the lands for cultivation among themselves.

Under the Ryotwar System every registered holder of land is recognised as its proprietor, and pays direct to Government. He is at liberty to sub-let his property, or to transfer it by gift, sale, or mortgage. He cannot be ejected by Government so long as he pays the fixed assessment, and has the option annually of increasing or diminishing his holding, or of entirely abandoning it. In unfavourable seasons remissions of assessment are granted for entire or partial loss of produce. The assessment is fixed in money, and does not vary from year to year, except in those cases where water is drawn from a Government source of irrigation to convert dry land into wet, or one into two-crop land, when an extra rent is paid to Government for the water so appropriated; nor is any addition made to the assessment for improvements effected at the Ryot's own expense. The Ryot, under this system, is virtually a proprietor on a simple and perfect title, and has all the benefits of a perpetual lease without its responsibilities, inasmuch as he can at any time throw up his lands, but cannot be ejected so long as he pays his dues; he receives assistance in difficult seasons, and is irresponsible for the payment of his neighbours.

The assessment is fixed on each field, and the mode in which this was done is as follows: a certain portion of the produce was first set aside from the gross produce as a joint contribution of the Ryot and Government for the pay of village officers, and the remainder divided in certain proportions, the share allotted to Government being commuted into money at the average value of the produce for a period of years antecedent to the settlement.

The "Annual Settlements" under Ryotwary are rendered necessary by the right accorded to the Ryot of diminishing or extending his cultivation from year to year. Their object is to determine how much of the assessment due on his holding the Ryot shall pay, and not to re-assess the land. In those cases where no change occurs in the Ryot's holding, a fresh Puttah or lease is not issued, and such parties are in no way affected by the annual settlement, which they are also not required to attend.

The greater portion of the Presidency is under Ryotwary.

The Oolungoo-renting System prevails only in Tanjore and Tinnevelly, and is not general in either; its peculiarity consists in the Government demand being dependent on the current price of grain. On the introduction of the system, a standard grain assessment was fixed on each village, and also a standard rate, according to which the grain demand was to be commuted into money; but it was, at the same time, arranged, that if current prices in any year rose more than 10 per cent. above the standard commutation rate, or fell more than 5 per cent. below it, the Government, and not the Ryot, was to receive the profit and to bear the loss. The profit up to 10 per cent. remains with the landowners, who also bear all loss by fall of price as far as 5 per cent. The advantages of the system are, that the Government participates with the Ryot in the benefit of high prices, while the latter is relieved from loss when prices are much depressed; its disadvantage consists in the difficulty that is experienced in obtaining accurate and fair returns of the current prices which are taken throughout the year.

Existing System in Bombay.

Under the Bombay Presidency, "the revenue management" may be described in general terms as "Ryotwary," implying that, as a general rule, the occupants of Government lands settle for their land revenue, or tax, with the Government officers direct, and not through a Middleman. It should be understood, however, that throughout the Presidency, instances not unfrequently occur in which the Government revenues of entire villages are settled for by individual superior holders, under various denominations, or by a co-partnery of superior holders; as instances of the former, the Khotee villages of the Konkan, and the Talookdaree* estates of Guzerat may

* So called from Talook, a proprietary estate, generally smaller than a Zemindary, but held on the same tenure.

be adduced, while the latter are exemplified in the Bhagdaree * and Neerwadaree tenures of the Broach and Kaira Collectorates.

In Sinde, not many years ago, the revenue throughout was collected in grain by actual division of the crop: the grain was then sold by reserved auction, at artificially high, and sometimes even at famine, prices by the Government, as the great grain dealers of the country. Great progress has been made in superseding this system by cash assessments, which have been already introduced into several districts of the province. In the Shirkarpore Collectorate generally, and in Larkhana particularly, the principle of cash-assessments has been successfully adopted.

A revision of assessment is now in progress throughout Bombay, by which the amount payable on each field is determined according to its quality, and the amount so fixed is not liable to alteration for a term of thirty years.

Existing System in the Punjaub

In the Punjaub one and the same man is usually absolute proprietor and generally the sole cultivator, though he may occasionally lease out a few fields to tenants. He is saddled with no rent. He has to provide for the cost of cultivation and for the Government demand; the rest of the produce he may devote to the maintenance of his family and the accumulation of his capital. But these men, while maintaining their individuality, do yet belong to Village Com-

* From *Bhagdar*, a sharer or partner.

munities. A village is not inhabited by a certain number of Ryots, each unconnected with the other, but by a number of persons of common descent, forming one large cousinhood, having their own headmen, accustomed to joint action and mutual support.

The British Government has from the first decided on levying the tax by money payments assessed for a term of years. The peasant proprietors compound with the State for a fixed period, such assessment and compounding being technically termed a Settlement. But the proprietors do not engage *individually* with the Government, but by *villages*. The brotherhood, through its headmen or representatives, undertakes to pay so much for so many years; and then, having done this, they divide the amount among themselves, assigning to each man his quota. Primarily each man cultivates and pays for himself, but ultimately he is responsible for his co-parceners and they for him; and they are bound together by a joint liability. The Punjaub System, therefore, is not Ryotwary, nor Zemindary; but the *Village System*. In the hills, and occasionally elsewhere, the Zemindary System, and near Mooltan, something approaching to the Ryotwary System, may be found. But the Village System is the prevalent one, especially in the most important districts.

The average rate of assessment per acre, per annum, in the Cis-Sutlej States is, in English money, 2*s*. 3½*d*.; in the Trans-Sutlej States, 3*s*. 11⅜*d*.; in the Upper Baree and Rechna Doabs, 2*s*. 9⅝*d*.; in the

Upper Chuch Doab, 2*s.* 3⅞*d.* It will be observed that the rate diminishes as the settlement progresses westward, the country being poorer; the same result will occur in the southern districts. It is estimated that a peasant proprietor cultivates, on an average, eight acres, and, at a mean rate of assessment, would pay 1*l.* 4*s.* per annum to the State. From searching and accurate inquiry in the Settlement Department, showing the exact yield and value per acre of every kind of crop, it has been ascertained that the Government demand does not exceed one-fifth of the gross value of the produce in rich tracts, and one-sixth, or one-eighth, in poor tracts.

Revenue-free Lands.

Large tracts of land in various parts of India are exempted from the payment of any Land Revenue.

These lands, known by various designations, but called generally Lakhiraj* lands, consist principally of those, the revenues of which were originally assigned by the Mogul Emperors to holders of offices in payment for their services, which lands are called Jaghires, or sometimes Maaffees.†

There is also another class of revenue-free lands, originally assigned either by the State, or by the Villages, or by opulent Mahommedans and Hindoos, for the keeping up of temples, shrines, and mosques, and for various other purposes, without any conditions. These Exempted Grants are called "*Inams,*"‡ and are subdivided into many classes.

* *Lakhiraj* signifies no tribute.

† *Maaffee* signifies forgiven, or remitted.

‡ *Inam* signifies a gift or benefaction.

There are also lands which have been the subjects of a permanent assessment, called Mocurreree* or Istamraree,* not liable under any circumstances to be increased.

The above-mentioned exemptions, which originated with the Native Governments which preceded us, have since been confirmed by the British authorities.

The amount of Land-Revenue actually received by the latest Government returns in each Collectorate in Bengal, the North-West Provinces, Madras, Bombay, the Punjaub, and in those Provinces of British India directly under the Governor-General in Council, which are for revenue purposes borne on the Bengal books, will be found in the statistical table appended to the revenue map which accompanies this volume.

Opium Revenue.

The Opium Tax, which forms the most considerable source of revenue in British India next to that derived from land, is levied in two forms :—

1. By an exclusive system of cultivation and sale carried on by the Government in Bengal.†

2. By a high export duty levied in Bombay on opium grown in the native States of Malwa and shipped from Bombay.

In Bengal the revenue from opium is realised by means of a Government monopoly. It is grown exclusively for the Government, under severe penalties for any infraction of the laws.

The cultivation of the poppy was prohibited in

* Both these words signify "established or agreed upon."

† Opium Farms are also established at Penang, Singapore, and Malacca.

Bengal by Regulation VI. of 1799, sect. 3, and in the North-West Provinces by Regulation XLI. of 1803, sect. 2.

The system now pursued in Bengal is as follows: Annual engagements are entered into by the Government with the Ryots in certain selected districts, to sow a certain quantity of land with the white poppy, under a system of pecuniary advances, the produce to be delivered in the form of opium to the Government at a fixed rate.

In the month of August contracts are entered into with the Ryots, and an advance of four rupees per beega (nearly two-thirds of an acre) granted by the Government. The sowings commence in November, when another advance is made of three rupees per beega. Again in January and February, when the crop arrives at maturity, a third advance of about three rupees per beega takes place to assist the cultivator in gathering the produce. The crop is collected by the end of March, when the poppy heads are cut or scratched with a sharp instrument, and a milky juice exudes, which becomes brown in colour and thick in consistency by exposure to the sun and air.

The opium in this crude form is delivered by the Ryots to the Agents of the Government, whose chief dépôts are at Ghazeepore and Patna for the Benares and Bahar Provinces respectively.

The opium is prepared by the Government Agents for the China market by rolling it into large balls covered with a coating of opium paste and poppy leaves, so as to exclude the air; it is then packed in chests—forty balls to a chest—and transferred to the Government warehouses in Calcutta, where it is put up to auction at the Government sales, of which there are four each season at intervals of a month, commencing with January. At these sales the opium sells at prices varying from 700 to 1600 rupees per chest containing 116 lbs. weight, and it is estimated that after deducting cost of production, charges of transport, and commission, a revenue is yielded to the Government by these sales of from 40*l.* to 120*l.* per chest. The merchants in India purchase the opium either on their own account or for mercantile houses in China, and it is then shipped for the Chinese coast or Hong Kong, in vessels capable of carrying from five hundred or one thousand chests.*

The total net receipts from the opium monopoly in Bengal amounted in 1856 to 2,767,136*l.*

A large additional revenue is derived from the transit of the opium of Malwa through the British territories to Bombay for exportation to China. Previous to the year 1831 the British Government reserved to itself, by separate treaties with the Native Princes of Central India, subsequently cancelled, a monopoly of the article, which was purchased by the British Resident at Indore, and sold by auction, either at Bombay or at Calcutta. But in that year it was deemed advisable, chiefly on account of the large quantity of opium smuggled to the Portuguese settlements of Demaun, &c., on the coast, to relinquish the

* *Vide* "What is the Opium Trade?" a pamphlet by Mr. Donald Matheson.

monopoly, to open the trade to the operations of private enterprise, and to substitute, as a source of revenue, in place of the abandoned system, the grant, at a specified rate, of passes to cover the transit of opium through the Company's territories to Bombay. In determining the amount of transit duty, it was proposed to be guided by a comparison of the cost of transit direct to Bombay, with that of the transmission of the drug to the coast by the cheapest of the more circuitous routes through the territories of Native States; and on the basis of such a comparison it was fixed at Rs. 175 per chest of 140 lbs. each. In 1835, the results of the preceding official year being unfavourable, the shipments of opium from Bombay having largely declined, while those from Demaun had greatly increased, the rate was reduced to Rs. 125 per chest.

The subjugation of Sinde afforded opportunity for the levy of a higher rate. Down to the period of that event, a large portion of the opium of Malwa had been conveyed through Sinde to Kurrachee, and thence onwards to the Portuguese ports of Diu and Demaun. That route was now closed, and it was reasonably expected that an advance might be made in the charge of passes, without risk of loss to the revenue from a diminished demand for them. The rate was accordingly increased, in October, 1843, from Rs. 125 to Rs. 200 per chest. Upon the principle that it was desirable to fix the price at the highest amount which could be levied, without forcing the trade into other channels, a further increase was made in 1845, when it was determined that the charge should be Rs. 300 per chest. On the same principle it was, in 1847, raised to Rs. 400 per chest.

It appears from recent returns, that from Pass Fees on Malwa opium exported through Bombay, a net revenue (after deducting all costs and charges) was received, in the financial year ending in the spring of 1856, of rather more than a million sterling.

The total gross revenues derived by the Government of India from this tax, in the two forms in which it is levied, amounted, by the last returns, to about four and a half millions sterling.

The Salt Tax has been, like the Land Revenue, inherited or instituted by the Government of British India from their predecessors in power. It was an ancient source of revenue to the Sovereigns of Asiatic countries. It was first applied by Warren Hastings, in 1773, to the payment of certain departments of the Civil Service.

Salt Revenue.

The Salt Tax now yields in India (exclusive of all Customs' duties on salt imported) about two and a half millions sterling, and is levied by different means in the different Presidencies.

All the salt produced in India, whether that obtained from the sea-water in Bengal by boiling, or in Madras and Bombay by a process of solar evaporation, or that obtained from the salt mines in the Punjaub, or from the salt lakes in Rajpootana, is subject to tax in one or other of the following forms.

In Bengal the Government have establishments for the manufacture of salt, the monopoly of which they retain in their own hands. It is manufactured by a system of advances to the Natives (about 100,000 of whom are thus employed in the Sunderbunds), and who, by contract, are bound to deliver at a fixed low price, all salt manufactured, which is sold by Government at public sales, at six principal agencies in Bengal. The price at which salt is sold, by the Government, is thus regulated. To the actual cost of producing the salt is added an amount equivalent to the duty levied on imported salt, which is now two and a half rupees per maund, or three farthings per lb., which makes the average retail price to the consumer about a penny per lb. The private manufacture of salt is permitted round Calcutta, subject to an excise of the same amount with the Customs' duty levied on imported salt. The system which has been adopted since 1837, in pursuance of the recommendations of a Select Committee of the House of Commons in the previous year, has been one of fixed prices, and open warehouses, at which the sales, instead of being as before periodical, are constantly going on. The duty on imported salt has been since three times reduced, and with such effect, that in 1853 half the salt consumed in Bengal appears to have been supplied from the port of Liverpool.

It is calculated that, taking the average annual consumption of salt, and the average earnings of the Bengal Ryots, the salt consumed by each absorbs about five days' wages per annum.

The salt agencies in Bengal are located along the head of the Bay; namely, at Hidgelee, Tumlook,

Chittagong, Arracan, Cuttack, Balasore, and Khoredah.

The supply of salt to the North-West Provinces is furnished partly from the Lower Provinces of Bengal, and partly from the Sambhur Salt Lake,* in Rajpootana, and other localities on the western side of India. The salt of Bengal, having paid the excise or import duty of Rs. 2 8a. per maund, passes free into the North-West Provinces. The Sambhur and other salt, on crossing the north-western frontier customs' line is subjected to a duty of two rupees per maund, and to a further duty of half a rupee † per maund, on transmission to the eastward of Allahabad, thus coming into competition with the salt of Bengal, under an equal duty of Rs. 2 8a. per maund.

At Madras salt is manufactured on account of Government, and sold for internal consumption at one rupee per maund, or under one farthing per lb. The duty on imported foreign salt was three rupees per maund, but it has been recommended by the home authorities that the import duty should (as in Bengal) be equal only to the difference between the selling price and the cost of manufacture; the difference between the cost price and the price at which

* The Sambhur Lake belongs to the native States of Joudpore and Jeypore.

† The Allahabad special duty was fixed by Act 14 of 1843 at one rupee per maund; but in 1847, and again in 1849, when reduction of duty on Bengal salt was effected, corresponding reductions were made in the Allahabad duty.

the salt is given out for consumption being the duty to be realised.

In Bombay the manufacture of salt is carried on by individuals, but subject to an excise duty of twelve annas (1*s.* 6*d.*) per maund, a similar duty being imposed on imported salt. In the Punjaub the salt-mines are worked by the Government. Salt is sold at the mines at two rupees per maund. Facilities are also afforded for the export of salt to Malabar, Travancore, Cochin, and other places.

Customs. The Customs' duties, which now amount to about two millions sterling per annum, are levied (not as formerly after the fashion of the native Indian States, in the shape of inland and transit tolls *), but under one generally uniform system throughout British India.

The Customs' duties now arise from two sources.

1. The Sea Customs on imports and exports—the latter chiefly on silk and indigo.

2. The Land Customs, levied on certain articles of produce passing the frontier lines between native States and British Territories.

Subsidies from Native States. The Revenues received from tributes and subsidies payable under existing treaties between the British Government and native States in India, amount, altogether, to about half a million sterling, per annum, as will appear from the following extract from the

* Transit or inland duties formerly levied at every town and on every road were abolished, in Bengal by Act 14, of 1836; in Bombay by Act 1, of 1838; and in Madras by Act 6, of 1844.

accounts of the territorial Revenues, for the year, ending in April, 1856.*

	£.	£.
BENGAL:		
Tributes from the under-mentioned States:		
Kotah	7,056	
Odeypore	18,516	
Mundy	9,375	
Jhalwar	7,500	
Banswarra	2,568	
Doongerpore	2,568	
Jeypore	37,500	
Serohee	1,269	
Various Petty States	4,320	
Nizam's Government on account of Mahratta Choute	10,133	
		100,805
MADRAS:		
Peishcush and Subsidy:		
Mysore Government	229,687	
Travancore ditto	74,666	
Cochin ditto	18,750	
		323,103
BOMBAY:		
Subsidy from the Cutch Government	15,795	
Kattywar Tribute	56,105	
Various Petty States	3,096	
		74,996
		£498,904

The remaining sources of Indian Revenue, not particularized above, are as follows.

Stamps, with reference to which it may be observed that in India stamped paper is required, not only as in England for bills of exchange, agreements, receipts and deeds, but for all judical proceedings, petitions, and papers of all kinds filed in Court. Stamps.

* The amount given in the estimate for 1857 under this head is 510,166*l*.

The gross Revenue derived from this source amounts to about half a million sterling, per annum.

Abkarree.

Another considerable item in Indian taxation is Abkarree,* the name given to the Revenue derived from the sale of monopolies to vend spirits. These licences are, in every large town or district, farmed yearly to the highest bidder, who sells his wares at his own price, but under Government regulations as to the position of his store and hours of business. From this Abkarree, and from another tax of the same nature on the (sale of certain drugs not strictly classed as spirits), and called Sayer,† a gross annual Revenue of about a million sterling, is obtained

The total residuary amount of the Indian Revenue is made up from the following various sources:—

Miscellaneous.

Post Office,‡ Mint, Marine, Pilotage, Judicial, Electric Telegraph receipts, and other miscellaneous items,§ adding altogether about a million sterling to the aggregate annual Revenue of British India, the gross amount of which (as estimated for the year, ending April 30, 1857) is 29,344,960*l.*

The detailed statistics of the income and expenditure of India are given fully in the accounts of the Territorial Revenues, annually laid before Parliament.

It may, however, be stated generally, that the chief items of expenditure of the Anglo-Indian Government,

* *Abkarree* signifies a tax on "waters."

† *Sayer* signifies the "remainder," or unclassified taxes.

‡ The postal rates are uniform throughout India from Cape Comorin to Peshawur. There is also a Book-post.

§ The Moturpha, a tax on shops, &c., was abolished in 1856.

on an average of four years, preceding the mutiny of 1857, have been, in round numbers, as follows:—

Charges incident to the Collection of the Revenue	about	£6,000,000 sterling.
Military and Naval Charges . .	"	11,000,000
Civil, Judicial, and Police	"	5,000,000
Public Works	"	1,500,000
Interest on Bond Debt in India .	"	2,000,000
Charges defrayed in England (including Interest on Home Bond Debt, Dividends to Proprietors of East India Stock,* Payments on account of Her Majesty's Troops, and Establishment.—Charges of the East India House and Board of Control	"	3,500,000
Allowances and Assignments to Native Princes under Treaties and other engagements . . .	"	1,000,000
Total about		£30,000,000 sterling.

In order to meet the exigencies from time to time arising from the excess of expenditure over revenue, two distinct modes of raising money in England and in India have been adopted by the Government.

In England the only mode in which money can be raised by the East India Company is by the process usually adopted by Corporations similarly circumstanced, namely, on bond. About one-fifth part of the debt now existing has been so contracted.

In India a different mode of borrowing money has been adopted by the Government, as follows.

When the Government wants money, it advertises

* Amounting in the last estimated Returns to 627,893*l*.

that the Treasury is open to receive money upon loan, at certain rates specified in the advertisement, and upon the conditions there contained. So long as the loan remains open, parties are admitted to make what payments they please, and to receive what are called loan notes in acknowledgment, and this to any amount. The money raised on loan is all raised in India.

The aggregate amount of the Indian Debt, as contracted in these two modes, is now about 60,000,000*l.* sterling.

In the accounts of the Territorial revenues of India for the four years preceding the mutiny of 1857, Bengal alone presents an uniform local deficit; the North-West Provinces alone an uniform local surplus.

The excess of expenditure over income on the estimate of the revenues, and charges of all the Presidencies and Provinces of British India, for the year ending April 30, 1857, is 1,981,062*l.*

CHAPTER VI.

ADMINISTRATION OF NATIVE STATES.

THE system of Government above described must be understood to apply to that portion only of British India, which is comprised within the Presidencies, and those Provinces which are directly subject to the Governor-General of India in Council.

The native States of India are not included in this system of administration; but are bound by treaties and engagements varying in their provisions, but generally entitling these States to British protection on the condition either of payment of tribute or providing a Military Contingent, except in those cases in which a commutation for other conditions has been arranged by cession of a portion of their territory to the British Government.

The stipulations contained in the various treaties are not uniform. The Rajah of Nepaul, for instance, though bound by the Treaty of 1815 to cede certain territories, undertook simply to accept British mediation in event of any differences arising between himself and the neighbouring Rajah of Sikkim.

In other cases again, as in that of the State of Mysore, and the smaller States of Kolapore, and Sawunt-Warree, engagements involving an absolute surrender of independence have been contracted, and the entire internal administration of these States has been assumed by the political agents of the British Government.

Subject to such exceptions, it may be stated generally, that the Native Princes of India are bound by their respective treaties to act in "subordinate co-operation" with the paramount power, some by maintaining a military force, others by the payment of a subsidy: and an article almost universally introduced into such treaties is one restraining the Native Contracting powers from the employment of Europeans or Americans, in their respective services.*

The relations of the British Government with the Native States of India are generally maintained through the medium of functionaries (who may be either civil or military officers), who are styled "Residents,"† and who are stationed at the metropolis of the State to which they are respectively delegated. The degree of interference actually exercised by the "Resident" in the internal affairs of each State (precluded, in some instances, by the terms of the treaties) depends, not so much on the instructions received from head-quarters, as on the personal energy and policy of each "Resident."

The Native States are, in their relations with the

* This stipulation arose probably from the circumstance that the Mahratta armies were at one time disciplined and commanded by French officers.

† The representative of the British Government in Mysore is called "Commissioner;" in Kolapore and Sawunt-Warree, "Political Agent."

British Government (with certain exceptions hereafter to be noticed), placed under the Supreme Authority of the Governor-General in Council, in whom the appointment of British Representatives at their several Courts is vested.

The aggregate military resources of all the Native Princes of India are estimated at about 400,000 troops, and their aggregate revenues at about thirteen millions sterling per annum. The obligations of these Native Princes to the British Government involve altogether a nominal military contingent of 32,000 troops, and an aggregate annual subsidy of about half-a-million sterling per annum.

The actually-subsisting relations between the Native States of India and the British Government will appear from the following summary :—

SUMMARY OF THE NATIVE STATES OF INDIA, AND OF THEIR RELATIONS WITH THE BRITISH GOVERNMENT.

	Residencies and Political Agencies.	Area in Sq. Miles.	Estimated Population.	Existing relations with the British Government.
The Nizam's dominions in the Deccan	Hyderabad.	95,337	10,666,080	Bound by treaty to maintain a contingent force.
Scindia's dominions in Central India	Gwalior.	33,119	3,228,512	Ditto, ditto.
Holkar's dominions in Central India	Indore.	8,318	815,164	Bound by treaty to furnish 1000 horse (not commanded by British Officers).
Bundelcund States (Central India)	...	7,404	824,000	Under various tributary and protective treaties.
Bhopal (Central India)	Sehore.	6,764	663,656	Bound to furnish a contingent force.
Mysore (Southern India)	Bangalore.	30,886	3,460,696	Mysore is administered by a Commissioner, two Assistants, and four Superintendents, exercising the powers of Judge, Magistrate, and Collector, at Bangalore, Ashtagram, Chitterdroog, and Nuggur, respectively. The Revenue, after defraying the expenses of the Commission, the Subsidy payable to the Company, and the fixed Stipend (one-fifth of the revenues) allotted to the Rajah, is appropriated to the purposes of the Mysore State.

Kolapore (Western India)......	Kolapore.	3,445	500,000	Under direct British management, similar to that of Mysore. Carried on through the Bombay Government.
Sawunt Warree (Western India)	...	800	12,000	
Travancore (Southern India)...	Trivandrum.	4,722	1,011,824	Under a Subsidiary Treaty. The management of Travancore and of Cochin is carried on through the Madras Government.
Cochin	Cochin.	1,938	288,176	
Gholeep Sing's dominions in Cashmere	...	60,000	3,000,000	Bound to pay tribute, but no returns.
Nepaul (Northern India)	Khatmandoo	54,500	1,940,000	Bound to accept British mediation in certain cases.
Bahawulpore (Northern India)	...	25,200	925,000	Under a protective treaty.
Bhurtpore (Northern India) ...	...	1,978	600,000	Ditto, ditto.
The Guicowar's dominions (North-Western India)	Baroda.	4,399	325,526	Bound by treaty to maintain a contingent.
Rajpoot States (North-Western India)	Aboo.	114,391	7,370,326	Jeysulmere and Alwar under protective—all the rest under Subsidiary Treaties.
Various States in Northern India—including Dholpore, Bhurtpore, Cis and Trans-Sutlej States, the Cuttack Mehals, and certain petty States contiguous to the Presidencies of Madras and Bombay	...	174,296	12,752,287	The Cuttack Mehals and Cis-Sutlej States, with few exceptions, are bound to pay tribute. The smaller States are, for the most part, simply entitled to British protection.
Total—Area and Population of Native States	...	627,910	48,376,247	

LIST OF TREATIES OR ENGAGEMENTS

BETWEEN THE BRITISH GOVERNMENT AND THE NATIVE PRINCES AND STATES OF ASIA, FROM THE EARLIEST PERIOD TO THE PRESENT TIME, ARRANGED CHRONOLOGICALLY.

1739, July 12th, Treaty with the Mahrattas.

1756, October 12th, Treaty with the Mahrattas.

1756, Treaty with the Prince of Cherrikal (Malabar).

1757, February 9th and 12th, Treaty and Agreement with Serajah Dowlah.

1757, March 31st, Perwannah from Serajah Dowlah.

1757, Treaty with Jaffier Ali Khan.

1757, Perwannah from Jaffier Ali Khan, for the Mint.

1757, Perwannah from Jaffier Ali Khan for Saltpetre of Behar.

1757, Sunnud from the Company's Zemindary, for lands given under the Seal of Allow-o-Dowlah, Meer Mahomed, Saddk Khan Bahadur Assud Jung, Dewan of the Sobah of Bengal.

1757, July 15th, General Sunnud from Jaffier Ali Khan.

1757, December 20th, Perwannah from Jaffier Ali Khan for the granted lands.

1758, Sunnud, for the free tenure of the town of Calcutta, &c., to the Hon'ble East India Company, given under the seal of the Nawab Allow-o-Dowlah, Meer Mahomed Saddk Khan Bahadur Assud Jung, Dewan of the Sobah of Bengal.

1758, Articles of the Firmaund granted by the Bringah Raja (Malabar), for granting to the Company the exclusive privilege of purchasing Pepper, &c., in his dominions.

1758, September 22nd, Perwannah, &c. from the Prince of Sinde, relative to the rate of Customs and Duties to be paid by the Company.

1759, March 4th, Articles of Agreement made with Meah Atchund, at Surat, for the confirmation of Faris Khan in the Naibship. Treaties with Native States.

1759, May 14th, Treaty with the Nizam for the Cession of Masulipatam to the Company.

1759, August 23rd, Articles of Agreement, offensive and defensive, relative to certain commercial arrangements with the King of Cotiote (Malabar).

1759, Perwannahs, &c., relating to Surat, &c.

1759, December 6th, Treaty and Accommodation and Ratification between the Dutch and English.

1760, August 23rd, Treaty between the Nawab Jaffier Ali Khan and the Dutch, guaranteed by the Governor and Council of Fort William.

1760, Sunnud under the seal of the Nawab Nusseer-ul-Mulk, Inteaz-o-Dowlah Nessaret Jung Meer Mahomed Cossim Ally Khan Behauder.

1760, December 24th, Firmaund from the Raja of Loundah (Malabar), for the purchase of Pepper in his country for one year.

1760, September 9th, Royal Grant of King Baddacalamcur, Regent of Colastria (Malabar), for the trade in Pepper, and agreement for the payment of certain debts.

1760, September 27th, Treaty between the Nawab Meer Mahomed Cossim Ally Khan and the Company, assigning to them the lands of Burdwan, Midnapore, and Chittagong.

1761, January 3rd, Articles of Agreement with Seiddee Hillol of Jinjerah, on the part of himself and the inhabitants of Jaffrabad, relative to commerce.

1761, April 22nd and 23rd, Three Perwannahs from the Prince of Sinde, relative to certain commercial privileges.

1761, September 14th, Articles of Agreement made with Seuram Punt Tatiah, in behalf of Madaroo Balajee, son of Balajee Badjeerow, of Poonah.

1761, December 30th, Articles of Agreement made with the King of Cartenadder (Malabar), for the purchase of Pepper in his country, and for mutual aid and assistance.

Treaties with Native States.

1763, April 12th, Articles of Agreement made with Shaik Saddoon, of Bushire, for the establishment of a Factory and other commercial privileges.

1763, May 27th, Articles of a Firmaund granted by the Nawab Hyder Ali Khan Bahadur, for the establishment of a Factory at Onore, and other privileges.

1763, July 2nd, Royal Grant from Kureem Khan of certain privileges of trade.

1763, July 10th, Articles of a Treaty and Agreement between the Governor and Council of Fort William on the part of the East India Company, and the Nawab Shujah-ul-Mulk, Hossain-o-Dowlah, Meer Mahomed Jaffier Khan Bahadur, on his restoration to the Sobahship.

1763, October 16th, Sunnud from the Nawab of Arcot, for the Seven Magans dependent upon the Soubah.

1764, September 16th, Nawab Meer Mahomed Jaffier Ali Khan's note for Rupees 500,000 per month, for the expenses of the army.

1764, November 22nd and December 6th, Proposals made and Articles executed by the Mogul, granting to the Company the Zemindary of Benares.

1765, February 20th, Articles of a Treaty and Agreement concluded between the Governor-in-Council of Fort William, on the part of the English East India Company, and the Nawab Nudjum-ul-Dowlah, on his accession.

1765, March 23rd, Agreement with the Prince of Cherrikal (Malabar), for the grant of the Province of Randoterrah to the Company.

1765, April 7th, Articles of Agreement of peace and friendship with the Boonshla, concluded at the Fort of Karee.

1765, August 12th, Firmaund from the King Shah Aulum granting the Dewannee of Bengal, Behar and Orissa to the Company.

1765, August 12th, Firmaund from the King Shah Aulum for the Dewannee of the Province of Bengal.

1765, August 12th, Firmaund from the King Shah Aulum for the Dewannee of the Province of Behar.

Treaties with Native States.

1765, August 12th, Firmaund from the King Shah Aulum for the Dewannee of the Province of Orissa.

1765, August 12th, Firmaund from the King Shah Aulum confirming the grants of Burdwan, and the rest of the Company's possessions in Bengal, to them.

1765, August 12th, Firmaund from the Mogul for the Northern Circars.

1765, August 12th, Firmaund from the Mogul, being a confirmation of the Nawab's grants to the Company in the Carnatic.

1765, August 16th, Treaty between the Nawab Shujah-ul-Dowlah, the Nawab Nudjum-ul-Dowlah, and the English Company, executed at Allahabad.

1765, August 19th, Articles of Agreement between the King Shah Aulum and the Company for the tribute of Bengal.

1765, August 28th and 30th, Grant from the Nawab of Arcot for the Company's Jaghire.

1765, September 30th, Agreement between the Nawab Nudjum-ul-Dowlah, and the Company for his stipend.

1765, Grants for Lord Clive's Jaghire and the Sunnuds for the reversion of the Jaghire to the Company.

1766, January 12th, Articles of Agreement made with the Ranee of Kattywar for the restoration of Fort Augustus and in regard to commerce.

1766, February 23rd, Grant from Hyder Ali Khan Bahadur of certain commercial privileges in Malabar.

1766, May 19th Articles of a Treaty and Agreement concluded between the Governor and Council of Fort William, on the part of the English East India Company, and the Nawab Syef-ul-Dowla on his accession.

1766, November 12th, Treaty with the Nizam for ceding to the Company the Northern Circars.

1768, February 23rd, Treaty of perpetual friendship and alliance with the Nawab of the Carnatic and the Sobah of the Deccan.

1768, November 29th, Treaty between the Company and the Vizier Shujah-ul-Dowlah, for the reduction of his army.

Treaties with Native States.

1769, April 3rd, Treaty of perpetual friendship and peace with Hyder Ali.

1770, March 21st, Articles of a treaty and agreement between the Governor and Council of Fort William, on the part of the English East India Company, and the Nawab Mobarek-ul-Dowlah, on his accession.

1770, August 8th, Treaty of peace with Hyder Ali.

1771, October 20th, Translation of a paper containing the articles agreed to by the Raja of Tanjore, for the discharge of the Peshcush.

1771, October 22nd, Agreement with the Nawab of Cambay for the eventual grant to the Company of a Factory at Gogo.

1771, Treaty with the Nawab of Cambay for the cession to him of the Fort of Tarrajah, taken from the Coolies.

1771, November 30th, Treaty of peace and friendship with the Nawab of Broach.

1772, Treaty with the Raja of Cooch Behar.

1773, January 12th, Treaty with Futteh Sing, for a participation of the Revenues of Broach.

1773, September 7th, Treaty of Subsidy with Shujah-ul-Dowlah.

1774, April, Articles of a treaty of peace with Deb Raja of Bootan.

1774, October, Treaty under the hands and seals of Nawab Shujah-ul-Dowlah Bahadur and Col. Champion.

1774, October, Treaty under the hands and seals of Fyzulah Khan and Col. Champion.

1775, March 6th, Treaty with Ragobah for placing him in the Peshwaship.

1775, May 21st, Proposed Articles of the Treaty with the Nawab Asuf-ul-Dowlah, for the cession of Benares to the Company.

1776, April 12th, Agreement with the Raja of Tanjore for subsidizing a body of the Company's troops for the protection of his country.

1776, April 15th, Sunnud granted to Raja Cheyt Sing for the Zemindary of Ghazeepore, Benares, &c.

Treaties with Native States.

1776, May, Treaty of peace between the Hon'ble the English East India Company and the Mahratta State.

1778, November 24th, Treaty with Ragobah for conducting him to Poonah, with a view of placing him in the Peshwaship.

1779, Convention of Wurgaon.

1779, April 27th, Treaty of alliance with Bazalet Jung, for renting the Guntoor Circar to the Company, and for receiving into his service a body of the Company's troops.

1779, December 2nd, Draft of a Treaty proposed between the Company and Maha Raja Luckindar Bahadur, Rana of Gohud.

1780, January 26th, Treaty of alliance and defence with Futteh Sing, Gwicowar, by General Goddard.

1780, January 26th, Treaty of alliance and defence with Futteh Sing, as amended and ratified by the Governor-General in Council.

1781, September 14th, Copy of the Pottah granted to Raja Mehipnarain Bahadur of Benares.

1781, September 19th, Agreement concluded by the Governor-General with the Vizier of Oudh, for the removal of the temporary Brigade.

1781, October 13th, Translation of a Copy of the Treaty entered into by Mobariz-ul-Mulk, Iftiker-ul-Dowlah, Colonel Muir, Behauder Mahabul Jung, on the part of the English East India Company, and the Maha Rajah Sahib Madhajee Rao Scindia Bahadur Sobahdar.

1782, May 17th, Treaty of Peace with the Mahrattas.

1784, March 11th, Treaty of perpetual peace and friendship with the Nawab Tippoo Sultan Bahadur.

1785, June, Preliminary Treaty and Agreement with the Nawab Mahomed Ali, for his proportion of the charges for the defence of the Carnatic.

1786, Agreement with the King of Queda for the cession of Prince of Wales' Island.

1787, February 24th, Treaty with the Nawab Mahomed Ali, for settling his proportion of the expences for the

Treaties with Native States.

protection of the Carnatic and for the adjustment of his private debts.

1787, April 10th, Treaty with the Rajah of Tanjore for settling his proportion of contribution towards the defence of his country, and for adjusting his private debts.

1787, April 15th, Treaty with Asuf-ul-Dowlah, Nawab of Oudh, fixing the whole of his payments at 50 lacs of rupees.

1788, August 12th, Agreement with the Raja of Travancore for two battalions to be stationed within his dominions.

1788, September 1st, Treaty of Commerce with the Nawab Asuf-ul-Dowlah.

1788, September 18th, Translation of the Nizam's Order to Seyf Jung, for the surrender of the Guntoor Circar to the Company, delivered to Captain Kennaway, the Resident at the Nizam's Durbar.

1789, July 7th, Copy of a letter from Earl Cornwallis to the Nizam deemed equal to a Treaty, being preliminary to that of 1790, June 5.

1790, June 5th, Treaty of Alliance between the Company, the Peshwa, and the Nizam, against Tippoo Sultan.

1791, February 2nd, Treaty of Alliance with the Raja of Cochin.

1791, May 1st, Treaty with the King of Queda for an annual quit-rent for Prince of Wales' Island.

1792, February 22nd, Preliminary Treaty with Tippoo Sultan.

1792, March 18th, Definitive Treaty with ditto.

1792, March 1st, Treaty of Commerce with Raja of Nepal.

1792, July 12th, Treaty with the Nawab Mahomed Ali, with a modification of the Treaty of 24th February, 1787, assigning certain districts as securities for payment of sums stipulated.

1793, January 28th, Agreement with the Raja of Travancore, commonly called the Pepper contract.

1793, February 28th, Commercial agreement with the Raja of Assam.

1794, June 12th, Agreement between Commodore Mitchell and Johannes Seberg, Councillor and Director of Batavia, for furnishing and equipping a vessel as a cartel ship to Mauritius.

Treaties with Native States.

1794, December 13th, Treaty with the Nawab Asuf-ul-Dowlah and the chief of the Rohillas, with Appendix.

1795-6, Captain Syme's Commercial Arrangement with the King of Ava.

1797, March 20th, Agreement with the Nawab Vizier Asuf-ul-Dowlah, for the pay of an additional regiment of cavalry.

1797, April 9th, Paper of Declarations for the management of Furrakabad.

1797, May 18th, Treaty with the Raja of Travancore, as originally proposed by the Government of Bombay, and afterwards amended, and finally concluded and ratified by the Governor-General of India in Council.

1798, February 7th, Engagement executed by the Nawab Saadut Ali Khan to the Bow Begum (mother of the late Nawab Asuf-ul-Dowlah), under the guarantee of the Company.

1798, February 21st, Treaty of Alliance and Subsidy between the Nawab Vizier Saadut Ali Khan Bahadur and the Hon'ble East India Company.

1798, September 1st, Treaty of Alliance, Defence, and Subsidy, with the Nizam, and for the dismission of the French troops from his service, and the reception of a body of British troops in lieu of them, with two separate articles.

1798, October 12th, Treaty with the Imaum of Muscat.

1799, June 22nd, Partition Treaty of Mysore for strengthening the alliance and friendship subsisting between the Company, the Nizam, and the Peshwa, and for effecting a settlement of the dominions of Tippoo Sultan.

1799, July 8th, Subsidizing Treaty with the Raja of Mysore.

1799, October 25th, Treaty with the Raja of Tanjore for transferring the sovereignty of his country to the Company.

1800, January 18th, Treaty of Friendship with the Imaum of Muscat.

1800, May 13th, Treaty with the Nawab of Surat for the cession of the City of Surat and the circumjacent country to the Company.

Treaties with Native States.

1800, August 26, Articles of Agreement for the adjustment of the Desh Cavelly and Talem Cavelly of the province of Tinnevelly.

1800, October 12th, Treaty of Alliance and Defence with the Nizam, and for the cession of territory in commutation of subsidy.

1801, January, Political Treaty with the King of Persia.

1801, January, Commercial Treaty with ditto.

1801, July 31st, Treaty with Azeem-ul-Dowlah for settling the succession to the Sobahdarry, and for vesting the administration of the Civil and Military Government of the Carnatic in the Company.

1801, October 30th, Treaty of Alliance with the Raja of Nepal.

1801, November 10th, Treaty with the Nawab Vizier Saadut Ali for ceding to the Company in perpetual sovereignty certain portions of His Excellency's territorial possessions in commutation of Subsidy.

1802, February 15th, Final arrangement with the Nawab Vizier Saadut Ali Khan.

1802, March, Articles of Convention between General Duncan and Rowjee Appajee, for and on behalf of Anund Rao Gwicowar Senakasskell Shumshere Bahadur, for the security of the dominion and government of the Gwicowar in Guzerat.

1802, April 12th, Commercial Treaty with the Nizam.

1802, July 6th, Treaty of Alliance and Subsidy with Anund Rao Gwicowar.

1802, July 24th, Treaty with the Nawab of Furruckabad for ceding to the Company, in perpetual sovereignty, the Province of Furruckabad and its dependencies, in commutation of Tribute.

1802, July 29th, Agreement concluded between the Resident at Baroda and Anund Rao Gwicowar.

1802, November, Treaty with the King of Queda for cession of territory on the coast of Queda.

1802, December 31st, Treaty of Alliance and Subsidy with the Peshwa, commonly called the Treaty of Bassein.

1803, January 25th, Agreement with Anund Rao Gwicowar, supplementary to the Treaties of March and June, 1802.

1803, August 14th, Treaty with Amrut Rao of Poonah. Treaties with Native States.

1803, August 24th, Instrument under the signature of the Governor General in Council, delivered to the Nizam (Secunder Jah) on his accession to the Musnud, recognising all the former treaties and engagements with Nizam Ali, deceased.

1803, September 4th, Agreement with Raja Himnut Bahadur.

1803, September 29th, Treaty of Alliance and Friendship with the Raja of Bhurtpore.

1803, November 14th, Treaty of Alliance and Friendship with the Raja Macherry.

1803, November 14th, Treaty with the Raja of Lunaward in Guzerat, declaratory of his allegiance to the Company.

1803, December 12th, Treaty of Amity and Alliance with the Raja of Gyepore (or Gyenagur).

1803, December 15th, Treaty with the Raja of Soonth in Guzerat, declaratory of his allegiance to the Company.

1803, December 16th, Treaty of Amity and Alliance with Raja Umbajee Rao (Gwalior and Gohud).

1803, December 16th, Supplementary Article to the Treaty of Bassein.

1803, December 17th, Treaty of Peace and Friendship with the Raja of Berar, commonly called the Treaty of Deogaum.

1803, December 22nd, Treaty of Amity and Alliance with the Raja of Joudhpore.

1803, December 29th, Supplementary Treaty with the Rajah of Mysore, for adjusting an exchange of certain districts, dated 29th December, 1803, with reference to the 15th Article of the Treaty of Mysore, concluded in 1799.

1803, December, Treaty of Peace and Friendship with Dowlut Rao Scindia.

1804, January 9th, Additional Article to the Treaty with the Nizam, of 12th October, 1800.

1804, January 17th, Treaty of Amity and Alliance with the Rana of Gohud.

1804, February 6th, Treaty with the Sobahdar of Jhansi.

1804, February 27th, Treaty of Alliance and mutual Defence with Dowlut Rao Scindia.

Treaties with Native States.

1804, March 15th, Treaty concluded with Rao Raja Pareecheet of Dutteea.

1804, April 28th, Partition Treaty of Hydrabad with his Highness the Sobahdar of the Deccan.

1804, May 14th, Partition Treaty of Poona with his Highness the Peshwa.

1804, July 17th, Political Treaty with Raja of Colapore.

1804, July 17th, Maritime Treaty with ditto.

1804, September 2nd, Ikrar-namah, or obligation of allegiance and fidelity executed on the part of Maha Raja Beekrumajeet, Bajee Bahader, Raja of Chukary.

1804, September 2nd, Sunnud granted to ditto.

1804, November 25th, Treaty with the Raja of Pertaubgurh declaratory of his allegiance to the Company.

1805, January 12th, Treaty of Friendship and Alliance with the Raja of Travancore.

1805, April 17th, Treaty of Amity and Alliance with the Raja of Bhurtpore.

1805, April 21st, Definitive Treaty with Anund Rao Gwicowar, in confirmation of former Treaties, and for augmentation of the Subsidiary Force.

1805, August 21st, Engagement on the part of Zeiboo Nissa Begum of Sirdanah.

1805, November 22nd, Definitive Treaty of Amity and Alliance with Dowlut Rao Scindia.

1805, December 24th, Treaty of Peace and Amity with Jeswant Rao Holkar.

1805, Treaty of Friendship and Amity with Sirdars Runjeet Sing of Lahore, and Futteh Sing, Allowallah.

1806, January 10th, Treaty with the Rana of Gohud, for the relinquishment to the Company of the Country and Fort of Gohud and others, and for the investiture of the Rana in the sovereignty of the districts of Dholepore, Baree, and Bajkera.

1806, February 6th, Agreement made with Shaik Abdoolla Bin Croosh on the part of the Joasmee Chiefs.

1806, March 1st, Sunnud granted to Raja Nerender Gier.

1806, April 1st, Agreement entered into by the Agents of Bhunga Sing.

1806. April 4th, Ikrar-nameh, or obligation of allegiance presented by, and Sunnud granted to Kooar Soonee Sah. Treaties with Native States.

1806, May 4th, Sunnud granted to Assud-oo-Dowlah Nujabut Ali Khan Bahadur.

1806, May 4th, Sunnud granted to Abdool Mahomed Khan.

1806, May 13th, Perwannah granted to Ahmud Buksh Khan Bahadur.

1806, July 25th, Sunnuds granted to the Officers and Chiefs of Raja Ragojee Bhooslah, to whom pensions were assigned.

1806, August 24th, Engagement with the Raja of Berar for the restitution of the Provinces of Sumbulpore and Patna by the British Government to the Raja.

1806, October 23rd, Treaty with the Rana of Calpee.

1806, November 22nd, Ikrar-nameh, or obligation of allegiance from Chobee Deriao Sing, Killadar of Calinger.

1806, December 9th, Ikrar-nameh, or obligation of allegiance from Duchmun Sing, Killadar of Adjyghur.

1807, January 10th, Political Treaty with the King of Persia.

1807, January 10th, Commercial Treaty with ditto.

1807, January 29th, Articles explanatory of the third article of the Treaty of Mysore, concluded in 1799.

1807, February 1st, Sunnud granted to Maharajah Kishore Sing.

1807, February 4th, Ikrar-namah, or obligation of Allegiance on the part of Marajah Kishore Sing, written 28th January.

1807, June 8th, Ikrar-nameh, or obligation of Allegiance, presented by, and Sunnud granted to Rajah Bukht Sing.

1807, June 21st, Ikrar-nameh, or obligation of Allegiance, presented by, and Sunnud granted to Rajah Mohun Sing.

1807, July 4th, Ikrar-nameh, or obligation of Allegiance, presented by, and Sunnud granted to Gopaul Lall.

1807, September 19th, Ikrar-nameh, or obligation of Allegiance, presented by, and Sunnud granted to Koar Luchmon Sing.

1807, September 22nd, Ikrar-nameh, or obligation of Allegiance, presented by, and Sunnud granted to Dewan Aperbul Sing and Dewan Chuthary.

1807, October 7th, Ikrar-nameh, or obligation of Allegiance, presented by, and Sunnud granted to Purseram.

Treaties with Native States.

1807, November 29th, Ikrar-nameh, or obligation of Allegiance, presented by, and Sunnud granted to Raja Ram.

1808, December 1807, January 1808, Agreements with the piratical Mahrattas.

1808, February 1st, Ikrar-nameh, or obligation of Allegiance, presented by, and Sunnud granted to Purtaub Sing.

1808, December 9th, Ikrar-nameh, or obligation of Allegiance, presented by, and Sunnud granted to, Dewan Deeraj Sing.

1809, March 11th, Ikrar-nameh, or obligation of Allegiance, presented by Laul Shew, Raja of Cucheerah and Nagode.

1809, March 12th, Treaty with the King of Persia.

1809, March 20th, Sunnud granted to Laul Shew, Raja of Cucheerah and Nagode.

1809, April 25th, Treaty of Alliance with the Raja of Lahore.

1809, May 3rd, Ittila-nameh, addressed to the Chiefs of the Country of Sirhind, on this side of the river Sutledge.

1809, May 6th, Treaty of perpetual Friendship and Subsidy with the Raja of Cochin.

1809, June 17th, Treaty of Alliance and Friendship with the King of Cabool.

1809, July 16th, Ikrar-nameh, or obligation of Allegiance, presented by Laul Amaun Sing, of Souhawal and Rygown.

1809, July 18th, Sunnud granted to Laul Amaun Sing.

1809, August 22nd, Promissory Agreement with the Ameers of Sinde.

1809, August 23rd, Ikrar-nameh, or obligation of Allegiance, from Dewan Joogul Purshaud.

1809, August 25th, Sunnud granted to Dewan Joogul Purshaud

1809, October 28th, Engagement with Dewan Hansraj of Mandavie.

1809, Agreement with Futteh Mahomed of Cutch.

1810, August 16th, Ikrar-nameh, or obligation of Allegiance, from Laul Doonierputt.

Treaties with Native States.

1810, August 17th, Sunnud granted to Laul Doonierputt

1811, January 7th, Sunnud granted to Dewan Jooggul Purshaud.

1811, March 22nd, Ikrar-nameh, or obligation of Allegiance, from Raja Kishore Sing, Bahader Raja of Punna.

1811, March 22nd, Sunnud granted to Raja Kishore Sing, Bahader Raja of Punna.

1811, March 25th, Sunnud granted to Raja Bajee, Bahader Raja of Churkary.

1811, March 26th, Ikrar-nameh, or obligation of Allegiance, from Raja Ruttun Sing, Raja of Bijawar.

1811, March 27th, Sunnud granted to Raja Ruttun Sing, Raja of Bijawar.

1811, July 16th, Engagement with the Raja of Macherry.

1811, August 22nd, Sunnud granted to Chiefs of the Country of Malwa and Sirhind, on this side of the river Sutlege.

1812, January 14th, Treaty with the Vizier of Oudh.

1812, February 24th, Sunnud granted to Dewan Gopaul Sing.

1812, March 14th, Treaty with the King of Persia.

1812, June 19th, Ikrar-nameh, or obligation of Allegiance, from Chobey Derrao Sing, late Killadar of Calinger.

1812, July 4th, Sunnud granted to Chobey Derrao Sing, late Killadar of Calinger.

1812, June 19th, Ikrar-nameh, or obligation of Allegiance, from Nawal Kishwur and the relic of Bherit Jew Chobey.

1812, Sunnud granted to Nawal Keshwur and the relic of Bherit Jew Chobey.

1812, June 19th, Ikrar-nameh, or obligation of Allegiance, from Chobey Chittersaul, and the mother of Chobey Chittersaul.

1812, July 4th, Sunnud granted to Chobey Chittersaul, and the Mother of Chobey Chittersâul.

1812, June 19th, Ikrar-nameh, or obligation of Allegiance, from Gya Purshaud Chobey.

1812, July 4th, Sunnud granted to Gya Purshaud Chobey.

1812, June 19th, Ikrar-nameh, or obligation of Allegiance, from Poker Purshaud Chobey.

Treaties with Native States.

1812, July 4th, Sunnud granted to Poker Purshaud Chobey.

1812, June 19th, Ikrar-nameh, or obligation of Allegiance, from Chobey Salagram.

1812, July 4th, Sunnud granted to Chobey Salagram.

1812, July 4th, Ikrar-nameh, or obligation of Allegiance, from Gopaul Lall.

1812, July 4th, Sunnud granted to Gopaul Lall.

1812, July 4th, Sunnud granted to Thakoor Doorjun Sing.

1812, October 1st, Agreement with the Raja of Colapore.

1812, October 3rd, Agreement with Raja Pond Sawunt Boonshla Bahadur, Dessye of Sawant Warree.

1812, October 5th, Treaty of Friendship and defensive alliance with the Raja Rewah and Mookundpore.

1812, December 23rd, Treaty of Friendship and Defensive Alliance with the Raja of Oorcha or Tehree.

1813, June 2nd, Second Treaty with the Raja of Rewah and Mookundpore with a supplemental Article.

1813, Engagement with the Raja of Rewah's son, binding himself to abide by the Treaties concluded with his father.

1814, March 11th, Third Treaty with the Raja of Rewah and Mookundpore, under the seals and signatures of the Raja and his son.

1814, July 12th, Engagement with the Vizier of Oudh.

1814, August 3rd, Counterpart of engagement with the Vizier of Oudh by the British Government.

1814, November 25th, Treaty with the King of Persia.

1815, March 6th, Sunnud granted to Raja Maha Chund, of Belaspore.

1815, September 3rd, 4th, and 21st, Sunnuds granted to Rana Juggut Sing, of Baghal, to Rana Bhoop Sing, of Koobhar; same date, to Rooder Paul, of Boojye; September 4th, 1815, to Sunsaroo Thakoor, same date; to Mann Chund, of Boojye, same date; to Roy Mungree Deo, same date; to Thakoor Jugrah, September 21st, 1815.

1815, September 21st, Sunnud granted to Raja Futteh Sing of Nahan.

1815, October 20th, Sunnud granted to Raja Ram Sing (or Ram Surrun) for Hindore Hindoreea.

Treaties with Native States.

1815, October 20th, Sunnud granted to Raja Ram Sing, (or Ram Surrun), for Burrowlee.

1815, October 20th, Sunnud granted to Raja Kurrum Sing, of Putteala, for Pergunnah Mahalee, &c.

1815, October 20th, Sunnud granted to Raja Kurrum Sing, for Bugghaut and Juggutgurh.

1815, November 6th, Sunnud granted to Mehendra, Sing, of Bussahir.

1815, December 2nd, Treaty and Peace with the Raja of Nepal.

1816, January 16th, Treaty of alliance with Rao Bharmuljee, of Cutch, with a supplemental article.

1816, March 4th, Ikrar-nameh, or obligation of Allegiance, executed on the part of the Rajah of Nepal.

1816, May 1st, Treaty with the Vizier of Oudh.

1816, May 27th, Treaty of defensive alliance with the Raja of Berar.

1816, June 18th, Treaty with the Rao of Cutch, supplemental to that of the 16th January, 1816.

1817, January 11th, Sunnud granted to Purtaub Sing.

1817, January 11th, Sunnud granted to Nawab Kishore.

1817, January 11th, Sunnud granted to the widow of Bhurtjoo Chobey.

1817, February 10th, Treaty with the Raja of Siccim.

1817, April 7th, Sunnud granted to the Raja of Siccim.

1817, April 11th, Sunnud granted to Subadar Major Hoolas Pundit.

1817, June 13th, Treaty with the Peshwa.

1817, November 1st, Engagement with Nana Govind Rao, of Calpee.

1817, November 5th, Treaty with Dowlut Rao Scindia.

1817, November 6th, Supplement to the Definitive Treaty with the Gwicowar.

1817, November 9th, Treaty with the Raja of Kerowlee.

1817, November 9th, Engagement with Nawab Ameer Khan.

1817, November 12th, Engagement with the Raja of Sumpthur.

1817, November 17th, Treaty with the Sobahdar of Jhansi.

1817, November 21st, Sunnud granted to the widow of Gooroo Giyraj Misser.

Treaties with Native States.

1817, December 26th, Treaty with the Raja of Kotah.

1818, January 6th, Treaty with Mulhar Rao Holkar.

1818, January 6th, Treaty with the Raja of Joudhpore.

1818, January 6th, Provisional Treaty with the Rajah of Berar.

1818, January 13th, Treaty with the Rana of Oudeypore.

1818, February 10th, Treaty with the Raja of Boondee.

1818, February 20th, Supplementary Article to the Treaty with the Raja of Kotah dated December 26th, 1817.

1818, February 26th, Treaty with the Nawab of Bhopal.

1818, March 9th, Treaty with the Raja of Bickaneer.

1818, March 26th, Treaty with the Raja of Kishenghur.

1818, April 2nd, Treaty with the Raja of Jyepore.

1818, July 25th, Engagement with Dowlut Rao Scindia.

1818, July 31st, Treaty with the Raja of Dutteeah.

1818, September 16th, Treaty with the Raja of Banswarra.

1818, September 16th, Supplementary Article to the Treaty with the Raja of Banswarra.

1818, October 5th, Treaty with the Raja of Dowleah and Purtaubghur.

1818, November 28th, Additional Article to the Supplementary Treaty with the Gwicowar.

1818, November 28th, Sunnud granted to Sujahut Khan.

1818, November 28th, Sunnud granted to Naumdhar Khan.

1818, December 11th, Treaty with the Raja of Doongerpore.

1818, December 12th, Treaty with the Raja of Jessulmere.

1818, December 12th, Treaty with the Petty Chiefs of Dewass.

1818, December 25th, Treaty with the Raja of Banswarra.

1819, January 10th, Treaty with the Raja of Dhar.

1819, Ikrar-nameh, or obligation of Allegiance from Ramchunder Buller.

1819, Sunnud granted to Ramchunder Buller, for villages in the district of Saugor.

1819, February 17th, Treaty with the Regency of Sawant Warree.

1819, April 22nd, Treaty with the King of Acheen.

1819, July 16th, Sunnud granted to Hurbullub Pundit.

1819, July 31st, Sunnud granted to Narain Pundit.

1819, July 31st, Sunnud granted to Nawab Saduk Ali Khan.

1819, August 13th, Sunnud granted to Kurreem Khan.

Treaties with Native States.

1819, August 13th, Sunnud granted to Khandee Buksh.

1819, September 25th, Treaty with the Raja of Satara.

1819, September 25th, Sunnud granted to Maha Rao Omeed Sing of Kotah.

1819, October 13th, Treaty with the Cutch Government.

1820, January 8th, Treaty with the Arab Tribes.

1820, January 8th, Preliminary Treaty with Hassan Bin Ramah.

1820, January 9th, Preliminary Treaty with Sultan Bin Sugger.

1820, January 9th, Preliminary Treaty with the Sheikh of Dubey.

1820, January 11th, Preliminary Treaty with Sheikh Shakhbool Bin Dyab, of Abon Dyabee.

1820, January 15th, Preliminary Treaty with Hassan Bin Ali.

1820, February 6th, Engagement with Dowlut Rao Scindia.

1820, February 14th, Sunnud granted to Raja Ayoon Sing of Sah Gurh.

1820, February 14th, Sunnud granted to Raja Surmeet Sing of Ramnugger.

1820, February 17th, Treaty with the Regency of Sawunt Warree.

1820, March 4th, Sunnud granted to the Raja of Gurhwal.

1820, April 3rd, Sunnud granted to Takoor Zorawur Sing, of Hindoreea.

1820, April 15th, Sunnud granted to Sreedhur Pundit.

1820, May 20th, Sunnud granted to Raja Sunker Sah, of Ajnee.

1820, November 9th, Treaty with the Ameers of Sinde.

1821, January 15th, Treaty with the Imaum of Senna.

1821, January 15th, Sunnud granted to Bhugwant Sing Sobahdar.

1821, March 14th, Sunnud granted to Raja Maharag Sahy, Raja of Sumbulpore.

1821, June 16th, Sunnud granted to Rana Govind Rao Sobahdar Major.

1821, December 18th, Treaty with the Raja of Dhar.

1822, May 21st, Treaty with the Government of Cutch.

1822, July, Treaty with the Raghojee Angria of Colaba.

1822, August 29th, Treaty with the Imaum of Muscat.

Treaties with Native States.

1822, December 12th, Treaty with the Nizam.

1823, February 11th, Agreement from Maha Rawul Sree Bhunwannee Sing, Rawul, of Banswarra.

1823, April 11th, Sunnuds conferred on the Husht Bhayeh Jageerdars, viz. to Rao Bahadur Bukut Sing of Chirgaong, Dewan Soorjun Sing of Bijna, Dewan Boodh Sing of Dhoorwye, Rooard Hurpersand of Foree, Dewan Bunka Esurree Sing of Puharee.

1823, Treaty with Rao Sheo Sing, Regent of Serohee, ratified 31st October, 1823.

1823, November 21st, Sunnud granted to Veetul Rao. Mulhar, Poorundary.

1823, November 21st, Sunnud granted to the widow of the late Madoo Rao Bhoskutta.

1823, December 9th, Agreement with Raja Pertaubghur.

1824, March 6th, Treaty with Raja Govind Chunder of Cachar.

1824, March 10th, Treaty with Raja Ram Sing of Jyntheea.

1824, April 20th, Sunnud granted to Raja Ghunsham Sing.

1824, August 2nd, Treaty with the Sultan and Tumongong of Johore.

1825, July 31st, Provisional Treaty with the King of Siam.

1825, August 17th, Agreement with the King of Oudh.

1825, December 30th, Agreement with the Raja of Colapore.

1826, February 24th, Treaty of Peace with the King of Ava, with additional article.

1826, June 20th, Political and Commercial Treaties with the King of Siam.

1826, November 23rd, Commercial Treaty with the King of Ava.

1826, November 30th, Agreement with Teerut Sing Acheembee, called the White Raja, Chief of Nungklow.

1826, December 1st, Treaty with the Raja of Nagpore.

1827, February 6th, Agreement with the Sheik of the Tribes of Hubberawal.

1827, October 23rd, Agreement with the Raja of Colapore.

1828, March 10th, Bond from His Royal Highness, the Prince Royal of Persia, annulling the 3rd and 4th articles of the Treaty dated 25th November, 1814.

Treaties with Native States.

1828, May 2nd, Sunnud granted to Teiz ool Khan Bungush.
Sunnud granted to Nubbee Buksh Khan, and Hyder Buksh Khan.

1828, August 22nd, Sunnud granted to Wolly Mahomed Sobahdar Major.

1829, May 1st, Treaty with the King of Oudh.

1829, July 15th, Agreement with the Raja of Colapore.

1829, September 25th, Sunnud granted to Khadim Hossein Khan, and Mahomed Hossein Khan.

1829, December 25th, Revised engagement with the Raja of Nagpore.

1831, September 20th, Engagement with the Nizam.

1832, April 4th, Treaty with the Government of Khyrpore.

1832, April 20th, Treaty with the Government of Hyderabad in Sinde.

1832, April 22nd, Supplementary Article to ditto.

1832, September 20th, Treaty with the Government of Cutch.

1832, December 26th, Indus Toll Treaty with Maharaja Runjeet Sing of Lahore.
Supplementary Article to ditto.

1833, February 22nd, Indus Toll Treaty with the Nawab of Bahawulpore.
Supplementary Article to ditto.

1833, March 2nd, Treaty with Raja Poorunder Sing.

1833, March 12th, Treaty between Maharajah Runjeet Sing and Shah Shoojah-ool-Moolk.

1833, June 21st, Agreement with the King of Oudh, concerning the deposit of 3 lacs of rupees for the poor of Lucknow.
Modified Treaty with the Raja of Mysore.

1834, July 2nd, Treaty with the Government of Hyderabad.

1834, July 5th, Treaty with the Government of Cutch.

1834, July 31st, Agreement with Deb Raja on the restoration of Dooar Booree Gooma.

1834, October 18th, Indus Toll Treaty with the Ameers of Sinde.

1834, November 3rd, Agreement with Toola Ram Seenaputty.
Articles proposed to be substituted for Articles 3rd, 4th, and 6th of the definitive Treaty with Persia.

Treaties with Native States.

1834, November 22nd, Proclamation by Government on Female Infanticide.

1835, January 24th, Supplementary Treaty with Maharajah Runjeet Sing, for abolishing a Toll on the Indus.

1835, March 5th, Supplementary Treaty with the Nawab of Buhawulpoor.

1835, December 7th, Engagement with the Raja of Joudhpore.

1836, January 18th, Bhownuggur, Engagements entered into by the Thakoor of Bhownuggur, exempting from Payment of Duty, Vessels putting into his Ports through stress of Weather.

1836, February 6th, Proclamation by the Ruo of Kutch, prohibiting Slave Trade.

1836, February 18th, Mahee and Rewa Kunta. Paper addressed to Acting Political Agent, by Maharaj Rithee Singjee Kururnsingjee.

1836, May 7th, King of Persia's Firman for British subjects trading with Persia.

1836, November 28th, Commercial Treaty with the Ameers of Sinde.

1837, September 11th, Treaty with the King of Oudh.

1838, January 3rd, Engagements by the Nawab of Joonaghur for the Suppression of Suttee.

1838, January 7th, Engagement by the Seedee of Jafferabad for the Suppression of Suttee.

1838, January 23rd, Preliminary Engagement with Sultan McHassan of Lahij, for the Transfer of Aden to the British Government.

1838, April 8th, Treaty with the Raja Rana of Jhullawur, when that State was formed into a separate Principality out of the Koto Territory.

1838, April 8th, Treaty with the Raj Rana Mudun Sing of Kotah.

1838, April 10th, Treaty with Maha Rao Ram Sing of Kotah.

1838, April 17th, Agreement with the Chief of Ras-ool-Khymah, for the Suppression of Slavery.

1838, June 26th, Tripartite Treaty between Shah Sooja ool Moolk of Cabool, Maha Raja Runjeet Singh of Lahore, and the English East India Company.

Treaties with Native States.

1838, April 20th, Treaty with the Ameers of Sind.

1838, September 15th, Agreement with the Sudesaee.

1838, October 5th, Treaty with the Nawab of Bahawulpore.

1838, December 24th, Treaty with His Highness Meer Roostum Khan of Khyrpoor.

1839, July 3rd, Agreement for the Suppression of Slavery in the Persian Gulf.

1839, February 2nd, Engagement with the Sultan of Lahij, on behalf of himself and the Abdallees.

1839, February 4th, Further Engagement with the Sultan of Lahij.

1839, May 31st, Commercial Treaty with the Imam of Muscat.

1839, June 18th, Bond of Peace and Friendship, entered into by the Sultan of Lahij.

1839, January 31st, Engagement with the Huzzabee Tribe.

1839, February 2nd, Engagement with the Chief of Wakeel, and all under him.

1839, February 4th, Engagement of Peace and Friendship with the Chiefs of Hagrabees.

1839, February 18th, Engagement entered into between Shaikh Iwas Bin Sallaam el Abbadee and his Tribe.

1839, February 18th, Engagement with Shaikh Maidee.

1839, February 18th, Engagement with Shaikh of Zaidee.

1839, February 29th, Engagements with the Shaikhs of the Muswadie Territory of the Subees.

1839, February 20th, Engagement of Peace and Friendship with Shaikh Mahomet Bin Alee Busalee, of the Southern Division of the Subees.

1839, February 21st, Engagement of Friendship and Peace, with Shaikh Arsel Bin Hydee Bin Ahmed Musaidee, of a District of the Yaffaaes.

1839, March 10th, Treaty with Shah Kannan of Herat.

1839, March 10th, Engagement of Friendship and Peace, with Asun Bin Yorsoof Shirzebee.

1839, March 11th, Treaty with the Ameers of Scinde.

1839, September 4th, Treaty with the Raja of Satara.

1839, September 30th, Treaty with the King of Cabool.

1839, December 17th, Additional Articles to Treaty, with the Imaum of Muscat for the Suppression of Slavery.

Treaties with Native States.

1839, September 23rd, Proclamation by the Raja of Sattara, against Suttee.

1839, September 23rd, Proclamation by the Raja of Sattara abolishing Transit Duties.

1839, February 3rd, Agreement with Punt Sucheo.

1839, March 11th, Treaty with the Ameers of Hyderabad.

1840, April 13th, Proclamation by the Gwickwar, abolishing Suttee.

1840, June 23rd, Agreement subscribed to by Meea Pretum Singh, of Koomharsain.

1840, September 8, Agreement with the Chief of Bhownuggur for relinquishing Land and Sea Customs.

1840, March 23rd, Renewed Engagement with Jhareja Chiefs for the suppression of Infanticide.

1840, April 16th, Egagement with the Chief of Soonawara.

1840, April 28th, Engagement with the Raja of Baria against Suttee.

1840, April 8th, Engagement by the Chief of Bhadurwa against Suttee.

1840, April 22nd, Engagement by the Chief of Chota Oodapoor against Suttee.

1840, May 9th, Engagement by the Raja of Rajpeepla against Suttee.

1840, May 12th, Engagement by Ranee Bhowanee Singjee of Soauth, against Suttee.

1840, May 8th, Engagement by Thakoor Sirdar Sing of Wankaneer, against Suttee.

1840, August 21st, Agreement entered into by Nawab Mohamed Syeed Khan.

1841, October 6th, Treaty with Meer Nusseer Khan, Chief of Kelat.

1841, March 11th, Proclamation by the Raja Kolhapoor, prohibiting Suttee.

1841, June 18th, Treaty between the British Government and the Ameer of Meerpoor, Meer Cher Mahomed Khan.

1842, August 13th, Proclamation by the Raja of Rajpeepla, against Suttee.

1843, June 1st, Maritime Truce for Ten Years from 1st June, 1843, by Arab Chiefs.

1843, February 11th, Engagement with the Sultan of Lahij. Treaties with Native States.

1843, September 11th, Agreement regarding the Levy of Duties of Merchandise in Transit through the Buhawulpoor Territory.

1844, February 20th, Further Bond entered into by the Sultan of Lahij.

1844, October 31st, Rules by His Highness the Gwickwar exempting Vessels trading between Bombay and Sind, forced into his Ports by stress of weather, from Payment of Duty at these Ports.

1844, November 8th, Treaty with the Sultan of Johanna for the Suppression of the Slave Trade.

1845, October 2nd, Further Agreement with the Imaum of Muscat for the Suppression of Slavery.

1846, March 19th, Engagement by His Highness the Nawab of Joonaghur, relative to the Customs on Vessels.

1846, March 22nd, Engagement by His Highness Jam Runmulgee of Nowanuggur, relative to the Customs on Vessels.

1846, March 9th, Treaty with the State of Lahore.

1846, March 11th, Agreement with the Lahore Durbar.

1846, March 16th, Treaty with Maharajah Golab Sing.

1846, December 16th, Agreement with the Lahore Durbar.

1846, April, Rules by the Imaum of Muscat regarding Duties to be charged on Cargoes of Vessels putting into his Highness's Ports.

1847, April 30th, with Shaik Sultan Bin Suggur, Chief of Ras-ool Kymah and Shurgah. Agreements for the Abolition of the African Slave Trade.

1847, April 30th, with Shaikh Muktoom, of Debaye.

1847, May 1st, with Shaikh Abdool Azeez, of Ejman.

1847, May 1st, with Shaikh Abdoollah Bin Rashid, of Amulgavine.

1847, May 3rd, with Shaikh Saud Bin Tohnoon, of Aboothabee.

1847, May 8th, Shaikh Mahomed Bin Khuleefa, of Bahrein.

1848, June 12th, Firmans by the Shah of Persia for the Suppression of the Slave Trade by Sea.

1849, May 22nd, Engagement with the Chief of Sohar for abolishing Slave Trade.

Treaties with Native States.

1849, May 7th, Final Treaty with the Sultan of Lahej.

1849, December 20th, Engagement by the Thakoor of Bhownuggur, relating to Customs on Vessels.

1849, March 29th, Terms granted to Maharajah Dulup Sing.

1850, June 3rd, Treaty of Friendship and Commerce with the Sultan of Johanna.

1851, October 8th, Rules by the Rao of Kutch, exempting, under certain circumstances, Vessels belonging to the Ports of Bombay from Payment of Duties on Goods.

1851, October, Agreement with the Persian Government for suppression of Slavery.

1853, February 22nd, Treaty of Friendship and Alliance with the Nawab of Buhawulpoor.

1853, May 4th, Perpetual Treaty of Peace, by Chiefs of the Arabian Coast.

1853, August 15th, Agreement with the Chiefs of Pahlunpoor for the Suppression of Infanticide.

1853, May 14th, Treaty with Meer Nusseer Khan, Chief of the Kelat.

1853, May 21st, Treaty with the Nizam.

1855, February 10th, Treaty with the Raja of Nepaul respecting the mutual surrender of Criminals.

1857, March 4th, Treaty of Peace between Her Majesty the Queen, and the Shah of Persia.

CHAPTER VII.

EXISTING GOVERNMENT INSTITUTIONS AND PUBLIC WORKS IN BRITISH INDIA.

SECT. I.—EDUCATIONAL INSTITUTIONS. SECT. II.—PUBLIC WORKS—CANALS—ROADS—RAILWAYS—TELEGRAPHS. SECT. III.—LIST OF GOVERNMENT MEASURES ADOPTED TO PROMOTE THE CULTURE OF COTTON. SECT. IV.—MEASURES ADOPTED TO PROMOTE THE WORKING OF IRON ORES.

SECT. I.—EDUCATIONAL INSTITUTIONS.

THE existing system of Government education in India is as follows:— Education.

There are Directors of Public Instruction in Bengal, the North-West Provinces, Madras, Bombay, and the Punjaub respectively, and under them are Inspectors and Sub-Inspectors of different grades, in numbers proportioned to the territories to be superintended.

There are three Universities constituted under Acts of the Legislature of India at Calcutta,* Madras,* and Bombay. These Institutions were (by a dispatch of the Court of Directors, dated July 19, 1854), directed to be framed on the model of the University of London, and empowered to grant degrees to all who should

* *Vide* Acts of the Indian Government, Nos. 2 and 27 of 1857.

Education. produce certificates from certain affiliated Institutions, comprising all the principal Colleges and Schools in India, as to a previous course of study.

The functions of these Presidency Universities are thus defined in the dispatch above alluded to:—

"The Universities in India will consist of a Chancellor, Vice-chancellor, and Fellows, who will constitute a Senate. The Senates will have the management of the funds of the Universities and frame regulations, under which periodical examinations may be held in the different branches of art and science by examiners selected from their own body, or nominated by them.

The function of the Universities will be to confer degrees upon such persons as having been entered as candidates according to the rules which may be fixed in this respect, and having produced from any of the "affiliated Institutions," which will be enumerated on the foundation of the Universities, or be from time to time added to them by Government, certificates of conduct, and of having pursued a regular course of study for a given time, shall have also passed at the Universities such an examination as may be required of them.

The examination for degrees will not include any subjects connected with religious belief; and the affiliated Institutions will be under the management of persons of every variety of religious persuasion. As in England, various Institutions in immediate connection with the Church of England, the Presbyterian College at Caermarthen, the Roman Catholic College at Oscott, the Wesleyan College at Sheffield, the Baptist College at Bristol, are among the Institutions from which the University of London is empowered to receive certificates for degrees;—so in India, Institutions conducted by all denominations of Christians, Hindoos, Mahommedans, Parsees, Sikhs, Bhuddists, Janis, or any other religious persuasions, may be affiliated to the Universities, if they are found to afford the requisite course of study, and can be depended upon for the certificates of conduct which will be required."

With respect to all existing vernacular and Anglo-vernacular Schools throughout India, whether established by individuals or societies, they are entitled, on certain prescribed conditions to grants in aid, on proof of attainment to a prescribed standard of secular instruction. Education.

Among the schools entitled under existing Government regulations, to grants in aid, are those established at various periods by Christian Missionary Societies.

The total number of these schools scattered throughout the various districts of India, including vernacular and English elementary schools, both for boys and girls, was in 1853, 1657 schools, containing 64,806 scholars of both sexes, as will appear from the following statistical table :—

Presidencies.	Boys' Schools.						Girls' Schools.			
	Vernac.		Boarding.		English.		Day.		Boarding.	
	Schools.	Boys.	Schools.	Boys.	Schools.	Boys.	Schools.	Girls.	Schools.	Girls.
Bengal .	140	6470	22	790	22	6005	24	669	29	830
North-W. Provinces	61	3707	10	191	22	1754	10	242	10	175
Bombay .	70	3480	2	21	7	1144	37	1222	6	101
Madras .	849	24,445	52	1165	41	4286	191	6639	52	1470
Total	1120	38,102	86	2167	92	13,189	262	8772	97	2576

These schools have been chiefly established by the

Education. twelve following Societies,* placed in the order of the commencement of their respective operations in India :—

1727. The Society for the Propagation of the Gospel.
1793. The Baptist Missionary Society.
1805. The London Missionary Society.
1812. The American Board of Missions.
1814. The Wesleyan Missionary Society.
1815. The Church Missionary Society.
1822. The General Baptist Missions.
1830. { The Established Church of Scotland. The Free Church of Scotland. The Basle Missionary Society. }
1834. The American Presbyterian Mission.
1840. The American Baptist Mission.

Bengal. The chief existing higher Government Educational Institutions in Bengal, which it is the object of the present system to affiliate to the University at Calcutta, are the following :—

1. The Madrissa, or Mahommedan College, at Calcutta, founded by Warren Hastings in 1782, for the study of Arabic and Persian (English having been since included). This institution contained in 1854, 314 pupils, all Mahommedans. The Hindoo College organized by a Native Committee for giving an English education to Hindoos in 1816, in which the pupils are taught Law, Medicine, and Civil Engineering;

* It appears that the total number of Missionaries employed by these twelve Societies in 1853 was 383, and the total number of native Christians returned as belonging to their various communions was 94,145.—*Vide* "Revised Statistics of Indian Missions," reprinted from the Calcutta *Christian Observer*, 1853.

the Sanskrit College at Calcutta, and which has also an English department. This College was founded in 1823, and contained, in 1854, 386 pupils, all Hindoos. There is also a Medical College and Hospital with ten classes at Calcutta. There are also Government Anglo-Vernacular Colleges at Hoogly, Dacca, Kishaghur, and Berhampore. Education.

There are other Collegiate Institutions in Bengal, some of which have been hitherto unconnected with, and unaided by, the Government, which it is the object of the present system to affiliate with the University, or Presidency College. Among these are the Oriental Seminary, conducted by East Indians, the Bishop's College, the General Assembly's Institution, Dr. Duff's College, and the Baptist College of Serampore.

North-West Provinces

In the North-West Provinces, there are Government Colleges at Delhi and Agra, and at Benares a Sanskrit College, established in 1792. The Vernacular Schools in the North-West Provinces, first established by Mr. Thomason in 1843, and now brought within the scope of the grants in aid, amounted, in 1856, according to the statement of Lord Dalhousie, to 3669 in number. Hospitals and Dispensaries were also established in the North-West Provinces by Mr. Thomason. In the Civil Dispensaries, Medicines and Instruments are provided and Salaries paid by the Government. In Bengal there are now fourteen, and in the North-West Provinces thirty-six, Dispensaries.

Bombay.

In Bombay, the two chief Government Educational Institutions, which it is proposed to affiliate to the

Education. University to be established in that Presidency, are the Elphinstone College at Bombay, and the College at Poonah.

There are also about 235 Vernacular and Anglo-Vernacular Schools in that Presidency.

Madras. In the Presidency of Madras, there were said to be, in Sir Thomas Munro's time, 733 Schools and Colleges, containing 3750 Students, mostly Brahmins.

There are also in the Presidency of Madras thirty Government Civil Dispensaries, on the same footing with those above alluded to in Bengal.*

SECT. II.—PUBLIC WORKS EXECUTED BY THE GOVERNMENT IN BRITISH INDIA.

Canals and Irrigation Works. The portions of Canals and Irrigation Works actually completed, are as follows:—

Ganges Canal.—449½ miles of the Ganges Canal were completed in April, 1856.

E. and W. Jumna Canals.—445 miles of the W. Jumna Canal are completed.

Punjaub Canals.—425 miles of the Baree-Doab Canal in the Punjaub, were executed in May, 1856.

Madras Irrigation Works.—Tanks, reservoirs, and "annicuts," or dams, across the beds of the Cauvery, Godavery, and Kistna Rivers.†

---

* It appears from Parliamentary returns that the total amount expended in aid of Native Education in India in 1853 was about 100,000*l.* sterling.

† *Vide* Memorandum of Public Works, &c., completed by the Government of India during the last thirty years.

The principal Trunk Roads in India now completed, are as follow:— Trunk Roads.

	Miles.		Cost.
From Calcutta to Peshawur	1,423	. . .	£1,423,000
„ Calcutta to Bombay .	1,002	. .	500,000
„ Madras to Bangalore	200	. .	37,121
„ Bombay to Agra . .	734	. .	243,676
„ Rangoon to Prome .	200	. .	160,000

The portions of Railroads in India now completed, under Government-guarantees are as follow:— Railroads.

	Miles.
From Calcutta to Burdwan	120
„ Bombay* to Wassind	50
„ Bombay to Campoolie	10
„ Madras to Vellore	81

The Electric Telegraphs now completed in India comprise about 4000 miles of telegraphic wire, namely:— Electric Telegraphs.

From Calcutta to Peshawur.
„ Agra to Bombay.
„ Bombay to Madras.

Other lines are in course of construction.

* Of the Great Indian Peninsular Railway two branches have been commenced—the North-Eastern to Mirzapore, the South-Eastern to Madras. Thirty-three miles of these two Railways, viz. from Bombay to Callianee, are on the same line.

SECT. III.—MEASURES ADOPTED AT DIFFERENT PERIODS BY THE GOVERNMENT TO PROMOTE THE CULTIVATION OF COTTON IN INDIA, CHRONOLOGICALLY ARRANGED.*

Cotton.

1788. The Court of Directors called the attention of the Indian Government to the cultivation of cotton in India, "with a view to affording every encouragement to its growth and improvement." 500,000 lbs. weight of cotton are ordered to be sent. Reports are called for from the Collectors of districts.

1789. Screws for compressing cotton are at this time established, both by the Company and by individuals.

1790. Cotton (422,207 lbs.) received from India. Ahmood cotton-seed directed to be sent to Bengal. Reports of culture at Bombay, Benares, and Dacca received; also from Collectors of Bengal and Behar. Dr. Anderson employed in distributing cotton-seeds, from the Mauritius and from Malta, throughout the Peninsula of India.

1794. A machine sent out for cleaning cotton from seed, and other impurities.

1797. A plantation, under Mr. M. Brown, established at Randatarra in Malabar, chiefly for spices; but Mauritius and Nankeen cottons were grown in 1801, and the produce sent to this country.

1799. Nagpore cotton-seed directed to be tried in the Circars, and a bounty offered to growers.

1802–3. Reports received on the cotton trade of Bombay and of the Gangetic Doab.

1809. Cotton ordered from India. 30,000,000 lbs. received in the following year.

---

* Extracted from "The Culture and Commerce of Cotton in India," by Dr. Forbes Royle. 1850.—See also "Essay on the Productive Provinces of India," 1840; and "The Fibrous Plants of India," 1855, by the same Author.—See also a Paper read before the Society of Arts in London by J. B. Smith, Esq., M.P., May 13, 1857.

1810. Samples of Georgian and Grenada cottons sent out, also seeds of West Indian and of American cottons. Directions sent out for the culture of cotton, prepared by Mr. R. Hunt and by the African Society. Cotton.

1811. Bourbon seed procured, and distributed to Collectors of Surat and Broach, with directions for cultivation.

1813. Mr. B. Metcalfe, a cleaner of cotton from Georgia and New Orleans, sent to Tinnevelly, with saw-gins. Mr. Bruce directed to send cotton-seed from Persia to India. Seed from Bourbon and Seychelles Islands procured.

1814. Two or three hundred bales of the best and cleanest *Toomil* cotton directed to be sent annually.

1816. Collector at Caranga cultivates Bourbon cotton there. Drawback allowed "of the whole internal and sea duties" on cotton exported to Great Britain. Two improved gins sent to Bombay, one for cleaning black-seed, the other for green-seed cotton.

1817. Mr. Assistant-Surgeon Gilder succeeds in cultivating Bourbon cotton at Kaira. Cotton culture attempted in Circars by Commercial Residents. The Court suggest that, in addition to Caranja and Salsette, Malwan should be tried.

1818. Satisfactory report from Malwan, Pernambuco seed asked for. Mr. Hughes successfully cultivates Bourbon cotton at Tinnevelly. Mr. Heath, having obtained instructions from Mr. Hughes, succeeds in Coimbatore. Memoir from Mr. Randall, Commercial Resident in Ceded Districts, proposing rewards for growing Brazil cotton in districts of Madras Presidency. Four cotton farms of 400 acres directed to be established at Tinnevelly, Coimbatore, Masulipatam, and Vizigapatam.

1819. Considerable success by Mr. Heath in Coimbatore. The cotton approved of in England, and 500 bales of 300 lbs. each, sent to China, and sold there.

1823. Barbadoes and Brazil cotton grown at Tittyghur, near Barrackpore.

1828. Attention again called to the subject of cotton culture by Lord Ellenborough, President of the Board of Control, "in different and distant parts of India;" also in a Paper by one of the Directors, H. St. George Tucker, Esq.

1829. The Court direct attention to the growth of new and

Cotton. better species; sent out machines for cleaning cotton; sent out seeds of Upland Georgia and of New Orleans Cotton; also Sea Island, Pernambuco and Demarara Cotton Seed, with accounts of methods of cultivation;—five of Whitney's saw-gins sent out to India, with twelve more made up in England, and metallic work for twelve sets to be made up in India.—A quantity of Surat Cotton (500 bales) also ordered to be sent, of the best quality and well cleaned.—Rewards to be offered both to Ryots and to Wakarias for clean picking, and cleaning.—The Agricultural Society of India had an allowance of 1000*l.* a year, exclusive of rents, until 1833, to attempt the culture of cotton.—20,000 rupees allowed for premiums for cotton and tobacco.

Dec. 31. Bombay Government report establishing a farm in Guzerat under Mr. Finney, another in Dharwar, &c., under Dr. Lush, another in Salsette. Land offered for cultivation of Cotton.

1830. Upland Georgia, Sea Island, Demarara, and other seed, also saw-gins received at Calcutta.—300 bales of Toomil Cotton sent, and 25 bales from Broach Farm.

1831. Partial success at Cotton farm established at Akra, near Calcutta.

1832. The Court direct that land appropriated to the growth of Cotton should not (as theretofore) be subject to a higher assessment.—3000 to 4000 bales ordered to be sent, if procurable, at 115 rupees per candy.—Disposal of Cotton grown in the experimental farm of Guzerat for 152 to 156 rupees per candy.

1833. Reports from Collectors of Caddapah, Guntoor, Arcot, Salem and Coimbatore Farms, subsidiary to that at Danda in Guzerat, established, to be cultivated by Ryots. Farms established at Segee Hullee in Bedare District under Dr. Lush. White-seeded perennial, also the Pernambuco and Egyptian succeeded.—Agency for the purchase of Cotton from Natives who had been instructed in picking it clean.—Screws and packing-sheds at Dharwar, Noulgond, and Gudduch. Natives had the option of paying their rents in kind, or receiving a remunerating price. Foreign Cotton-seeds also tried in Dharwar, Poona, and the Concan.

1834. Egyptian Cotton-seed and Egyptian cleaning machine applied for and supplied.

1836. Report of the proceedings of the East India Company in regard to the production of cotton wool, published. Cotton.

1839. The Court of Directors first propose to procure planters from America, with a view to further experiments. Minute by Lord Auckland on this subject, with reports from Madras and Bombay, giving an account of the results of former experiments, as well as proposals for the present one.

1840. Mr. Elphinstone, Collector of Rutnagerry, succeeds in cultivating Sea-Island and Bourbon cotton.

Captain Bayles returns with ten planters from Cotton States of North America, bringing with him seeds and saw-gins, ploughs and hoes, with model of a gin-house. A hand saw-gin, prepared in Liverpool, where experiments are made, and three planters are sent to Broach, in Bombay.

1841. Three Planters sent to Madras, first stationed at Tinnevelly, then at Coimbatore. Four planters sent to Calcutta, and stationed in the Doab and Bundelcund. Dr. Burns appointed to the charge of the experiments in Broach.

1842. An Engineer sent to each of the three Presidencies, to repair and put up machinery. Mr. Shaw and Mr. Hadow, Collectors, cultivate New Orleans and Bourbon cotton, in Dharwar. Mr. Mercer is stationed at Dharwar. Mr. Finnie explores the North-West for suitable sites.

1843. Unsuccessful experiments in Gorruckpore, and at Agra, by Mr. Blount and Mr. Finnie. Successful trial of New Orleans cotton by Mr. Wroughton, Collector of Coimbatore.

1845. Messrs. Simpson and Blount appointed to conduct experiments in Candeish. Cotton Committee appointed at Bombay.

1847. Mr. Landon appointed to carry on experiments in Broach.

(November.) Court of Directors order the following six queries to be sent out and circulated among the Collectors in the Presidencies, and the Political Agents in such Native States as are known to produce cotton.*

1. What is the price of cotton, freed from seed, at the principal mart or marts in your district?

---

* For replies to several of these queries, *vide* Report presented to the Board of Trade by Dr. Forbes Royle. in 1857.

Cotton. 2. At what prices does the Ryot sell his cotton, cleaned or uncleaned, and with or without advances?

3. What is the expense of cleaning cotton by the churka, or foot roller, or by any other method which may be in use?

4. What are the expenses of conveying cotton to the nearest port for shipment?

5. What is the average produce of cotton per beegah, or acre?

6. What is the quantity of land under cultivation with cotton, and to what extent is it probable that the cultivation could be carried in the event of an increased demand?

1848. Mr. Blount, having returned from America, is engaged to take charge of the culture in Dharwar.

1849. Mr. Simpson is engaged to prosecute the experiments in Candeish,

200 cottage saw-gins, prepared under the superintendence of the Manchester Commercial Association and of Mr. Petrie, sent by the Court of Directors to the three Presidencies. Seeds and saws sent at various times during these experiments.

1850. The Indian Government offers, through the Agricultural Society of India, a reward of 5000 rupees for an improved cotton-cleaning machine.

SECT. IV.—MEASURES ADOPTED BY THE GOVERNMENT TO PROMOTE THE WORKING OF IRON ORES IN INDIA.

1850. In a Dispatch dated December 11, relating to the introduction of railways into India, the Court of Directors called the attention of the Government to the manufacture of iron in Bengal, pointing out several localities as most eligible for carrying on those works.

In the same year the Court addressed a Dispatch to the Government of Madras, calling attention to the subject of iron works within that Presidency.

The Madras Government observed, in reply, that the various reports for seventeen years on the affairs of the Porto Novo Iron Company, would have put the Court in possession of the means and operations of that Company, which were then manufacturing superior ores at Beypoor. It was added, that additional capital alone was wanting to develope the resources of the Presidency as regards iron, the locations of which were stated to have been sufficiently shown in the correspondence which had taken place relating to the collection of specimens for the Great Exhibition. Iron Ores.

Subsequently an arrangement was concluded with "The Indian Iron Company," the leading feature of which was the grant of fresh leases for thirty years to a new Company of the districts held on lease by the Old Iron Company, such leases to contain provisions for securing the due working of the iron ores on an enlarged scale.

In the same year the Court directed the institution of inquiries with regard to the capabilities of Western India, as regards the production of iron.

The reports received in reply show that iron ore exists in many parts of the Presidency of Bombay, and that in those districts iron is manufactured to a small extent by the natives for their own use. In consequence, however, of the general scarcity of fuel, and the wasteful manner in which the process of smelting is conducted, the iron imported from England seems to have the advantage both as regards quality and price. With reference to the iron of Belgaum, Professor Oldham observes, "the absence of economical fuel and the scattered mode of occurrence of the ores appear to be abundantly sufficient to preclude the profitable extraction of the metal."

1853. Mr. Jacob, and afterwards Professor Oldham, were deputed to examine reports upon the mineral resources of the valley of the Nerbudda.

1854. (The existence of iron mines in the Province of Kumaon having been long known) Lieutenant-Colonel Drummond of the Bengal Establishment was deputed to this Province to carry on the investigations necessary to satisfy the British public that sufficient inducement existed for the investment of capital in iron works in India. Colonel Drummond entered on his duties on the 18th October, 1854, and continued his researches for a period of about seven months. His inquiries appear to have been principally directed to the Bhabur district of Kumaon, and the results may be briefly summed up as follows:—

Iron Ores. In order to obviate the necessity of carriage through a mountainous country, it became an object of importance to trace the existence of iron as near the plains as possible, and Colonel Drummond's first inquiries were consequently directed to the tract of country at the foot of the hills. At Dechouree the most western point of Colonel Drummond's route, a rich iron ore was discovered associated with clay. Here the deposits are stated to be readily discoverable not only by the large masses lying on the surface, but also by the beds being extensively exposed by deep ravines. In one part the solid bed of ore is exposed to a thickness of 30 ft.; in another it measured 24 ft.; in a third it exceeded the depth of 50 ft. Where "a bed of such rich material," says Mr. Sowerby, one of the civil engineers connected with the East India Railway Company, "is ascertained to be at least 50 ft. thick—a few feet more or less cannot be of much importance." The extent of ground examined at Dechouree was about a mile, and the quantity of ore at and near the surface was estimated to yield, if smelted, 100,000 tons of pig iron.

From Dechouree Colonel Drummond pursued his course in an easterly direction, passing by Loha Bhurbur, Kaleedoongee, Chowsilla, Beejapore, Jham, Burgote, and Burragur. The length of the route was about sixty miles, and rich deposits of iron ore were discovered at most of these places, varying in thickness from 25 ft. to 50 ft. At Loha Bhurbur the ore is associated with clay, not mere clay impregnated with iron, but solid iron stone. Huge blocks are here represented as lying exposed on the surface: several of these were measured, and found to be upwards of 10 ft. long, 6 ft. broad, and 4 ft. in thickness, each of which, it is said, if smelted into pig iron, would yield upwards of three tons of metal. These blocks were not occasional, but frequent, and common over the whole distance traversed, which was a mile in length, by a width of 175 yards. It was estimated, that upwards of 60,000 tons of metal could be obtained from the ore lying on the surface. The beds in the route, pursued by Colonel Drummond, fully show that an inexhaustible supply of workable iron ore yielding the quality of iron which is most useful for railway purposes can be obtained in an accessible tract, along the outer face of the lower Himalaya ranges, close to the plains.

1855. A Report on the Iron Ores of India, from Lieutenant-Colonel Goodwyn, Chief Engineer of the Lower Provinces of Bengal, in the Public Works Department, dated Fort William, June 27, contains the following passage:— Iron Ores.

"That the Indian Iron can not only be successfully worked, but structurally applied, was proved many years ago, by Colonel Presgrave, formerly Mint-Master at Saugor, who smelted the iron in the neighbourhood, rolled it in the mint rollers, fashioned it into bars and rods, and then erected an excellent suspension bridge, near Saugor, entirely from the ore in the vicinity. Its manufacture in India is a subject of prominent importance, and scarcely less so than the establishment of railways and electric telegraphs.

"I will not here enter into details of the profits or percentage gained by native processes, or the nature of those processes: suffice it to notice here, that the result is most satisfactory, as a guarantee to enterprise, whilst the specimens that I have seen, and which are extant, show the metal to be of superior quality, where attention has been paid to locality, and if the postulates I have advanced are admitted, I deem that the Government would do well to expend a certain sum to place the matter beyond all possible doubt.

"As regards Central India, the Gwalior and Jubbulpore districts and the neighbourhood of Hazareebaugh, place the question of the existence of good iron beyond doubt; but for the more ready consumption of the Presidency and its vicinity, it would, probably, be worth while to enter on experiments in the Valley of the Damooda, near Raneegunge, on the Brohming in Cuttack, in Assam, and near Palamoas; and an outlay of from one lac to four lacs of rupees according to the extent of the operations, would, I am sure, end in the most advantageous results.

"Its *modus operandi* will be to call upon the authorities for an immediate brief return of the general character of the iron; information which has, at various times, been obtained on each district in which it is found; to select from these, under advice, two, three, or four districts, with especial reference to local facilities for the object in view, and, if possible, of after conveyance; to decide to spend not exceeding Rs. (400,000) four lacs upon the whole; to erect, at once, moderate-sized blast furnaces, at each place, the blast engines, &c., being constructed in Cal-

N 2

Iron Ores. cutta, while the furnaces are being built, the iron stone, or ore, fuel, and flux, being simultaneously collected in quantity, in readiness for the starting, and keeping up the supply, and placing each furnace in charge of some person who has been used to the work, and who may be found in the Calcutta foundries, giving to them certain latitude, to vary the proportions, and record the results, and give a large premium to the most successful, to send down the first pigs made to Calcutta; and, upon the result of this examination, and the reports of the blast furnace operations, and local supplies, there will be no difficulty in making over the whole to those who will complete the scheme by supplying all the rolling mills, puddling furnaces, and continuing the manufacture through all its stages, either returning the outlay to the Government, if made a condition or not, as may be considered most equitable at the time.

"I believe that no complete analysis by a regularly-trained iron-viewer and smelter has yet been faithfully obtained, and it is very probable that greater value may, on the result of such analysis, be found in some localities, that will materially affect the prospect of working them; and I would fain hope, that, under effective and scientific management, our public works may, at no distant period, receive that aid from native iron, without which their energies must be comparatively circumscribed."

1856. (March and April.) A blast furnace was erected at Deckouree, 50 miles from Moradabad in Kumaon; and, upon the works being completed, two experiments were made to test its efficacy for the smelting of iron ore, which were partially successful. The metal which was taken out of the furnace, when remelted, flowed out in a very liquid state into small pigs, which, when fractured, showed them to be iron of the best quality.—(*Vide* Mr. Sowerby's Report, April, 1856.)

CHAPTER VIII.

LAWS AND PUBLIC DOCUMENTS RELATING TO BRITISH INDIA.

SECT. I.—BENGAL REGULATIONS, AND ACTS OF THE GOVERNOR-GENERAL IN COUNCIL. SECT. II.—ORDERS IN COUNCIL. SECT. III.—ACTS OF THE IMPERIAL PARLIAMENT. SECT. IV. —PARLIAMENTARY REPORTS, ACCOUNTS, AND PAPERS.

SECT. I.—BENGAL REGULATIONS AND ACTS OF THE GOVERNOR-GENERAL IN COUNCIL.

(Those previous to 1834 being styled "Regulations"—those of a subsequent date, "Acts.")

*** The initials placed before the titles signify—R. Revenue—J. Judicial—M. Miscellaneous.

Regulations.	For what Provinces enacted.	Subject of the Regulation.
1793.		
1	Bengal.	R. The Revenue Settlement of Bengal, Behar and Orissa declared permanent.
2	,,	R. Powers and duties of Collectors and of the Board of Revenue.
3	,,	J. Constitution and jurisdiction of Zillah Courts.
4	,,	J. Rules for receiving, trying, and deciding Civil Suits.
5	,,	J. Rules for receiving Appeals, and the

Regulations.	For what Provinces enacted.	Subject of the Regulation.
1793.		relation of the Court of Appeal to the Court of original jurisdiction.
6	Bengal.	J. Jurisdiction, powers and duties of the Sudder Dewanny Adawlut.
8	"	R. Rules for the decennial settlement of Bengal, Behar, and Orissa.
9	"	J. Powers and duties of Magistrates, the Courts of Session, and the Nizamut Adawlut—Rules of Mahommedan law, modified.
10	"	R. Powers and duties of the Court of Wards.
11	"	R. Succession to estates of intestate proprietors.
12	"	J. Appointment and responsibilities of Mahommedan & Hindoo law officers.
13	"	J. Appointment, removal, and duties of ministerial Officers of Courts.
14	"	R. Recovery of arrears of revenue.
15	"	J. Rates of interest to be allowed on loans and mortgages.
16	"	J. Reference of Suits to arbitration and to the Nazim.
17	"	R. Recovery of arrears of rent.
18	"	J. Preservation of judicial records, civil and criminal.
19	"	R. Validity of La-Khiraj Titles, not Badshahee.
21	"	R. Preservation of revenue records.
22	"	J. Establishment of police.
24	"	R. Payment of pensions charged of the land revenues.
26	"	M. Fixing the age at which landholders attain majority.
27	"	R. Resumption and abolition of Sayer.
33	"	M. Embankments, reservoirs, and water-courses.
35	"	M. Coinage.
36	"	J. Registry of deeds and wills.
38	"	M. Revenue and judicial covenanted servants forbidden to lend money to natives.
39	"	J. Appointment, removal and duties of the head and town Kazis.

Regulations.	For what Provinces enacted.	Subject of the Regulation.
1793.		
41	Bengal.	M. Enactment and authority of regulations.
43	"	M. Allotment of lands to native invalid officers and soldiers.
44	"	M. Limitation of term for grant of leases by proprietors.
48	"	M. Formation and continuance of quinquennial register.
49	"	M. Affrays respecting disputed rights in land.
50	"	R. Court of Wards may admit females to manage estates.
1794.		
3	"	R. Recovery of arrears of revenue—Recovery of money or accounts from public servants—Expediting the settlement of revenue accounts.
8	"	R. Reference of revenue accounts by Courts to collectors for report.
1795.		
1	Benares.	R. Permanent settlement of the land revenue of Benares.
2	"	R. Rules of the temporary settlement preceding the permanent, enactment, authority, and construction of regulations.
3	"	R. Prohibition of the collection of internal duties.
5	"	R. Powers and duties of the collectors of land revenue.
6	"	R. Recovery of arrears of revenue.
7	"	J. Constitution—Duties—Powers and jurisdiction of Zillah Courts.
8	"	J. Rules for the institution and trial of civil suits—Privileges of the Raja of Benares.
9	"	J. Rules for the institution of and trial of appeals.
10	"	J. Jurisdiction of the Sudder Dewanny Adawlut in Appeals.
11	"	J. Appointment and duties of law officers.
12	"	J. Appointment and duties of ministerial officers of Courts.

Regulations.	For what Provinces enacted.	Subject of the Regulation.
1795.		
15	Benares.	J. Reference of suits to arbitration and to the Raja.
16	"	J. Administration of criminal justice.
17	"	J. Establishment of police.
18	"	J. Preservation of judicial records.
19	"	R. Formation and continuance of quinquennial register of lands.
21	"	M. Prevention of infanticide.
22	"	J. Record of judicial rules anterior to the judicial code.
27	"	R. Rights of proprietors under the permanent settlement.
28	"	J. Registry of deeds and wills.
30	"	R. Preservation of revenue records.
33	"	R. Record of rules respecting the cultivation of indigo by British subjects.
35	General.	R. Recovery of arrears of rent.
36	"	J. Rule to provide against loss of criminal trials in route to the Nizamut Adawlut.
41	Benares.	R. Validity of La-Khiraj Titles.
42	"	R. Validity of La-Khiraj Titles. Badshahee Titles.
43	"	M. Allotment of land to invalid native officers and soldiers.
44	"	R. Succession to estates of intestate proprietors.
45	"	R. Recovery of arrears of rent.
46	"	M. Embankments, reservoirs, and watercourses.
48	"	M. Revenue and judicial covenanted servants forbidden to lend money to natives.
49	"	J. Appointment, removal and duties of head and town Kazis.
50	"	R. Limitation of term for grant of leases by proprietors.
51	"	R. Rules respecting Ryotty Pottahs.
55	Bengal.	R. Constitution and duties of the Court of Wards.
58	"	R. Commission granted to Collectors, on La-Khiraj resumed.

Regulations.	For what Provinces enacted.	Subject of the Regulation.
1795.		
61	Bengal.	M. Mint Master to furnish Collectors with money-weights.
62	”	M. Abolition of the Mint at Moorshedabad.
1796.		
2	General.	J. Procedure of Magistrates against offenders, being European British subjects.
3	Bengal.	R. Limitation of the operation of the Court of Wards Regulation.
4	General.	J. Provisions for the absence of Judges and Magistrates.
7	Bengal.	R. Court of Wards—Contumacy and profligacy not grounds of disqualification.
9	General.	J. Appearance of prisoner's witnesses before the Court of Sessions.
10	”	J. Provisions in case of difference between judicial officers on the construction of Regulations.
11	”	J. Procedure against persons resisting or evading process of criminal Courts.
13	”	J. Court of Appeal to adjudge interest in decrees and to punish litigious appeals.
1797.		
2	Benares.	J. Police Responsibilities of landholders and farmers.
4	General.	J. Administration of Mahommedan law—Procedure on charges of sorcery—Examination of witnesses in criminal cases.
6	”	J. Appropriation of police funds.
7	Local.	J. Zillah of Bakungunge constituted.
8	Benares.	J. Prosecutions for recovery of losses by theft to be civil suits.
13	General.	J. Powers and duties of assistant Magistrates.
14	”	J. Levy of fines—Equivalent imprisonment—Restitution of stolen property.

Regulations.	For what Provinces enacted.	Subject of the Regulation.
1797.		
15	General.	R. Fees on divisions and transfer of estates—Definition of "Jumma."
16	"	J. Appeals to Her Majesty in Council.
19	"	J. Translations—Rescissions of previous rules.
1798.		
1	"	R. Procedure in cases of conditional sale, or Bye-bil-Wuffa.
2	"	J. Bewastas or Futwas—Their weight in civil cases—Petition to superior on procedure of inferior Courts.
3	"	J. Vacations of the Courts.
5	"	J. Security in appeals—Preservation of judicial records.
1799.		
1	Local.	M. Freedom of trade on the frontiers of Sylhet.
2	General.	J. Administration of Mahommedan law.
9	"	J. Procedure on resistance of process of Civil Courts.
10	"	J. Reference of trials to the Nizamut Adawlut.
1800.		
1	"	J. Appointment of guardians to minors, being proprietors not subject to the jurisdiction of the Court of Wards.
2	Benares.	R. Use of stone quarries at Chunar.
5	"	R. Extension to Benares of Regulation 7, 1799.
8	General.	R. Establishment of Pergunnah registers.
10	Bengal.	R. Succession to landed estates.
1801.		
1	Bengal, and partly Benares.	R. Realization of revenue—Amendment of Regulation 7, 1799. Separation of Talooks from Zemindaries.
2	General.	J. Constitution and powers of the Courts of Sudder Dewanny and Nizamut Adawlut. Powers of single judges.

Regulations.	For what Provinces enacted.	Subject of the Regulation.
1801.		
3	General.	J. Procedure on charges of perjury preferred by parties against witnesses.
7	Local.	R. Duties on dhonies and vessels navigating the Hooghly.
8	General.	J. Administration of Mahommedan law —Reference of trials to the Nizamut Adawlut.
9	"	J. Procedure in cases of resistance of process of Criminal Courts.
1802.		
2	"	R. Duties on spirits manufactured at distilleries worked in the European manner.
3	"	J. Securities to be taken in civil suits and appeals.
6	"	J. Prevention of infanticide at Saugor and elsewhere.
1803.		
1	Ceded Provinces.	J. Enactment and authority of Regulations.
2	"	J. Constitution, jurisdiction, and powers of Zillah Courts.
3	"	J. Institution and trial of civil suits.
4	"	J. Institution and trial of appeals.
5	"	J. Jurisdiction powers and duties of the Sudder Dewanny Adawlut.
6	"	J. Powers and duties of Magistrates.
7	"	J. Powers and duties of Courts for holding Sessions.
7	"	J. Jurisdiction of Court of Nizamut Adawlut.
11	"	J. Appointment and removal of Mahommedan and Hindoo law officers.
12	"	J. Appointment and duties of ministerial officers of Courts.
13	"	J. Preservation of judicial records.
17	"	J. Registry of wills and deeds.
19	"	M. Revenue and judicial covenanted servants forbidden to lend money to natives.
20	"	J. Procedure in cases of crimes against the State.

Regulations.	For what Provinces enacted.	Subject of the Regulation.
1803.		
21	Ceded Prov.	J. Reference of suits to arbitration.
22	,,	J. Procedure in cases of difference between judicial officers on the construction of Regulations.
23	,,	R. Preservation of revenue records—Fees on divisions of estates.
24	,,	R. Rules respecting pensions assessed on the land and payable from the Treasury.
25	,,	R. Powers and duties of Collectors—Board of Revenue — Transfer of estates.
26	,,	R. Rules for sales of malguzary lands.
27	,,	R. Recovery of arrears of revenue and instructions respecting a Triennial Settlement.
28	,,	R. Recovery of arrears of rent.
30	,,	R. Rules respecting ryotty pottahs.
31	,,	R. Validity of La-Khiraj Titles not Badshahee.
33	,,	R. Recovery of money and accounts from Revenue servants.
34	,,	J. Rate of interest on loans, mortgages, and conditional sales.
35	,,	J. Establishment of police — Responsibilities of landholders.
36	,,	R. Validity of La-Khiraj Titles — Badshahee.
42	,,	R. Quinquennial and pergunnah registers.
44	,,	R. Embankments, reservoirs, water-courses.
46	,,	J. Appointment, removal, and duties of head and town Kazis.
47	,,	R. Powers of landholders to grant leases.
50	General.	J. Attendance of witnesses before Court of Session.
52	Ceded Prov.	R. Powers and Duties of the Court of Wards.
53	General.	J. Mahommedan law — Dacoity or gang robbery — Security for good behaviour—Transportation — Escape of convicts.

Regulations.	For what Provinces enacted.	Subject of the Regulation.
1804.		
1	General.	R. Invalid jaghires and pensions.
3	Ceded Prov.	J. Evasion or resistance of process—Bailable offences—Infanticide.
4	Cuttack.	J. Administration of justice in criminal cases—the laws in force in Bengal, Behar, and Orissa, extended to Cuttack.
5	General.	M. Appointment and removal of public servants—Oath of revenue officers.
6	Ceded Prov.	R. Salt—Rescinds XXXIX.—1803.
9	Conquered Provinces.	J. Division territorial and judicial—Magistrates, police and administration of criminal justice.
10	General.	J. Suppression of crimes against the State.
1805.		
2	„	J. Limitation of time for suits, and for recovery of arrears of rent, fines, and penalties—Devices in Government suits—Calculation of period for appeal.
3	„	J. Punishment of gang robbery and theft.
5	Ceded Prov.	R. Modifying the terms for the second settlement of Fussily, 1213 to 1215.
8	Con. Prov.	M. Extension of Regulations of 1803 to the Conquered Provinces.
9	„	M. Proclamation of the terms of settlement after Fussily, 1212.
12	Cuttack.	R. Proclamation of settlement—Extension of Regulations.
13	„	J. Administration of police — Amendment of IV.—1804.
14	„	J. Administration of civil justice.
17	Bengal and Cuttack.	J. Management of joint undivided estates.
19	Bengal.	M. Address to the Nazim of Bengal.
1806.		
1	Local.	J. Sudder Dewanny Adawlut authorised to dispense with vacations—Abolition of Zillah of Beerbhoom.
2	General.	J. Modification of rules of practice—

Regulations.	For what Provinces enacted.	Subject of Regulation.
1806.		Security — Process — Subsistence money—Satisfaction of decrees by instalments.
6	General.	R. Repairs of embankment.
7	Bengal.	J. Establishment and jurisdiction of Courts of twenty-four Pergunnahs.
10	General.	J. Security to be required on preferring charges of corruption against law officers and ministerial officers of Courts.
11	"	M. Assistance to troops and travellers passing through districts, military guards and escorts.
12	Agra.	J. Annexation of Pergunnahs resumed from Bhurtpore to Zillah of Agra.
14	"	J. Abolition of Zillah of Saharunpore.
15	General.	J. Procedure on committal of European British subjects — Estates of deceased Europeans.
16	Bengal.	M. Relating to the Nawab Nazim.
17	General.	R. Rules respecting interest and conditional sales.
18	Bengal.	R. Collection of Tolls on boats on the Hooghly.
21	General.	R. Appointment and responsibilities of Tehsildars.
22	"	R. Payment of pensions charged on the land revenue.
1807.		
1	"	J. Powers of single Judges of the Sudder Dewanny Adawlut.
2	"	J. Punishment of perjury and forgery.
7	Benares.	R. Payment by Zemindars of their revenues into the Moolky Treasury.
9	General.	J. Process in criminal cases — Powers and appointment of magistrates—Bail—Calendars and reports.
10	Ceded Prov.	R. Appointment of a commissioner (superseded).
11	General.	R. Transportation of arms of European manufacture beyond the Company's territories forbidden without a Government pass.

Regulations.	For what Provinces enacted.	Subject of Regulation.
1807.		
13	General except Bengal.	R. Regulation of currency of certain coins.
14	Ceded Prov.	J. Police—Amendment of the system.
1808.		
4	"	R. Appointment and duties of Canongoes.
5	"	R. Explanation of certain rules respecting the settlement.
6	Cuttack.	R. Settlement for Umlee, 1216—1219.
7	Ceded Prov.	R. Registry of La-Khiraj's lands.
8	General.	J. References of trials for Dacoity to the Nizamut Adawlut—Powers of single Judges.
10	Bengal.	J. Appointment and powers of superintendant of police for Calcutta, Dacca, and Moorshedabad
11	General.	R. Adjustment of rent payable by heirs of invalid jaghirdars.
13	"	J. Security for staying execution of decrees pending appeal.
1809.		
2	"	J. Power to convene courts-martial on foreign service.
3	"	J. Police in military cantonments and bazaars.
8	"	M. Appointment and Removal of native officers in civil departments.
1810.		
1	"	J. Power to dispense with futwas in criminal cases.
4	Cuttack.	J. Abolition of the office of Commissioner of Cuttack.
6	General.	J. Responsibilities of Zemindars to give notice of crimes.
8	"	J. Appointment of a superintendant of police for Patna, Benares, and Bareilly.
9	"	R. Collection of Government Customs.
13	"	J. Powers of the single judges of the Sudder Dewanny Adawlut.
14	"	J. Remission and mitigation of punishment—Pardon.

Regulations.	For what Provinces enacted.	Subject of the Regulation.
1810.		
16	General.	J. Appointment of Magistrates, assistant Magistrates, and joint Magistrates—Remuneration of Police for meritorious services.
19	,,	R. Endowments — Public Buildings — escheats.
20	,,	J. Amenability of camp-followers to Martial laws — Limits of Cantonments—Police in Military Bazaars.
1811.		
1	Bengal.	J. Punishment for housebreaking — Search for stolen property.
2	General.	R. Support of invalid Native Military Officers.
6	Bengal.	R. Close of period for allowing compensation in lieu of Sayer resumed.
7	General.	J. Duties of Police.
9	,,	R. Division of lands—Rights of Shareholders.
10	,,	M. Importation of Slaves prohibited.
11	,,	R. Extension of the period for correcting errors in apportioning the jumma on division of estates
12	,,	J. Constitution of the Sudder Dewanny and Nizamut Adawlut.
13	Bengal and Cuttack.	R. Constitution and powers of the Sudder Board of Revenue.
14	General.	J. Punishment by Transportation—office of Magistrate of the Twenty-four Pergunnahs.
1812.		
1	Bengal.	R. Modification of Customs' Duties
2	General.	R. Coinage and Mints.
3	,,	J. Preliminary investigations and Magistrates—Responsibilites of Landowners as to crimes on their estates.
4	,,	J. Conduct of suits of Native Princes before British Courts.
5	,,	R. Realization of revenue.
7	Bengal.	R. Abolition of the house-tax.
9	Ceded Prov.	R. Declaration that the settlements will not be made permanent.
10	Con. Prov.	Same.

Regulations.	For what Provinces enacted.	Subject of the Regulation.
1812.		
11	General.	M. Removal of suspicious immigrants.
14	Ceded Prov.	R. Period for which leases may be granted by landholders.
15	Ceded Prov. and Benares.	J. Extension of rules respecting house-breaking.
16	Bengal.	J. Execution of decrees of Court of Requests in Calcutta, by Court of Twenty-four Pergunnahs.
18	General.	R. Limitation of time for leases.
19	"	R. Collection of customs.
20	"	J. Registry of deeds—Indigo contracts.
21	Bengal.	J. Police—Rescission of rules respecting licences to certain trades.
22	Bundlecund.	R. Exemption of certain jaghires in Bundlecund from tribute.
1813.		
1	Cuttack.	R. Modification of rules respecting settlement.
2	General.	J. Punishment of Native Officers for abuse of trusts by using public monies.
6	"	J. Reference of suits to arbitration.
7	"	R. Reference of revenue accounts by courts to Collectors.
9	"	J. Prosecution for perjury—Translation of regulations.
10	"	J. Transportation restored—Transfer of convicts—Consolidated Abkarry regulation.
11	"	R. Modification of rules respecting payment of pensions.
12	"	R. Collection of customs.
14	"	R. Rescinds rules about duties on horses.
15	"	R. Abolition of the office of Dewan to Collectors.
1814.		
2	"	J. Rules for the conduct of suits against public officers.
4	"	R. Duty on saltpetre.
6	"	R Rates of *ad-valorem* duties.
8	"	J. Responsibilities of landholders to give notice of crimes.

Regulations.	For what Provinces enacted.	Subject of the Regulation.
1814.		
11	General.	J. Modification of the rules for the punishment of housebreaking.
13	Local.	J. Abolition of the office of Cutwal in Dacca Patna and Moorshedabad.
15	General.	J. Punishment by the Sessions Court for two offences conjointly.
17	"	R. Recovery of arrears from Abkarry manufacturers or venders.
19	"	R. Rules for the division of estates.
20	Bengal.	M. College of Fort William abolished.
21	General.	J. Judicial and revenue officers not to employ their native creditors in public duties.
23	"	J. Jurisdiction, powers, and duties of Moonsiffs and Sudder Ameens.
24	"	J. Rules of practice in Zillah Courts.
25	"	J. Powers of single Judges of Sudder Dewanny and Nizamut Adawlut.
26	"	J. Modification of rules of practice in Civil Courts.
27	"	J. Rules respecting the office and duties of pleaders.
28	"	J. Consolidated rules respecting pauper suitors.
29	Beerbhoom.	R. Settlement of the lands of Ghautwals in Beerbhoom.
1815.		
1	Ceded Prov.	R. Rules for dealing with Mocurreree and Istimraree tenures.
3	Cuttack.	R. Settlement for Umlee, 1223.
4	General.	R. Collection of Customs.
1816.		
2	Part of Behar.	R. Re-establishment of the office of Canoongoe.
3	Serampore.	J. Relinquishment of administration of justice in Serampore.
4	General.	J. Prisoners in civil suits may petition on unstamped paper.
5	Cuttack.	R. Re-establishment of the office of Canoongoe.
6	"	R. Settlement of Umlee, 1224 to 1226.
7	Bundlecund.	R. The estate of Amrut Rao exempted from the Regulations.

Regulations.	For what Provinces enacted.	Subject of the Regulation.
1816.		
9	Sunderbunds.	R. Appointment and powers of Commissioners of Sunderbunds.
11	Cuttack.	R. Rules for the administration of certain estates by a superintendent.
12	Chittagong.	R. Establishment of a Custom House at Cox's Bazaar.
13	General.	R. Consolidated opium regulation.
14	"	J. Management of gaols and control over the employment of prisoners.
15	"	J. Facilities to native officers and soldiers in the prosecution and defence of civil suits.
16	Ceded Prov.	R. Settlement for Fussily, 1225 to 1229.
17	General.	J. Regulation and control of police and gaol establishments — Powers of Superintendent of Police.
18	Allahabad.	J. Annexation of Pergunnah Handys to Zillah Allahabad.
22	General.	J. Consolidated rules respecting Chokeydars of Police.
1817.		
2	Behar.	R. Re-establishment of the office of Canoongoe.
4	Dehra and Dhoon.	J. Annexation of Dehra Dhoon to Saharunpore.
5	General.	R. Discovery of hidden treasure.
6	Ceded Prov.	R. Explanation of a rule in XXIV., 1803 —Pensions.
7	General.	J. Payment of Chokeydars of Police.
9	Midnapore.	J. Repeals 5, 1815—Pergunnah Bogree.
12	Ceded Prov.	R. Appointment and duties of Putwarries.
13	Midnapore.	R. Establishment of the office of Canoongoe.
16	General.	R. Duty on importation of opium.
17	"	J. Administration of criminal justice—Mahommedan law.
18	"	J. Oaths of native judicial officers — Proceedings in case of corruption or embezzlement.
19	"	R. Recovery of arrears of rent.
20	"	J. General consolidated Police Regulation.

Regulations.	For what Provinces enacted.	Subject of the Regulation.
1817.		
21	General.	R. Rescinds a section of Regulation 9, 1810.
24	"	R. Powers of a single member of the Board of Revenue.
1818.		
1	Bengal.	R. Establishment of the office of Canoongoe.
2	Bundlecund.	J. Annexation of the Elakeh of Khundeh to Zillah of Bundelcund.
3	General.	J. Authority to confine state prisoners without taking judicial proceedings.
4	Seharunpore.	J. Re-establishing a Court, Civil and Criminal, in the north district of Seharunpore.
5	Cuttack.	R. Establishing the office of Commissioner of Cuttack.
6	General.	J. Rules of practice in Courts of Magistrates and Sessions—Detention of prisoners—Bail—Recovery of penalties from securities.
7	"	R. Foreign trade.
8	"	J. Security for good behaviour.
9	Con. Prov.	R. Settlement, 1228 to 1232—Fussily.
10	Cuttack.	R. Realisation of the revenue.
11	General.	R. Modification of the opium regulations.
12	"	J. Powers of magistrates in cases of housebreaking, theft, and receiving stolen goods, and of prisoners escaping from confinement—Police.
13	Cuttack.	R. Settlement of Cuttack, 1227 to 1229—Umlee.
14	General.	R. Coinage.
819.		
1	Bengal.	R. Modification of Regulation 12, 1817.
2	General.	R. Resumption of unauthorized La-Khiraj.
3	"	J. Security to be taken from notorious robbers, not Dacoits.
5	"	R. Coinage and mints.
6	"	R. Management of ferries.
7	"	J. Increased powers of magistrates in certain cases.

Regulations.	For what Provinces enacted.	Subject of the Regulation.
1819.		
8	Bengal and Midnapore.	J. Rules regarding putnee talooks and leases—Recovery of rent.
10	Bengal and Cuttack.	R. Consolidated Salt Regulation.
1820.		
1	Bengal and Midnapore.	R. Sales for realisation of rent—Putnee talooks.
2	Chandernagore.	J. Trial of offences committed in Chandernagore.
3	General.	J. Prohibiting the pressing of Coolies and Begarees.
4	"	J. Magistrates to give effect to the sentences of Courts Martial—Jurisdiction and powers of Magistrates.
5	"	R. Frontier duties on tobacco.
7	"	J. Punishment of Dhurna.
1821.		
2	"	J. Practice of Civil Courts.
3	"	J. Powers of assistant magistrates, of native law officers, and Sudder Ameens—Chokeydarry assessment—Immigration of suspicious foreigners.
4	"	J. Power to blend the offices of Collector and Magistrate.
5	"	R. Value of certain rupees in revenue payments.
1822		
1	"	J. Powers of magistrates in cases of affrays.
2	"	R. Collection of customs.
3	"	R. Powers of the Board of Revenue.
4	"	J. Administration of Mahommedan law.
6	Benares.	J. Extension of Court of Wards Regulation to Benares, and limit of discretionary power of interference in case of minors.
7	N. W. Prov.	R. Settlement of the North-Western Provinces and Cuttack—Powers of Collectors — Making and revising Settlements.
8	General.	J. Power to remove criminal trials from one court to another.

Regulations.	For what Provinces enacted.	Subject of the Regulation.
1822.		
10	Garrow Hills.	J. Special rules for the administration in the Garrow Hills.
11	General.	J. Administration of estates purchased on account of Government—Government declared not liable for errors of Courts of Justice.
1823.		
2	"	J. Punishment of affrays.
4	"	J. Judges not to try prisoners committed by themselves as Magistrates—Employment of convicts in Allypore gaol.
5	Bengal.	R. Frontier duties.
6	General.	M. Enforcement of indigo contracts.
7	"	M. Covenanted civil servants forbidden to borrow from natives subject to their authority or influence.
1824.		
1	"	R. Power of Government to obtain land for roads or other public purposes.
2	Ceded Prov.	R. Abolition of the mint at Furruckabad.
3	General.	J. Powers of Principal Sudder Ameens and Sudder Ameens appointed to out-stations.
4	"	J. Registry of deeds—Rules modified.
5	Bengal.	R. Extension of the indigo contract Regulation 6, 1823.
6	General.	J. Procedure of Magistrates in cases of persons charged with two or more offences.
7	"	R. Amended rules for the Abkarry and Opium Departments.
8	Bengal.	R. Tolls on the Hooghly.
9	General.	R. Modification and amendment of Regulation 7, 1822.
10	"	J. Magistrates empowered to tender pardons.
11	"	J. Magistrates to depute assistants to make local investigations.
13	"	J. Enlarged powers of Sudder Ameens.
14	"	R. Jurisdiction of Collectors in summary suits for arrears of rent.

Regulations.	For what Provinces enacted.	Subject of the Regulation.
1825.		
1	General.	J. Execution of process, civil and criminal.
2	,,	J. Rules respecting review of judgment and pauper special appeals.
4	,,	J. Rules respecting security for keeping the peace.
5	,,	J. Provision for the union of the offices of Judge and Collector.
6	,,	R. Rules for the supply of troops on march, in modification of Regulation 11, 1806.
7	,,	J. Sales of land in satisfaction of decrees—Attachment of lands.
8	,,	J. Public servants not to be employed in private business, nor private in public duties.
9	,,	R. Extension of provisions of 7, 1822—New provisions in several subjects of revenue administration.
11	,,	R. Rules respecting gains and losses of land by alluvium or dereliction.
12	,,	J. Corporal punishment—Power of single Judges of the Nizamut Adawlut.
13	,,	R. Rules respecting Canoongoe and other La-Khiraj lands—Settlement of resumed lands.
14	,,	R. Validity of La-Khiraj grants.
15	,,	R. Duties and drawbacks.
16	,,	J. Punishment of dacoity by Sessions Court.
18	Chinsurah.	J. Annexation of Chinsurah to Zillah Hooghly.
19	Bengal.	J. Rules for the exercise of certain judicial rights by the Nazim.
20	General.	J. Constitution and jurisdiction of the Military Courts of Requests.
21	Dehra Doon.	J. Administration of the Dehra Doon.
1826.		
2	Ceded Prov.	R. Settlement, 1235 to 1239.
3	General.	J. Control of civil gaols.
5	Agra.	J. Annexation of Pergunnah Goberdhun to Agra.

Regulation.	For what Provinces enacted.	Subject of the Regulation.
1826.		
6	Futtehpore.	J. The Zillah of Futtehpore constituted.
8	General.	R. Amended rules respecting opium.
9	"	R. Local jurisdiction of the custom authorities.
10	Bengal.	R. Manufacture of noonchye prohibited —Retail sale of salt allowed.
11	"	J. Appointment of Hindoo and Mahommedan law officers.
12	Calcutta.	R. Stamp duties in Calcutta.
1827.		
1	Bhaglepore.	J. Administration of criminal justice in Bhaglepore.
3	General.	J. Procedure against law and ministerial officers of Courts for Corruption.
5	"	J. Management of estates under attachment by Zillah Courts.
1828.		
1	"	J. Transportation—Convicts in Allypore gaol.
2	Sylhet.	R. Free trade in Sylhet.
3	General.	R. Appointment of special commissioners for La-Khiraj resumptions.
4	"	R. Powers of collectors under 7, 1822—enlarged and defined.
6	"	J. Punishment of affrays—Modification of Regulation 2, 1823.
7	Benares.	R. Administration of the Raja's Jaghire Mehals.
8	General.	J. Powers of Magistrates in punishing affrays—Amendment of 1, 1822.
1829.		
1	"	R. Appointment and powers of Commissioners of Revenue and Circuit.
3	"	J. Denomination of Judges of the Sudder Court—Employment of copyists—Oaths—Abolition of law officers of Provincial Courts.
4	"	R. Modification of rules respecting commissioners under 3, 1828.
5	Dehra Doon.	R. Administration of the district.
6	General.	J. Powers of magistrates in cases of theft.
7	"	M. Modification of rules respecting returns, reports, calendars, &c.

Regulation.	For what Provinces enacted.	Subject of the Regulation.
1829.		
10	General.	J. Consolidated stamp regulation.
11	"	R. Repair of embankments.
12	"	J. Punishment for wounding with intent to murder—Revision by Superior Courts.
13	"	J. Suits against public officers—Government Vakeels.
14	"	J. Security in civil suits to be given by residents in foreign territories.
17	"	M. Abolition of Suttee.
1830.		
1	Midnapore.	J. Administration of Midnapore.
2	General.	R. Trade with foreign countries.
3	"	R. Export duties.
4	"	J. Temporary employment of Mahommedan law officers.
5	"	R. Indigo crops and contracts.
6	"	J. Allowance to prisoners in civil gaols.
7	Bengal and Benares.	R. Rescission of rule for levying of interest on arrears of revenue.
8	General.	J. Examination before Magistrates.
1831.		
1	"	J. Punishment of dacoity.
2	"	J. Trial of cases removed from one jurisdiction to another.
5	"	J. Modifications of authority in the jurisdiction of Courts and officers in civil cases.
6	"	J. Establishment of a Sudder Court for the North-Western Provinces—
7	"	Zillah Judges empowered to hold Sessions.
8	"	R. Cognizance of summary suits for arrears of rent transferred to Collectors.
9	"	J. Powers of single Judges of the Sudder Dewanny and Nizamut Adawlut.
10	"	R. Establishment of a Sudder Board of Revenue for North-Western Provinces.

Regulation.	For what Provinces enacted.	Subject of the Regulation.
1831.		
11	Con. and Ceded Prov.	J. Employment of Tehsildars as Darogahs of Police. Appointment and removal of police officers.
1832.		
2	General.	J. Power of search—Powers of law officers and Aumeens to punish Chokeydars.
3	"	M. Emancipation of slaves.
4	"	R. Transport of salt.
5	Delhi Ter.	J. Administration of the Delhi Provinces.
6	General.	J. Native agency in Civil and criminal Courts as jury, assessors, or punchayet—Administration of Mahommedan law.
7	"	J. Administration of justice in the Zillah Courts by the uncovenanted Judges.
8	Calcutta.	J. Abolition of Zillah "Suburbs of Calcutta" — Establishment of Zillah Twenty Four Pergunnahs.
1833.		
1	General.	R. Extended Powers of the Sudder Board of Revenue for North-Western Provinces.
2	"	J. Abolition of the Provincial Courts of Appeal.
4	"	R. Superintendence and employment of convicts on public works.
5	Dacca.	J. Union of Zillahs Dacca and Dacca Jelalpoor into one district.
6	General.	R. Duties on imports by sea.
7	"	R. Coinage.
8	"	J. Appointment of occasional Assistant Judges.
9	"	R. Enlargement of certain provisions of 7, 1822—Appointment of uncovenanted Deputy Collectors.
13	Ramghur, &c.	J. Special rules for the administration of those districts.
1834		
2	General.	J. Abolition of corporal punishment and labour—Prison discipline.

LIST OF THE ACTS OF THE GOVERNOR-GENERAL OF INDIA IN COUNCIL.

Act.	For what Provinces enacted.	Subject of the Act.
1834.		
1	General.	M. Certain Acts of the Governor General in Council declared valid.
2	„	M. Authority of Secretaries to Government.
1835.		
2	Assam, Arracan, and Tenasserim.	J. Administration of those territories.
3	Con. and Ceded Prov.	R. Dissolution of the Special Commission to rectify errors in the assignment of proprietary possession.
6	Cossya Hills and Cachar.	J. Administration of those districts.
7	General.	J. Extended employment of Zillah Judges as Session Judges.
7	„	R. Sales of land for arrears of revenue or rent to be effected by Collectors, not by Judges.
9	Bengal and Cuttack.	R. Administration of salt chokies—Appointment of uncovenanted superintendents.
10	General.	M. Notification in the Government Gazette, declared to be proof of the "Acts."
11	„	M. Regulation of printing presses.
16	„	R. Enforcement of indigo contracts.
17	„	R. Coinage.
18	„	M. Restrictions on wearing badges, uniforms, &c.
21	„	R. Coinage.
1836.		
5	„	J. Zillah Judges may employ Principal Sudder Ameens to execute decrees.
8	„	J. Appointments of Principal Sudder Ameen, Sudder Ameen, and Moonsiff, declared open to all persons—their responsibilities.

Act.	For what Provinces enacted.	Subject of the Act.
1836.		
9	General.	J. Commanding officers and military stations empowered to administer oaths.
10	"	R. Enforcement of indigo contracts.
11	"	J. No person exempt by reason of birth, &c. from jurisdiction of Civil Courts.
12	Ceded Prov.	J. Execution of decrees of the Nawab of Furruckabad.
13	"	R. Coinage.
14	"	R. Consolidated customs regulation—Abolition of inland and town duties.
17	Beg. Sumro's Jaghire.	J. Provision for the administration of the resumed Jaghire.
20	General.	R. Rules respecting divisions of estates.
21	"	J. Governor General in Council may create new, and alter limits of existing Zillahs.
22	Bengal.	R. Collection of tolls on the Hooghly.
25	General.	R. Rules for warehousing ports.
26	"	J. Appointment of a Superintendent of Police in the camp of the Governor-General.
30	"	J. Punishment for belonging to a gang of Thugs.
32	"	R. Importation of sugar.
1837.		
3	"	J. Transfer of suits and appeals from one Zillah to another.
4	"	R. British subjects empowered to hold land.
6	Cuttack.	R. Responsibilities of Mulguzars for their jumma.
15	General.	J. Levy and appropriation of police tax.
16	"	R. Levy of *ad-valorem* duties.
17	"	M. Post-office regulations.
18	"	J. Committal and trial for Thuggee.
19	"	J. Convicted persons admissible to give evidence.
21	"	J. Declarations substituted for oaths not judicial.
24	"	J. Re-appointment of superintendent of police—Powers of Session Judges—Revision of proceedings.
25	"	J. Jurisdiction and powers of the several Civil Courts.

Act.	For what Provinces enacted.	Subject of the Act.
1837		
28	General.	M. Uncovenanted officers may be appointed in the Stamp Department.
29	"	J. Language of proceedings, judicial and revenue.
31	"	R. Coinage.
38	"	R. Who may be appointed local agents under 19, 1810.
1838.		
7	"	J. Powers of Zillah Judges in the hearing of appeals.
10	Kumaon.	J. Administration of the Province.
11	General.	R. Remuneration of Ameens effecting partition of estates.
20	"	M. Amended Post-office regulations.
21	"	R. Coinage.
22	"	J. Summary appeals from Moonsiffs to Zillah Judges.
27	"	J. Jurisdiction and powers of Principal Sudder Ameens.
29	Bengal and Cuttack.	R. Prevention of illegal traffic in salt.
30	General.	J. Establishment of additional offices for registry of deeds.
32	"	J. Powers of Justice of the Peace.
1839.		
1	"	R. Commissioners for sale of property distrained for rent.
2	"	J. Levy of fines by magistrates under the Acts.
3	"	R. No one exempt from jurisdiction of Revenue Courts, or Moonsiffs, in matter of rent.
9	"	J. Practice in pauper suits.
11	"	J. No stamps required for proceedings in appeals to Her Majesty in Council.
14	"	M. Emigration.
17	"	M. Rates of postage.
18	"	J. Thuggee, where may be tried.
23	"	J. Punishment of soldiers dismissed by Courts Martial.
26	"	J. Rescission of previous rules respecting charges against public officers.

Act.	For what Provinces enacted.	Subject of the Act.
1839.		
27	General.	J. Execution of the decrees of the Court of the Twenty-four Pergunnahs by the Court of Requests of Calcutta.
32	„	J. Extension of certain English laws of interest to India.
1840.		
2	„	J. Sentences of imprisonment passed by Courts Martial, to be executed by officers in charge of gaols.
4	„	J. Powers of magistrates in disputes respecting land likely to lead to affrays.
5	„	J. Declaration substituted for oaths of Hindoos and Mahommedans.
7	„	J. Power to appoint uncovenanted Deputy Registers to the Sudder Courts.
10	„	R. Abolition of Pilgrim tax at Juggernauth, Gaya, &c.
16	„	J. Treatment of convicts at the places of punishment.
19	„	J. Procedure in pauper appeals.
21	„	M. Act 4, 1840, declared not retrospective.
22	„	J. Punishment of vagrants.
23	„	J. Execution of process of Mofussil authorities within the limit of the Supreme Court.
25	„	R. Administration of the Abkarry Department.
1841.		
1	„	R. Realization of Revenue—Putteedarry estates.
5	„	J. Trial of offences against the State.
6	„	R. Importation of rum and rum shrub.
7	„	J. Rules for taking examination of absent witnesses.
9	„	R. Abkarry—Amendment of Act 25, 1840.
10	„	M. Registry of ships.
11	„	M. Constitution and powers of Military Courts of Requests.
12	„	R. Repeal of sundry laws respecting arrears of revenue.

Act.	For what Provinces enacted.	Subject of the Act.
1841.		
13	General.	R. Import duties on wines and spirits.
15	"	J. Residents in Calcutta exempted from giving security in Mofussil Courts.
16	"	J. Qualification of Justices of the Peace.
17	"	J. Duties of Registrars of the Sudder Courts.
18	"	R. Exportation of military stores.
19	"	J. Protection of the property of intestates.
20	"	J. Collection of debts of deceased Hindoos and Mahommedans.
21	"	J. Prevention of local nuisances.
28	"	J. Punishment of camp followers.
29	"	J. Dismissal of suits and appeals for non-prosecution.
30	"	J. Repression of obstructions to justice—Contempts.
31	"	J. Appeals and revisions of proceedings in Criminal Courts.
1842.		
7	"	J. Rules respecting translations.
8	"	J. Designation of "Sudder Courts" applied to the Sudder Dewanny and Nizamut Adawlut.
11	"	R. Importation of foreign sugar.
12	"	M. Regulation of military bazaars—Liabilities of camp followers.
15	"	M. Emigration—Order of Her Majesty in Council, January, 1842.
16	N. W. Prov.	R. Term for which proprietors may grant leases.
1843.		
1	General.	J. Effect of registration on titles of land.
2	"	J. Decisions in appeals, how to be given by one or more judges.
3	"	J. Rules for special appeals.
4	"	J. Appeals from justices of the peace.
5	"	J. Amendments in the law of slavery.
6	"	J. Procedure in the Courts of Principal Sudder Ameens, Sudder Ameens and Moonsiffs.
12	"	J. Language in which decrees are to be written.

Act.	For what Provinces enacted.	Subject of the Act.
1843.		
14	N. W. Prov.	R. Manufacture of salt and custom duties thereon.
15	General.	J. Appointment of uncovenanted Deputy Magistrates.
16	„	J. Offers of reward for apprehension of offenders.
18	„	J. Procedure against persons charged with Thuggee and Dacoity committed in States in alliance.
19	„	J. Effect of registration—Amendment of 1, 1843.
21	„	M. Emigration.
22	„	J. Repeal of Section 17—Regulation 3, 1793.
23	General.	J. Jurisdiction of Zillah Courts.
24	„	J. Punishment of Dacoity.
25	„	R. False marks on foreign goods subject them to confiscation.
1844.		
2	„	J. Preparation of proceedings for transmission to Privy Council.
3	„	J. Modification of rules respecting corporal punishment.
4	„	J. Repeal of certain rules respecting Dacoity.
5	„	M. Suppression of lotteries.
9	„	J. Institution of suits before Principal Sudder Ameens and Sudder Ameens.
13	„	R. Coinage.
14	„	J. Punishment by transportation.
18	„	J. Superintendence of gaols vested in magistrates.
21	„	M. Emigration.
22	„	R. Coinage
1845.		
1	„	R. Realization of arrears of revenue.
3	„	J. Requisition of security for costs in appeals declared to be discretionary.
4	„	J. Amended rules respecting registry of deeds.
5	„	J. Appointment of law officers.
6	„	J. Issue of commissions of the peace.
7	N. W. Prov.	R. Tolls on canals, &c.

Act.	For what Provinces enacted.	Subject of the Act.
1845.		
9	General.	R. Amended rules for levy of import duties.
10	„	J. Issue of warrants when summons could not be served.
14	„	J. Appointments of Nazirs to Moonsiff's Courts.
15	„	J. Privileges of soldiers in judicial and revenue proceedings.
16	„	J. Dismissal of appeals for non-prosecution.
17	„	J. Attendance of witnesses in Moonsiff's Courts.
18	„	J. Punishment of offences committed by convicts.
20	„	M. Preamble to articles of war.
21	Cuttack.	J. Suppression of Meriah sacrifices.
27	General.	J. Powers of assistant Magistrates.
1846.		
1	„	J. Amended rules for Pleaders.
4	„	J. Sales of land in execution of decrees.
6	Bhuttee Ter.	J. Administration of the Bhuttee territory.
7	General.	J. Diet money of witnesses in petty cases.
8	N. W. Prov.	R. Settlement of the N. W. Provinces.
10	General.	J. Duration of procedure in certain cases of arrears of rent.
1847.		
1	N. W. Prov.	R. Establishment and maintenance of boundary rents.
2	General.	J. Operation of the Oath Act 5, 1840.
5	„	J. Execution of sentences of certain Courts established in territories not subject to general regulations.
9	Bengal.	R. Assessment of lands gained by alluvion or dereliction.
10	General.	J. Punishment of Thuggee—Amendment of 30, 1836.
12	„	J. Moonsiffs and Sudder Ameens declared not liable to fines.
13	„	M. Emigration.

Act.	For what Provinces enacted.	Subject of the Act.
1847.		
14	General.	J. Rescission of the rule for the transcription of plaints.
17	"	J. Remedy in cases of default in prosecution of suits and appeals.
18	"	J. Remedy of certain informalities in registry of deeds.
19	"	M. Articles of war.
20	"	M. Regulation of copyright.
1848.		
1	"	J. Amended procedure in cases of forgery.
3	"	J. Definition of "Thug" and "Thuggee."
5	"	J. Rules respecting penal recognizances.
6	"	R. Equalization of British and Foreign bottoms.
7	"	R. Drawbacks on exportation.
8	"	R. Realization of revenue and rent.
11	"	J. Punishment of wandering gangs of thieves and robbers.
13	"	R. Limitation of time for contesting Collector's awards under 7, 1822, &c.
16	"	R. Modification of certain rules respecting salt.
19	"	J. Revision of sentences and proceedings of criminal courts.
20	Gen. except N. W. Prov.	R. Attendance of landholders before Collectors.
23	General.	M. Correction of a clerical error in 25, 1840.
1849.		
1	"	J. Punishment of offences committed in foreign States.
2	"	J. Abolition of the punishments of branding and exposure.
4	"	J. Custody of criminal lunatics.
5	"	R. Duties of customs and excise.
6	"	M. Military and naval pensions and superannuations.
11	Calcutta.	R. Abkarry revenues in Calcutta.
13	"	R. Prevention of smuggling salt in Calcutta.

Act.	For what Provinces enacted.	Subject of the Act.
1849.		
14	General.	J. Punishment for tampering with the Army or Navy.
1850.		
1	Calcutta.	R. Title to lands taken for public purposes.
4	General.	J. Amended procedure in appeals to the Sudder Court.
5	"	R. Rules for the coasting trade in India.
6	"	M. Commander-in-Chief empowered to pardon military offences.
7	"	J. Removal of prisoners from one gaol to another.
8	"	J. Powers of Zillah Judges and principal Sudder Ameens in confirming appeals.
9	"	J. Establishment of powers of Small Debts Court.
10	"	R. Aden declared a free port.
11	"	M. Registry of ships—Amendment of 10, 1841.
12	"	R. Responsibility of public accountants.
13	"	J. Punishment of breaches of trust by public officers.
15	"	J. Practice in Moonsiff's Courts.
16	"	J. Restitution of the value of stolen property.
18	"	J. Protection of officers acting judicially.
19	"	M. Rules for binding apprentices.
20	Cuttack.	J. Trial of boundary questions.
21	General.	J. Rights of inheritance not affected by religion of the parties.
23	Calcutta.	R. Security of the land revenue in Calcutta.
25	General.	R. Sales of land.
26	"	M. Improvements in towns.
27	"	M. Registry of merchant seamen.
28	"	M. Encouragement of merchant seamen.
30	"	J. Practice in Civil Courts — Amendments of Acts 1, 1846, and 4, 1850.
32	Subathoo.	J. Administration of Civil Justice in the Province.
33	Bengal and Midnapore.	R. Sales of Putnee tenures under 8, 1819.
34	General.	J. Custody of state prisoners.

Act.	For what Provinces enacted.	Subject of the Act.
1850.		
36	General.	M. Amendment of an article of war.
37	"	R. Inquiries into the conduct of public servants.
38	"	J. Counsel and pleaders allowed for defence in criminal cases.
42	"	M. Facilities for public works.
44	Lower Prov.	R. Consolidation of the Board of Revenue and Board of Customs, salt and opium.
45	General.	J. Jurisdiction of coroners.
1851.		
2	"	J. Powers of Judges of the Sudder Dewanny Adawlut.
3	Bengal.	R. Administration of the salt laws.
8	General.	R. Levy of tolls on public roads and bridges.
10	"	J. Administration of estates of deceased persons.
11	"	J. Custody of registers of deeds, &c.
16	"	J. Trial of receivers of stolen property.
1852.		
4	"	M. Emigration.
8	"	J. Execution of Mofussil process within the jurisdiction of the Supreme Court.
9	Cawnpore.	J. Administration of Bajee Row's Jaghire.
18	Lower Prov.	J. Modification of the rules respecting pleaders.
22	General.	R. Summary suits for arrears of rent.
24	"	J. Prevention of crimping—Emigration.
25	"	J. Execution of decrees in appeals to Her Majesty in Council and other jurisdictions.
26	"	J. Amended procedure in the Courts of Sudder Ameens and Moonsiffs.
30	"	M. Naturalization of aliens.
31	"	J. Rescission of a rule respecting remuneration of Darogahs.
32	"	J. Prosecution of public servants for corruption.
33	"	J. Execution of decrees.
35	Arracan.	R. Poll-tax and house-tax

Act.	For what Provinces enacted.	Subject of the Act.
1853.		
2	General.	R. Responsibilities of British subjects holding lands.
6	,,	R. Sales of lands for recovery of arrears of rent.
7	,,	J. Powers of Magistrates in respect of certain offences not felonies.
9	,,	R. Limitation of Act 6, 1853.
10	Bengal.	R. Navigation of boats on the Hooghly.
1854.		
1	Madras.	J. An Act to amend the law for facilitating the acquisition of land for public purposes within the local limits of the jurisdiction of the Supreme Court of Judicature at Madras.
2	Bombay.	J. An Act to abolish the Office of Assessor to the Court of Petty Sessions at Bombay.
3	General.	M. An Act to amend the 38th Article of War for the Native Army.
4	Bombay.	J. An Act relating to the execution of sentences in petty cases by superintendents of Bazaars in the Presidency of Bombay.
5	Bengal.	M. To amend Act 5 of 1838 relating to the Bengal Bonded Warehouse Association.
6	General.	J. To amend the practice and course of proceeding on the Equity side of Her Majesty's Supreme Courts of Judicature at Fort William, in Bengal, Madras, and Bombay.
7	,,	J. For the apprehension within the territories under the Government of the East India Company, of persons charged with the commission of heinous offences beyond the limits of the said territories, and for delivering them up to justice, and to provide for the execution of warrants in places out of the jurisdiction of the authorities issuing them.

Act.	For what Provinces enacted.	Subject of the Act.
1854.		
8	General.	J. To explain and amend Act 10 of 1851, and Act 22 of 1841.
9	„	J. Relating to appeals in the Civil Courts of the East India Company.
10	„	J. For regulating the powers of Assistants to Magistrates and of Deputy Magistrates appointed under Act 15 of 1843.
11	„	R. To amend Act 21 of 1835, and Act 22 of 1844, and to authorize the issue of Half Pice.
12	Madras.	J. For conferring Criminal Jurisdiction upon District Moonsiffs in the Presidency of Madras.
13	Straits' Settlements.	M. To repeal Act 6 of 1852, and to make provision for defraying the cost of the Light House on Pedra Branca, and for maintaining the same, and also a Floating Light established in the Straits of Malacca, to the west of Singapore, and for the establishment and maintenance of such further Lights in or near to the said Straits as may be deemed expedient.
14	General.	J. To continue the operation of Act 19 of 1845, until the 30th day of April, 1855.
15	„	M. To facilitate the proceedings of the Commissioners appointed to inquire into certain matters connected with the position of Sir James Brooke, Her Majesty's Commissioner and Consul General in Borneo.
16	Bengal.	J. To amend Regulation 11 of 1831, of the Bengal Code.
17	General.	M. For the management of the Post Office, for the regulation of the duties of Postage, and for the punishment of offences against the Post Office.
18	„	M. An Act relating to Railways in India.

Act.	For what Provinces enacted.	Subject of the Act.
1854.		
19	General.	R. For removing the prohibition against the importation of Foreign Sugar.
20	Bengal.	J. To amend Regulation 13 of 1833, of the Bengal Code.
21	General.	J. To amend the Law relating to the several Banks of Bengal, Madras, and Bombay.
22	Bengal and Madras.	J. To repeal certain parts of the 53 George 3, c. 155, of Section 2, Regulation 15 of 1806, of the Bengal Code; and of Regulation 4 of 1809 of the Madras Code.
23	Madras.	J. For the suppression of the Outrages in the District of Malabar, in the Presidency of Fort St. George.
24	,,	M. To prohibit the possession of certain offensive Weapons in Malabar.
25	General.	R. For discontinuing the practice of issuing Warrants for the payment of money from the Treasuries of the Collectors.
26	,,	J. For making better provision for the education of male minors, subject to the superintendence of the Court of Wards.
27	,,	J. To amend the law relating to the Nazim of Bengal.
28	Bengal.	M. To continue the Commissioners for the Improvement of the town of Calcutta, pending the consideration of an Act to amend Act 10 of 1852.
29	General.	R. To prohibit the Exportation of Saltpetre to certain Ports in Europe.
30	Tenasserim Provinces.	R. To provide for the levy of Duties of Customs in the Arracan, Pegu, Martaban, and Tenasserim Provinces.
31	General.	J. To abolish real actions and also fines and common recoveries, and to simplify the modes of conveying land in cases to which the English law is applicable.

Act.	For what Provinces enacted.	Subject of the Act.
1854.		
32	Madras.	J. To facilitate inquiries respecting the alleged use of Torture in the Presidency of Fort St. George.
33	General.	J. To extend the provisions of Act 12 of 1843.
34	"	M. For regulating the establishment and management of Electric Telegraphs in India.
1855.		
1	"	M. For providing for the exercise of certain powers by the Governor-General during his absence from the Council of India.
2	"	J. For the further improvement of the law of evidence.
3	"	J. For the better prevention of desertion from the Indian Navy.
4	"	M. For incorporating for a further period, and for giving further powers to the Assam Company.
5	"	J. To assimilate the process of execution of all rules of Her Majesty's Supreme Courts, and to extend and amend the provisions of Act 25 of 1841.
6	"	J. To extend the operation of, and regulate the mode of executing writs of execution in Her Majesty's Supreme Courts of Judicature.
7	"	J. To amend the Law of Arrest on mesne process in civil actions in Her Majesty's Courts of Judicature, and to provide for the subsistence of prisoners confined under the civil process of any of the said courts.
8	"	J. To amend the law relating to the office and duties of the Administrator General.
9	Madras.	J. For the amendment of Procedure in cases of regular appeal to the Sudder Court in the Presidency of Fort St. George.

Act.	For what Provinces enacted.	Subject of the Act.
1855.		
10	Madras and Bombay.	J. To amend the Law relating to the attendance and examination of witnesses in the Civil Courts of the East India Company, in the Presidencies of Fort St George and Bombay, and to amend the provisions of Section 40, Act 19 of 1853.
11	General.	J. An Act relating to mesne profits and to improvements made by holders under defective titles in cases to which the English law is applicable.
12	"	J. To enable executors, administrators, or representatives, to sue and be sued for certain wrongs.
13	"	J. To provide compensation to families for loss occasioned by the death of a person caused by actionable wrong.
14	Madras.	M. For the better regulation of military bazaars in the Presidency of Fort St. George.
15	Bombay.	J. To amend Regulation 3 of 1833 of the Bombay Regulations.
16	"	J. To amend the law in force in the Presidency of Bombay concerning the use of badges.
17	Straits' Settlements.	R. To improve the law relating to the copper currency in the Straits' Settlements.
18	General.	J. To remove doubts relating to the power to grant pardons, reprieves, and remissions of punishments in India.
19	Madras.	J. To amend the law relating to District Moonsiffs in the Presidency of Fort St. George.
20	"	M. For the establishment and maintenance of boundary-marks in the Presidency of Fort St. George.
21	"	J. For making better provision for the education of male minors, and the marriage of male and female minors subject to the superintendence of

Act.	For what Provinces enacted.	Subject of the Act.
1855.		
		the Courts of Wards in the Presidency of Fort St. George.
22	General.	R. For the regulation of ports and port-dues.
23	„	J. To amend the law relating to the administration of the estates of deceased persons charged with money by way of mortgage.
24	„	J. To substitute penal servitude for the punishment of transportation in respect of European and American convicts, and to amend the law relating to the removal of such convicts.
25	Madras.	J. To empower the Session Judge of Coimbatore to hold sessions at Ootacamund on the Neilgherry Hills.
26	General.	M. To facilitate the payment of small deposits in Government savings' banks to the representatives of deceased depositors.
27	„	M. To enable the banks of Bengal, Madras, and Bombay to transact certain business in respect of Government securities and shares in the said banks.
28	„	M. For the repeal of the Usury Laws.
29	„	M. For amending Act No. 6 of 1844.
30	„	M. To repeal section 7 of Act No. 28 of 1839.
31	„	M. Act relating to the emigration of native labourers to the British Colonies of Saint Lucia and Grenada.
32	„	M. Relating to embankments.
33	„	R. To prohibit the exportation of Saltpetre, except in British vessels bound to the ports of London or Liverpool.
34	„	M. To explain and amend Act No. 33 of 1852.
35	Bengal.	R. To abolish the levy of Customs Duty on the import of cotton into the

Act.	For what Provinces enacted.	Subject of the Act.
1855.		North-Western Provinces of the Presidency of Bengal.
36	N. W. Prov.	R. To empower Officers of Customs and Land Revenue to search houses and other enclosed places for contraband salt in the North-Western Provinces
37	Sonthal Districts.	M. To remove from the operation of the general laws and regulations certain districts inhabited by Sonthals and others, and to place the same under the superintendence of an officer to be specially appointed for that purpose.
38	General.	J. To provide for the trial and punishment of rebellion and other offences committed within certain districts in which martial law has lately been proclaimed.
1856.		
1	"	J. To prevent the sale or exposure of obscene books and pictures.
2	"	J. To enable magistrates and certain other officers to take cognizance of certain offences without requiring a written complaint.
3	"	M. To amend Act No. 11 of 1849, and Act No. 19 of 1852.
4	"	J. To prevent the malicious or wanton destruction of cattle.
5	Madras.	M. To give effect to Act 23 of 1854, from the time of its promulgation in the district of Malabar, and to extend the application thereof in future.
6	General.	M. For granting exclusive privileges to Inventors.
7	Bombay.	M. To enable the Bombay Government to provide for a due supply of Water for public use in the islands of Bombay and Colaba.
8	Bombay and Madras.	J. For the better control of the Gaols within the Presidencies of Fort St. George and Bombay.

Act.	For what Provinces enacted.	Subject of the Act.
1856.		
9	General.	R. To amend the law relating to Bills of Lading.
10	"	M. To repeal the 122nd Article of War for the Native Army, and to substitute a new Article in lieu thereof.
11	"	M. For the better prevention of desertion by European soldiers from the Land Forces of Her Majesty, and of the East India Company in India.
12	Bengal.	J. To amend the law respecting the employment of Ameens by the Civil Courts in the Presidency of Fort William.
13	General.	J. For regulating the Police of the towns of Calcutta, Madras, and Bombay, and the several stations of the Settlement of Prince of Wales' Island, Singapore, and Malacca.
14	"	M. For the conveniency and improvement of the towns of Calcutta, Madras, and Bombay, and the several stations of the Settlement of Prince of Wales' Island, Singapore, and Malacca.
15	"	J. To remove all legal obstacles to the marriage of Hindoo widows.
16	"	R. To authorize the levy of Port-dues, and Fees at the present rates, for the further period of twelve months.
17	"	J. To provide for the execution of criminal process in places out of the jurisdiction of the authority issuing the same.
18	Bengal.	R. An Act relating to the administration of the public Revenues in the town of Calcutta.
19	General.	M. To enable the Governor-General of India in Council to suspend the operation of certain Acts relating to the emigration of native labourers.
20	Bengal.	J. To make better provision for the appointment and maintenance of police chowkeydars, in cities, towns,

Act.	For what Provinces enacted.	Subject of the Act.
1856.		stations, suburbs, and bazaars in the Presidency of Fort William, in Bengal.
21	Bengal.	R. To consolidate and amend the law relating to the Abkaree Revenue in the Presidency of Fort William, in Bengal.
22	"	R. For establishing a toll on boats and timber passing through the Kurratiya River, in the district of Bogra.
23	Madras.	R. For the better recovery of arrears of revenue under Ryotwar Settlements in the Madras Presidency.
24	Bengal.	M. To provide for the dissolution of the Bengal Mariners' and General Widows' Fund Society, and the distribution of the funds belonging thereto.
25	General.	R. To comprise in one Act the provisions necessary for the assessment and collection of Municipal rates and taxes in the towns of Calcutta, Madras, and Bombay, and the several stations of the Settlement o. Prince of Wales' Island, Singapore, and Malacca.
26	Madras.	R. For appointing Municipal Commissioners, and for levying rates and taxes in the town of Madras.
27	Straits' Settlements.	R. For appointing Municipal Commissioners, and for levying rates and taxes in the several Stations of the Settlement of Prince of Wales' Island, Singapore, and Malacca.
28	Bengal.	R. For appointing Municipal Commissioners, and for levying rates and taxes in the town of Calcutta.
29	General.	J. Concerning the taking of oaths of office by Registrars of Deeds.
1857. 1	Bengal.	M. To prevent over-crowding of vessels carrying native passengers in the Bay of Bengal.

Act.	For what Provinces enacted.	Subject of the Act.
1857.		
2	Bengal.	M. To establish and incorporate an University at Calcutta.
3	General.	J. An Act relating to trespasses by cattle.
4	Bombay.	R. To amend the law relating to the duties payable on tobacco, and the retail sale and warehousing thereof in the town of Bombay.
5	General.	M. To confer certain powers on the Oriental Gas Company, limited.
6	"	R. An Act relating to acquisition of land for public purposes.
7	Madras.	M. For the more extensive employment of uncovenanted agency in the Revenue and Judicial Departments in the Presidency of Fort St. George.
8	General.	M. To amend Act 19 of 1847.
9	"	M. To repeal Act 6 of 1856.
10	"	M. To amend Act 37 of 1855.
11	"	J. For the prevention, trial, and punishment of offences against the State.
12	Straits' Settlements.	J. To authorise the arrest and detention within the Ports of the Settlement of Prince of Wales' Island, Singapore, and Malacca, of junks or native vessels suspected to be piratical.
13	Bengal.	R. To consolidate and amend the law relating to the cultivation of the Poppy, and the manufacture of Opium, in the Presidency of Fort William, in Bengal.
14		J. To make further provision for the trial and punishment of certain offences relating to the Army, and of offences against the State.
15		M. To regulate the establishment of Printing-presses, and to restrain in certain cases the circulation of printed books and papers.
16		J. To make temporary provision for the trial and punishment of heinous offences in certain districts.

Act.	For what Provinces enacted.	Subject of the Act.
1857.		
17		J. To provide temporarily for the apprehension and trial of native officers and soldiers for mutiny and desertion.
18		J. Relating to the issuing of writs or process against certain members of the family, household, and retinue of His late Highness, the Nabob of the Carnatic.
19		M. For the incorporation and regulation of Joint-Stock Companies and other Associations, either with or without limited liability of the members thereof.
20		M. To amend Act 19 of 1850.
21		J. To make better provision for the order and good government of the suburbs of Calcutta, and of the station of Howrah.
22		M. To establish and incorporate an University at Bombay.
23	General.	M. To provide for the good order and discipline of certain Volunteer Corps, and to invest them with certain powers.
24	"	R. To authorise the levy of port dues and fees at the present rates for a further period of six months.
25	"	J. To render officers and soldiers in the Native Army liable to forfeiture of property for mutiny, and to provide for the adjudication and recovery of forfeitures of property in certain cases.
26	Straits' Settlements.	M. For regulating ferries in the Settlement of Prince of Wales' Island, Singapore, and Malacca.
27	Madras.	M. To establish and incorporate an University at Madras.
28	General.	R. Relating to the importation, manufacture, and sale of arms and ammunition, and for regulating the right to keep or use the same.

Act.	For what Provinces enacted.	Subject of the Act.
1857. 29	Bombay.	R. To make better provision for the collection of Land Customs on certain foreign frontiers of the Presidency of Bombay.

ORDERS IN COUNCIL RELATING TO BRITISH INDIA.

Year.	Orders in Council.
1613	(June 13.) For regulating the trade to the East Indies.
1614	(January.) For ordering certain criminals to be transported to the East Indies.
1615	(July.) For delivering J. Gates and other reprieved convicts to the Governor of the East India Company to be sent to India.
1617	(March 20.) For delivering John Browne, now a prisoner in the Castle of Canterbury, convicted of felony, unto Sir J. Smith, Knight, Governor of the East India Company, to be sent beyond the seas to the East Indies.
1618	(May 28.) Ordering the East India Company to advance, in connection with the Muscovy Company, a loan of 100,000 rubles to the Emperor of Russia.
1619	(February 28.) For separating the financial affairs of the East India Company from the Muscovy Company.
1622	(January 31.) For declaring the will of King James concerning certain points in dispute between the East India Company and the Dutch, and for ordering payment of 20,000*l.* to the Company in reals.
1626	(January 29.) For permitting the East India Company to export bullion.
1627	(January 25.) For ordering vessels belonging to the East India Company to be prepared for Government service.

Year.	Orders in Council.
1631	(September 23.) Ordering strict observance of the Proclamation regulating the East India Company's officers at various outports.
1638	(May 25.) For appointing Committee to inquire into the present state of the trade to the East Indies, and to receive propositions for the better regulation thereof.
——	(September 2.) For declaring His Majesty's answer to four propositions of the East India Company touching the regulation of their trade.
1661	(February 7.) Ordering certain munitions of war to be sent to Bombay.
1662	(March 13.) Ordering Lord Treasurer to send 1000*l.* sterling to Bombay for the present supply of His Majesty's forces there.
1663	(October 21.) Appointing Committee to adjust the differences between the East India Company and the Dutch.
1667	(March 20.) For reforming abuses at Bombay, Surat, and other factories in the East Indies.
1668	(March 6.) Ordering a patent for granting Bombay to the East India Company, to be engrossed, and to pass the seals.
1677	(October 26.) Ordering Mr. Barry at Lisbon to solicit about the quiet possession of the island of Bombaine (Bombay).
1681	(November 23.) Licensing the East India Company to transport sixty-six pieces of iron ordnance to Fort St. George.
1691	(February 4.) Granting Commissions to ships of the East India Company against the French.
1693	(November 2.) Approving the East India Company's Charters, with twenty-six regulations set forth in the Order.
1702	(June 11.) Approving the Indenture uniting the two East India Companies.
1721	(October 2.) Prohibiting ships going to the East Indies from trading to the Plantations.
1726	(August 9.) For passing letters patent granting the Company further privileges and franchises.
1735	(December 18.) Approving proclamation prohibiting all persons from trading to the East Indies, contrary to the privileges granted to the East India Company.
1760	(November 26.) Approving Charter to the East India Company to erect courts of justice near Bencoolen, in the island of Sumatra.

Q

Year.	Orders in Council.
1806	(August 5.) Approving Charter for establishing courts of judicature in the Prince of Wales's Island, and for trial of piracies.
1808	(October 15.) For permitting the East India Company to export stores to their settlements at Canton and St. Helena.
1809	(March 27.) Authorising the East India Company to permit the sale, by public auction, of several articles, the produce and manufacture of China.
1813	(August 14.) For regulating the trade between the United Kingdom and the East Indies.
1827	(March 14.) For submitting for His Majesty's approval a table of fees to be taken in the Supreme Court of Judicature at Bombay.
—	(June 30.) For allowing to the officers of the Bombay Marine, within the limits of the East India Company's Charter, the privilege of taking rank agreeably to their several degrees, with the officers of the Royal Navy.
1828	(March 5.) Approving the report of Committee on certain Rules relating to juries in the Supreme Court of Judicature at Fort William in Bengal.
1829	(June 10.) Approving report of Committee on the petition of Sir Peter Grant, the only surviving justice of the Supreme Court of Judicature at Bombay; also on a memorial from the East India Company.
1830	(June 28.) Approving report of Committee on certain variations in the times of holding Sessions of Oyer and Terminer in the Supreme Court of Bombay.
1832	(July 11.) Approving report of Committee for dismissing petition of certain Hindoos of Bengal, complaining of the suppression of the practice of Suttee by a regulation of the Governor-General of India in Council.
1833	(July 3.) Approving report of Committee on petition of Major-General Sir Lionel Smith on the subject of the Deccan booty.
1836	(April 13.) Approving report of Committee respecting certain rules and orders for the plea, equity, and Crown sides of the Supreme Court of Judicature at Bombay.
—	(November 30.) Approving certain rules proposed by the Commissioners for the affairs of India, relating to the preparation of the annual prospective estimates of vacancies in the Indian establishments under sections 103 and 106 of statute 3 and 4 Will. IV. cap. 85.

Year.	Orders in Council.
1838	(January 23.) Approving report of Committee on certain rules and tables of fees established by the Supreme Court of Judicature in Bengal.
—	(April 10.) Establishing certain rules in appeals from Her Majesty's Supreme Courts in India and elsewhere to the eastward of the Cape of Good Hope.
—	(July 30.) Confirming certain statutes framed by the Commissioners for the affairs of India, under statute 1 and 2 Vict. cap. 22, for the good government of the East India Company's College at Haileybury.
1839	(October 21.) Approving report of Committee on certain alterations in the statutes of the East India Company's College at Haileybury.
1840	(May 7.) For allowing the importation of sugars, the produce of the Presidency of Fort St. George, at a duty of *1l. 4s.* per cwt.
1841	(May 8.) For reducing the duties payable on the produce and manufactures of the British possessions in India on their importation into certain colonies therein named; to wit, Australia, Ceylon, and the Cape of Good Hope.
1842	(April 27.) Confirming certain rules and orders made by the Supreme Court of Judicature at Fort William, October 22, 1841.
1847	(June 17.) For granting Charter of Incorporation to the Eastern Archipelago Company.
—	(July 22.) Approving rules of November 7, 1846, and April 22, 1847, of the Supreme Court of Judicature of Bombay.
1848	(June 27.) Confirming certain rules of October 25, November 15, and December 10, 13, and 22, 1847, and of January 2 and February 2, 1848, of Supreme Court of Judicature of Bengal.
1849	(May 21.) Confirming rules of the Court of Judicature of the Prince of Wales's Island, Singapore, and Malacca, of November 6, 1848.
1850	(June 19.) Disallowing certain rules of the Supreme Court of Judicature of Bengal, confirmed by the Legislative Council of India, under statute 3 and 4 Vict. cap. 34.
1852	(August 18.) For apprehending, within the territories of the East India Company, seamen, being deserters from Russian, Swedish, Norwegian, and Peruvian merchant ships.

ACTS OF THE IMPERIAL PARLIAMENT RELATING TO BRITISH INDIA.

Royal Assent.	Acts of Parliament.
1698	9 and 10 Wm. III. cap 44.—An Act for raising a sum not exceeding two millions upon a fund for payment of annuities after the rate of 8 per cent. per annum, and for settling the trade to the East Indies.
1707	6 Anne, cap. 17.—An Act for assuring to the English Company trading to the East Indies, on account of their United Stock, a larger interest in the fund and trade therein mentioned, and for raising thereby 120,000*l.* for carrying on the war.
1711	10 Anne, cap. 28.—An Act for continuing the trade of the East India Company.
1744	17 Geo. II. cap. 17.—An Act for continuing the trade of the East India Company for a further period.
1754	27 Geo. II. cap. 9.—An Act for punishing mutiny and desertion of officers and soldiers in the service of the United Company of Merchants trading to the East Indies, and for the punishment of offences committed in the East Indies or at the Island of St. Helena.
1767	7 Geo. III. cap. 57.—An Act for establishing an agreement for the annual payment of 400,000*l.* for a limited time, by the East India Company in respect of the territorial acquisitions and revenues lately obtained in the East Indies.
1769	9 Geo. III. cap. 24.—An Act for continuing for five years, the provisions of Statute 6 Geo. III. cap. 57.
1773	13 Geo. III. cap. 63.—An Act to regulate the government of India.
——	13 Geo. III. cap. 64.—An Act to authorise the issue of 1,400,000*l.* in Exchequer Bills, to be applied in relief of the East India Company.
1781	21 Geo. III. cap. 65.—An Act for establishing an agreement with the United Company of Merchants trading to the East Indies, for the payment of the sum of 400,000*l.* in full discharge and satisfaction of all claims of the public, from the time the bond debt of the Company was reduced to 1,500,000*l.* till March 1, 1781.

Royal Assent.	Acts of Parliament.
1784	24 George III. cap. 25.—An Act to provide for the government of India.
1788	28 Geo. III. cap. 8.—An Act to provide for the expense of raising, transporting, and maintaining, such troops as may be required for the security of the British territories in the East Indies.
1793	(June 11.) 33 Geo. III. cap. 52.—An Act for continuing in the East India Company, for a further term, the possession of the British territories in India, together with the exclusive trade under certain limitations; for appropriating to certain uses the revenues and profits of the said Company, and for making provision for the good order and government of the towns of Calcutta, Madras, and Bombay.
1799	39 Geo. III. cap. 89.—An Act for regulating the manner in which the East India Company shall hire and take up ships for their regular service. (Amended by 50 Geo. III. cap. 86.)
1800	(July 28.) 39 & 40 Geo. III. cap. 79.—An Act for establishing further regulations for the government of the British territories in India, and for the better administration of justice within the same.
1802	(March 24.) 42 Geo. III. cap. 29.—An Act to authorise the East India Company to make their settlement at Marlborough, in the East Indies, a factory subordinate to the Presidency of Fort William, in Bengal, and to transfer the servants who, on the reduction of that establisnment, shall be supernumerary, to the Presidency of Fort St. George.
1803	(August 11.) 43 Geo. III. cap. 107.—An Act to enable the Court of Directors of the East India Company to make allowance to the owners of certain ships in their service.
——	(December 15.) 44 Geo. III. cap. 3.—An Act to regulate the bonds issued by the East India Company, with respect to the rate of interest and duty payable thereon.
1805	(April 10.) 46 Geo. III. cap 36.—An Act to enable the East India Company to appoint the Commander-in-Chief on the Bengal establishment to be a member of the Council of Fort William, in Bengal, notwithstanding the office of Governor General of Fort William and of Commander-in-Chief of the forces being vested in the same person.

Royal Assent	Acts of Parliament.
1807	(August 8.) 47 Geo. III. cap. 41. (Sess. 2).—An Act to enable the East India Company to raise money on bond, instead of increasing their capital stock.
——	(August 13.) 47 Geo. III. cap. 68. (Sess. 2).—An Act for the better government of the settlements of Fort St. George and Bombay, for the regulation of public banks, and for amending so much of statute 33 Geo. III. cap. 52, as relates to the periods at which the civil servants of the East India Company may be employed in their service abroad.
1810	(June 15.) 50 Geo. III. cap. 87.—An Act to provide for the raising of men for the service of the East India Company.
——	(June 20.) 50 Geo. III. cap. 114.—An Act for granting to His Majesty a sum of money to be raised by Exchequer Bills, and to be advanced and applied in the manner and on the terms therein mentioned, for the relief of the United Company of Merchants trading to the East Indies. (Amended by 52 Geo. III. cap. 10.)
1811	(June 10.) 51 Geo. III. cap. 64.—An Act to enable the East India Company to raise a further sum of money upon bond, instead of increasing their capital stock.
1812	(July 13.) 52 Geo. III. cap. 121.—An Act to authorise the transfer to the East Indies of debts originally contracted there on the part of the East India Company, payable in England.
——	(July 18.) 52 Geo. III. cap. 135.—An Act for advancing two millions and a half sterling to the East India Company, to enable them to discharge part of the Indian debt.
1813	(July 21.) 53 Geo. III. cap. 155.—An Act for continuing in the East India Company, for a further term, the possession of the British territories in India, together with certain exclusive privileges; for establishing further regulations for the government of the said territories, and the better administration of justice within the same; and for regulating the trade to and from places within the limits of the Company's charter.
1814	(May 17.) 54 Geo. III. cap. 56.—An Act to repeal the duties on teak wood and other ship timber imported from the East Indies.
——	(July 23.) 54 Geo. III. cap. 105 —An Act to remove

Royal Assent.	Acts of Parliament.
	doubts as to the duties and taxes heretofore imposed and levied under the authority of the several Governments in the East Indies.
1815	(May 25.) 55 Geo. III. cap. 64.—An Act to explain and amend 53 Geo. III. cap. 115 so far as relates to the granting gratuities by the East India Company.
——	(June 14.) 55 Geo. III. cap. 84.—An Act to make provision for the Judges in the East Indies in certain cases.
1817	(June 20.) 57 Geo. III. cap. 36.—An Act to regulate the Trade to and from the places within the limits of the Charter of the East India Company, and certain possessions of His Majesty in the Mediterranean.
——	(July 10.) 57 Geo. III. cap. 95.—An Act to exempt the territories within the limits of the East India Company's Charter from certain of the Navigation Laws.
1818	(June 5.) 58 Geo. III. cap. 83.—An Act to amend and reduce into one Act the several laws relating to the manner in which the East India Company are required to hire ships.
——	(June 5.) 58 Geo. III. cap. 84.—An Act to remove doubts as to the validity of certain marriages had and solemnized within the British territories in India.
1820	(July 21.) 1 Geo. IV. cap. 99.—An Act to enable the East India Company to raise and maintain a Corps of Volunteer Infantry.
——	(July 24.) 1 Geo. IV. cap. 101.—An Act to enable the examination of Witnesses to be taken in India in support of Bills of Divorce on account of adultery committed in India.
1822	(July 30.) 3 Geo. IV. cap. 93.—An Act for carrying into execution an agreement between His Majesty and the East India Company.
1823	(July 11.) 4 Geo. IV. cap. 71.—An Act for defraying the charge of retiring pay, pensions, or other expenses of that nature of His Majesty's forces serving in India; for establishing the pensions of the Bishops. Archdeacons, and Judges; for regulating ordinations; and for establishing a Court of Judicature at Bombay,
1824	(June 21.) 5 Geo. IV. cap. 88.—An Act to authorise the East India Company to trade direct from China to the British Colonies and Plantations in America.
——	(June 24.) 5 Geo. IV. cap. 108.—An Act for trans-

Royal Assent.	Acts of Parliament.
	ferring to the East India Company certain possessions, newly acquired, in the East Indies, and for authorising the removal of convicts from Sumatra.
1825	(July 5.) 6 Geo. IV. cap. 85.—An Act for further regulating the payment of the salaries and pensions to the Judges of His Majesty's Courts in India, and the Bishop of Calcutta; for authorising the transportation of offenders from St. Helena, and for more effectually providing for the administration of justice in Singapore and Malacca, and certain colonies on the coast of Coromandel.
1826	(May 5.) 7 Geo. IV. cap. 37.—An Act to regulate the appointment of juries in the East Indies.
——	(May 26.) 7 Geo. IV. cap. 52.—An Act for defraying the expense of any additional naval force to be employed in the East Indies.
1828	(June 27.) 9 Geo. IV. cap. 33.—An Act to declare and settle the law respecting the liability of the real estates of British subjects, and others within the jurisdiction of His Majesty's Supreme Courts in India as assets in the hands of executors and administrators to the payment of the debts of their deceased owners.
——	(July 19.) 9 Geo. IV. cap. 73.—An Act to provide for the relief of insolvent debtors in the East Indies until March 1, 1833 (continued by 4 & 5 Wm. IV. cap. 79, 6 & 7 Wm. IV. cap. 47, and 3 & 4 Vict. cap. 80).
——	(July 20.) 9 Geo. IV. cap. 74.—An Act for improving the administration of criminal justice in the East Indies.
1829	(June 24.) 10 Geo. IV. cap. 62.—An Act to exclude persons accepting offices in the East Indies from being Members of the House of Commons.
1832	(August 16.) 2 & 3 Wm. IV. cap. 117.—An Act to amend the law relating to the appointment of Justices of the Peace and of Juries in the East Indies.
1833	(August 28.) 3 & 4 Wm. IV. cap. 85.—An Act for effecting an arrangement with the East India Company, and for the better government of His Majesty's Indian territories, till April 30, 1854.
——	(August 28.) 3 & 4 Wm. IV. cap. 93.—An Act to regulate the trade of China and India.
——	(August 29.) 3 & 4 Wm. IV. cap. 101.—An Act to provide for the collection and management of the duties on tea.

Royal Assent.	Acts of Parliament.
1834	(July 25.) 4 & 5 Wm. IV. cap. 33.—An Act to repeal so much of several Acts as requires deposits to be made on teas sold at the sales of the East India Company.
1835	(August 31.) 5 & 6 Wm. IV. cap. 52.—An Act to authorise the Court of Directors of the East India Company to suspend the provisions of 3 & 4 Wm. IV. cap. 85, so far as they relate to the government of Agra.
1836	(August 13.) 6 & 7 Wm. IV. cap. 53.—An Act for enabling His Majesty to grant Admiralty Jurisdiction to the Courts of Judicature of Prince of Wales' Island, Singapore, and Malacca.
1837	(July 12.) 7 Wm. IV. & 1 Vict. cap. 47.—An Act to repeal so much of certain existing Acts as prohibits the payment of salaries of the East India Company's officers during their absence from their respective stations in India.
1839	(July 29.) 2 & 3 Vict. cap. 34.—An Act to confirm certain rules and orders of the Supreme Courts of Judicature at Fort William and Madras, and to empower the same Courts, and the Supreme Court of Judicature of Bombay to make rules and orders concerning pleadings.
1840	(August 4.) 3 & 4 Vict. cap. 37.—An Act to consolidate and amend the laws for punishing mutiny and desertion of officers and soldiers in the service of the East India Company, and for providing for the observance of discipline in the Indian Navy.
—	(August 7.) 3 & 4 Vict. cap. 56.—An Act further to regulate the trade of ships built and trading within the limits of the East India Company's Charter.
1841	(April 6.) 4 Vict. cap. 8.—An Act to reduce the duty on rum and rum shrub, the produce of and imported from certain British possessions in the East Indies into the United Kingdom.
1842	(August 10.) 5 & 6 Vict. cap. 101.—An Act for extending to the Governors of the East India Company the powers given by statute 5 Geo. IV. cap. 113, for suppressing the importation of slaves into India by sea.
—	(August 12.) 5 & 6 Vict. cap. 119.—An Act to enable Her Majesty to grant furlough allowances to the Bishops of Calcutta, Madras, and Bombay, who shall return to Europe for a limited period, after residing in India a sufficient time to entitle them to the highest rate of pension.

Royal Assent.	Acts of Parliament.
1844	(June 6.) 7 Vict. cap. 18.—An Act to remove doubts as to the power of appointing and confirming the sentences of courts-martial in the East Indies.
1849	(July 28.) 12 & 13 Vict. cap. 43.—An Act for punishing mutiny and desertion of officers and soldiers in the service of the East India Company, and for regulating, in such service, the payment of regimental debts and the distribution of the effects of officers and soldiers dying in the service.
1851	(July 24.) 14 & 15 Vict. cap. 40.—An Act relating to marriages in India.
——	(August 7.) 14 & 15 Vict. cap. 81.—An Act to authorise the removal from India of insane persons charged with offences, and to give better effect to inquisitions lunacy taken in India.
1853	(August 20.) 16 & 17 Vict. cap. 95.—An Act to provide for the government of India.
1854	(August 7.) 17 & 18 Vict. cap. 77.—An Act to provide for the mode of passing letters patent and other Acts of the Crown relating to India.
1855	(July 16.) 18 & 19 Vict. cap. 53.—An Act to relieve the East India Company from the maintenance of Haileybury College.
——	(August 14.) 18 & 19 Vict. cap. 93.—An Act to amend certain Acts relating to the Court of Judicature of Prince of Wales's Island, Singapore and Malacca.

PARLIAMENTARY REPORTS, ACCOUNTS, AND PAPERS RELATING TO BRITISH INDIA.

Year.	Sessional Number.	Parliamentary Reports, &c.
1772		(May 26.) First and second reports of the Committee (House of Commons) appointed to inquire into the nature, state and condition of the East India Company, and of the British affairs in the East Indies.

Year.	Sessional Number.	Parliamentary Reports, &c.
1772		Third, fourth and fifth reports of the same Committee (presented April 8, and 21, and June 9 of the following year.
——		(Dec. 7.) First and second reports from the Committee of Secrecy, appointed to enquire into the state of the East India Company.
1773		Third, fourth, fifth, sixth, seventh, eighth and ninth reports of the same Committee, presented Feb. 9, March 24, March 30, April 26, May 6, June 11, and June 30 of the same year respectively.
1781		First and second reports of the Committee of Secresy appointed to inquire into the causes of the war in the Carnatic, presented on the 27th of June and 5th July in the same year.
1782		Third, fourth, fifth and sixth reports of the same Committee, presented on the 4th and 6th of Feb., and 1st and 6th March, respectively.
——		First, second, third, fourth, fifth and sixth reports from Select Committee appointed to take into consideration the state of the administration of justice in the Provinces of Bengal, Behar, and Orissa, presented Feb. 5, June 6, June 12, June 18, and July 11 in the same year, respectively.
1783		Seventh, eighth, ninth, tenth and eleventh reports from the same Committee, presented April 23, June 13, June 25, July 10, and November 18 of that year respectively.
——		Report from Committee to whom the petition of the Honourable Company of Merchants trading to the East Indies was referred.
1801	64	Accounts of the annual revenues and disbursements of Bengal, Fort St. George, Bombay, Bencoolen, and Prince of Wales' Island.
——	122	Papers respecting private trade between India and Europe.
1801-2	126	Accounts of annual revenues, &c.
1802-3	60	Accounts of annual revenues, &c.
1803-4	111	Accounts of annual revenues, &c.
——	116	Papers relative to the Mahratta war.

Year.	Sessional Number.	Parliamentary Reports, &c.
1805	40	Papers respecting Prince of Wales' Island.
——	48	Treaties, engagements, and correspondence between the British Government and the Mogul.
1806	158	Accounts of annual revenues, &c.
——	205	Political correspondence relative to Oude.
1806–7	94	Papers relating to the affairs of the Carnatic.
1807	2 24 54	Accounts of annual revenues, &c.
1808	42	Correspondence of Marquess Cornwallis with the Court of Directors.
——	194 240	Accounts of annual revenues, &c.
1809	91	Report of Committee on East India patronage.
——	268	Return of writers and cadets sent to India by the Company.
——	275	Accounts of annual revenues, &c.
1810	227 228	
1810-11	165 200	Accounts of annual revenues, &c.
1812	186 343	
——	377	Fifth report of Committee on Land Revenues, &c.
1813	122	Report of Committee appointed to consider the affairs of the East India Company, and to whom the several petitions relating to the trade and shipping of the said Company, and the renewal of their Charter were referred, and also the petitions of the East India Company, praying to be heard by counsel before the said Committee.
——	194	Papers relating to the Christians in Malabar, Roman Catholic Chapels temple of Juggernaut, missionaries in Bengal, &c.
——	264	Return of answers of circuit judges respecting the religion of the Hindoos; also respecting missionaries, and the first introduction of Christianity into India.
1813–14	188	Accounts of annual revenues, &c.

Year.	Sessional Number.	Parliamentary Reports, &c.
1814-15	39	Regulations passed by the Governments of the three Presidencies.
——	323	Accounts of annual revenues, &c.
1816	381	
1817	310	
——	389	Papers relating to the war in Nepaul.
1818	65	Regulations passed by the Governments of the three Presidencies.
——	302	Accounts of annual revenues, &c.
1819	299	
1820	89 91	
1821	596-618	
1822	433-446	
1823	406-431	
1824	346-460	
1825	315-354	
——	360	Papers relating to the Burmese war, and to discussions with that Government.
——	450	Accounts relating to exports.
——	508-18	Papers relating to the burning of Hindoo widows, and voluntary immolation.
1826	158	Regulations passed by the Governments of Bengal, Fort St. George, and Bombay.
——	276	Returns of shipping and tonnage entered inwards and cleared outwards between the United Kingdom and the Asiatic dependencies.
——	349	Accounts of annual revenues, &c.
	410	
1826-27	330	
1828	325	
——	129	Regulations of the Governments of the three Presidencies.
——	390	Rules relating to juries in the Supreme Court of Judicature at Fort William, in Bengal.
1829	201	Regulations of the Governments in the three Presidencies.
——	240	Accounts of annual revenues, &c.
1830	60-682	Regulations of the Governments at the three Presidencies.
——	398	Accounts of Annual Revenues, &c.
——	633	Returns of East India civil offices.

Year.	Sessional Number.	Parliamentary Reports, &c.
1831	4	Accounts of annual revenues, &c.
——	211	Returns of number and names of persons appointed to judicial stations in British India since January 1, 1801, specifying dates and emoluments, and whether from the English, Irish, or Scotch bar.
——	450	Accounts of annual revenues, &c.
1831	731–5	Reports from Select Committee appointed to consider the present state of the affairs of the East India Company, with an Appendix on the state of society among the Asiatic subjects of Great Britain.
1833	125, 126, 370, 378, 549	Correspondence and papers respecting the renewal of the East India Company's Charter.
——	271	Accounts of annual revenues, &c.
——	277, 754	Regulations of the Governments of the three Presidencies.
1836	518	Report on salt monoply in India.
1837–8	51	Accounts of annual revenues, &c.
——	156	Regulations of the Governments of the three Presidencies.
——	673	Copy of the penal code prepared by the Indian Law Commissioners, published by command of the Governor-General in Council.
1839	40	Treaty with Runjeet Singh and Shah Shujah-ool-Moolk at Lahore, June 26, 1838.
——	55, 125	Return of the number of ecclesiastics of all denominations in the Colonies and territories of the East India Company maintained by grants of public money.
——	431	Various papers relating to the present state of steam communication with India by the various routes, and expenses incurred.
——	552	Accounts of annual revenues, &c.
1840	527	Minute by the Governor-General of India on the cultivation of cotton in the East Indies, and comparative cost of producing cotton-yarn in England and in India.

Year.	Sessional Number.	Parliamentary Reports, &c.
1840 1841	614 22	Accounts of annual revenues, &c.
——	39	Acts of the Government of India.
——	86	Correspondence between the Government of India and the Court of Directors relative to contributions to Hindoo temples.
——	97 428	Statements showing the pay and allowances of Her Majesty's troops serving in India.
1841	328	Dispatch from the Court of Directors on the further severance of Government from all connection with the idolatry and superstition of Mahommedans and Hindoos.
1842	58	Acts of the Government of India.
——	200	Accounts of annual revenues, &c.
——	585	Special reports of the Indian Law Commissioners.
1843	30 85	Proclamations of the Governor-General of India respecting the gates of the temple of Somnauth and the evacuation of Affghanistan.
——	300	Special reports of the Indian Law Commissioners.
——	313 489 490	Treaties with the Ameers of Scinde and other conventions, and correspondence relating thereto.
——	613	Papers relating to infanticide in India.
—— 1844	367 506	Accounts of annual revenues, &c.
1845	272	Special report of the Indian Law Commissioners.
1846	18	Acts of the Government of India.
——	406	Accounts of annual revenues, &c.
1847	14	Special reports of the Indian Law Commissioners.
——	68	Reports relating to railways in India.
——	190	Papers relating to Scinde.
——	439	Return of papers in possession of the East India Company showing the measures taken to promote the cultivation of cotton in India since 1836.
——	712	Report relating to cotton in Bombay.
1847-8	19 330	Special reports from the Indian Law Commissioners.

Year.	Sessional Number.	Parliamentary Reports, &c.
1847-8	123, 137, 167, 184, 206, 230, 245, 361	Eight reports from Select Committee on sugar and coffee planting in the East Indies, with minutes of evidence, appendix, and index.
——	431	Return of register of ships built in the Hooghly from 1781 to 1846.
——	481	Accounts of annual revenues, &c.
——	511	Reports from Select Committee on the growth of cotton in India, with minutes of evidence, appendix, and index.
——	974	Statistics of education in India.
1849	452	Accounts of annual revenues, &c.
——	621	Communications on the connection of the Government of British India with idolatry or Mahommedanism.
1850	479	Accounts of annual revenues, &c.
——	669	Documents relative to the revenue and expenditure of the State of Sattara since the death of the rajah, under the administration of the East India Company.
——	693	Correspondence between Her Majesty's Government and the East India Company and others respecting steam communication viâ Suez to the East Indies, &c.
——	752	Treaties, Acts, and Ordinances, relating to the Roman Catholic Church.
——	1203	Report of Commissioners on law of marriage in the East Indies.
1851	17	Laws passed by the Governor-General in Council in India, in 1847, 1848, and 1849, with indexes.
——	86	Account of exports to, and imports from, the East Indies in 1848.
——	90	Correspondence between the Government of India and the Court of Directors, and the Government of Bombay and the resident Commissioner at Sattara, relative to the annexation and government of that territory.
——	112	Statement showing the cost of postal communication with the East Indies.

Year.	Sessional Number.	Parliamentary Reports, &c.
1851	180, 498	Returns of postage charged on letters to the East Indies, and revenue and expenditure of the several post-offices for the three years ending January 5, 1848.
—	219	Reports and statements relative to the grand trigonometrical survey of India.
—	276	Communications relating to the connection of the Government of British India with idolatry or Mahommedanism.
—	326	Accounts repecting the annual revenues for the last three years.
—	372	First report of Select Committee on steam communication with the East Indies, &c.
—	385	Home accounts of the East India Company.
—	583	Returns showing nature of examination of cadets before appointment or promotion in the Service of the East India Company.
—	605	Second report from Select Committee on steam communication with India.
—	622	Return of all roads, bridges, factories, docks, and all other public works, completed in India by the East India Company within the last ten years, with cost thereof.
—	659	Statement of nature and locality of maritime surveys undertaken by the East India Company since 1820.
1852	41	Lords' report on Indian territories.
—	60	Copies of all documents furnished by the Resident at Sattara to the Bombay Government, showing revenues of Sattara, and charges thereon, under the administration of the East India Company.
—	73	Papers relating to Meer Ali Morad.
—	249	Copies of all tenders, letters, or statements relating to steam communication to the East Indies, &c.
—	338	East India Acts for 1850, with index.
—	87	Returns relating to postal communication in India.
—	361	Return of number of Scholars in the several Educational Establishments of the several Presidencies of British India, dis-

Year.	Sessional Number.	Parliamentary Reports, &c.
		tinguishing Christian, Mussulman, and Hindoo scholars, and whether the Christian Scriptures are used in such Schools.
1852	437	Accounts of annual revenues, &c.
—	484	Home accounts of the East India Company.
—	533	Report from the Select Committee on Indian territories, with minutes of evidence, appendix, and index.
—	561	Correspondence between the Bombay Government and the authorities at home on the trade of Scinde and the establishment of an annual fair at the port of Currachee.
1852-53	41	Report from the Select Committee (House of Lords) on Indian territories, with index.
—	73	Papers relating to Meer Ali Morad and the affairs of Sinde.
—	87	Report respecting postal communications in India, with Despatches from Court of Directors, authorising new regulations.
—	120	Correspondence relating to the departure of East India mail steamers from Southampton.
—	341	Documents relating to the irrigation on the Godavery and Kiatna Annicuts, in the Presidency of Madras.
—	358	Papers relating to appeals from the Courts of India to the Judicial Committee of the Privy Council.
—	369	Statistical papers, recently prepared, relating to India.
—	407 987	Reports and returns relative to public works in Bengal, Madras, and Bombay,
—	426 479 556 692 768 897	First, second, third, fourth, fifth, and sixth reports from Select Committee on Indian territories, with appendix and index.
—	437	Letter dated Nov. 21, 1852, signed by nine Proprietors of East India stock, and the Court's answer thereto (Sattara).
—	439	Papers relating to the Rajah of Sattara.
—	505	Accounts respecting the annual territorial revenues and disbursements of the East

Year.	Sessional Number.	Parliamentary Reports, &c.
		India Company for three years, 1848-9, 1849-50, 1850-1.
1852-53	545	Correspondence and official reports relating to the Madras Railway.
———	555	Statistical Reports on the health of the Navy on the Indian station.
———	560	Home accounts of East India Company.
———	615	Despatches relating to corrupt practices at Baroda.
———	627	First, second, and third reports from the Lords' Committee on Indian territories.
———	632	Correspondence respecting the Government of India, between the Board of Control and Directors.
———	634	Despatches, minutes, and reports from the Madras Government, respecting the origin and transactions of the Porto Novo Iron Company.
———	645	Return respecting calicos, muslins, cotton goods, and cotton yarn, exported from, and imported into India.
———	681	Returns relating to East India Proprietors, their voting, and the patronage of Directors since 1834.
———	741	Correspondence between Court of Directors and Board of Control respecting the India Bill.
———	770	Instructions to the Governor-General of India respecting Sir James Brooke.
———	787	Correspondence relating to railways in India.
———	789	Letter to Secretary to the Government of Bengal, and Minute thereupon by the Governor-General, respecting the revenue on salt.
———	883	Returns of the subjects of the Guicowar enjoying the British guarantee.
———	884	Papers relating to public works, and financial letters from Madras, containing also Instructions from the Court of Directors to the Government of India respecting public works.
———	897	Index and appendix to reports on Indian territories.

Year.	Sessional Number.	Parliamentary Reports, &c.
1852–53	928	Returns of East Indian importations.
——	948	List of covenanted and uncovenanted servants on the East India Civil Service.
——	975	Monies disbursed by way of gratuities in the East Indies at the three Presidencies.
——	988	Despatch respecting the allowance to the temple of Juggernaut from the Treasury.
——	996	Papers relating to the case of Viccajee, Merjee, and Pertonjee Merjee.
——	999	Papers illustrative of the revenue survey and assessment of Bengal and Bombay, with plans.
——	1608	Further papers relating to hostilities with Burmah.
1853	87	Reports from Bengal, and Despatches respecting the establishment of electric telegraphs in India.
——	182	Report of Admiralty surveyors on Calcutta mail packet.
——	407	Reports of Commissioners on public works at Bengal, Madras, and Bombay.
——	692	Regulations respecting batta allowance to military officers in India.
1854	21	Report of Commissioners on public works in Bengal and Bombay.
——	29	Return of sums spent on education in India since 1834.
——	80	Papers relative to Sir Charles Napier's resignation.
——	131	Memorandums of Major Kennedy, with plan respecting railways in India.
——	188	Correspondence respecting the claims of Meer Oomaid Sing.
——	213	Return relating to public works in India.
——	224	Return of the quantity of land under cultivation in the East Indies, and papers respecting public works.
——	247	Correspondence respecting the China expedition.
——	251, 272	Accounts of annual revenues, &c.
——	292	Home accounts of East India Company.
——	318	Correspondence relating to railways in India.

Year.	Sessional Number.	Parliamentary Reports, &c.
1854	393	Despatch relating to education in India.
——	413	Letter from Court of Directors respecting public works in India.
——	416	Correspondence and Treaty relating to the Rajah of Berar.
——	418	Papers relative to the Nizam's territory.
——	483	Reports on the administration of Sinde.
——	497	Correspondence respecting postage in India.
——	513	Despatch from the Court of Directors respecting military appointments in India.
——	514	Number of divisional and brigade commands of the army under each Presidency, distinguishing those held by Queen's and by Company's officers.
——	1843	Payments into the Exchequer from the East India Company.
——	0.5	General report on the administration of the Punjaub for the years 1849-50, and 1850-51.
1855	34	Regulations by Board of Control for examination of candidates for Civil Service.
——	77	Regulations for examination of candidates for assistant surgeons.
——	174	Return of total land forces and police corps commanded by British officers in India.
——	183	Return respecting torture by the police in India.
——	226	Return of sums paid and remaining due for Carnatic debts.
——	242	Receipts and charges from 1850 to 1854 respecting Sattara.
——	243	Reports respecting telegraphs in the East Indies, with a plan.
——	248	Estates to which the Registrars have administered in the Supreme Court of Calcutta.
——	253	Territorial accounts of the East India Company.
——	272	Abstract of correspondence respecting railways in India.
——	279	Amount of four per cent. Stock of the East India Company, accepted by holders of the various five per cent. Stocks.

Year.	Sessional Number.	Parliamentary Reports, &c.
1855	300	Home accounts of the East India Company.
—	325	Revenue accounts.
—	336	Gross revenue derived annually from all sources of taxation in India.
—	346	Despatch respecting an alleged case of torture.
—	356	Army school regulations at Madras.
—	420	Report of Commission for the investigation of alleged cases of torture at Madras.
—	423	Documents under the title "Selections from the records of Government."
—	431	Treaty between the Sobadah of Jhansi and the British Government concluded in the year 1817, relating to the annexation of that territory.
—	435	Letters relative to the alleged use of torture by the native officers of the Government at Madras.
—	455	Despatches relating to the annexation of Kerowlee.
—	513, 514	Reports of examiners of candidates for assistant-surgeons for the Civil Service.
1856	46	Names of all officers commanding brigades in the last Burmese war.
—	48	Despatch relating to judicial establishments in India.
—	63	Copy of an Act for the administration of the estate of the Nawab of Surat.
—	82	Correspondence relating to the annexation of Berar.
—	102	Return of sums borrowed from the king of Oude between the year 1811 and 1855.
—	104	Territorial revenues for three years.
—	133	Returns of territories annexed to the British dominions since the close of the Punjaub war by the Governor-General of India.
—	168	Account of gross and net revenues of India.
—	245	Copy of minute by Marquis of Dalhousie.
—	265	Minutes of evidence before Select Committee on Nawab of Surat Treaty Bill.
—	267	Returns of pensions exceeding 200*l.* a year granted to Governors and ex-Governors

Year.	Sessional Number.	Parliamentary Reports, &c.
		General of India since Stat. 33 Geo. III. cap. 52.
1856	271	Home accounts of East India Company.
——	284	Resolution of Court of Directors granting pension to Marquis of Dalhousie.
——	288	Names of all officers who were honourably mentioned in the despatches of Lord Gough.
——	305	Copies of treaties with the Nawab of Baroda, Surat, and others.
——	317	Correspondence relating to examinations for Civil Service.
——	341	Copies of all treaties and connections made with the Native States of India since May 1, 1834.
——	362	Prices for making up regimental clothing in India.
——	2086	Papers relating to Oude.
——	2035	First, second, third, and fourth reports of commissioners on reform of judicial establishments and laws of India.
——	2036	
——	2097	
——	2098	
——	2084	Report of commissioners on manufacture, sale, and tax on salt in British India, with maps and plans.
——	2089	Ships and emigrants dispatched from Calcutta to the West Indies, from the West to the East Indies, and from Madras to the Mauritius.
1857	12	Despatch of Directors relating to Government of Oude.
——	31	Papers relating to the Nawab of Surat.
——	33	Returns relating to opium.
——	41	Territorial revenues of East India Company for 1854–5.
——	51	Circular of Governor-General in Council, dated February 28, 1856, calling for opinions on the Law Commission—Reports on judicial establishments, also Memorial of missionaries of Bengal on the state of that province, with the reply of the Government.
——	52	Papers relating to military education at Addiscombe.
——	60	Returns of charges to East India Government in growth and monopoly of opium—

Year.	Sessional Number.	Parliamentary Reports, &c.
	•	Return by the East India Government of the charges incurred in the growth and monopoly of opium.
1857	63	Correspondence relating to expedition to Persia.
—	71	Papers relating to the Nawab of Surat.
—	79	Correspondence relating to the Hindostan and Tibet-road-project, with the several Reports of Major Kennedy and Lieut. Briggs relating thereto.
—	81	Returns of capital due to various East Indian railways from East India Company.
—	82	Return of law expenses in England charged on revenues of East India Company. or to be charged thereon for the years 1855 and 1856.
—	85	Return showing value of silver coinage at mints of Calcutta. Madras, and Bombay.
—	110	Home accounts of East India Company.
—	111	Despatch from Court of Directors relating to memorial of Missionaries.
—	112	Return showing under which tenure and subject to which land-tax lands are held in the several Presidencies.
—	117	Correspondence relating to torture in India.
—	118	Despatches relating to confiscation of territories of Ameer Ali Morad.
—	120	Returns of outlay by East India Company on Indian railways and canals.
—	127	Despatch relating to police system in Bengal Presidency.
—	135	Territorial accounts of East India Company.
—	140	Returns of all creditors on State of Oude.
—	166	Despatch relative to Bengal Military Fund.
—	167	Estimate of sum to be voted in 1857, for the Persian expedition.
—	177	Estimate of extraordinary expenditure—Persian expedition.
—	191	Account of expenditure by East India Company on China War.
—	193	Supplemental estimate ditto.

Year.	Sessional Number.	Parliamentary Reports, &c.
1857	194	Correspondence respecting European troops.
—	198	Despatch relating to police in Bengal.
—	209	Memorandum on Indian railways, with map.
—	215	Return of area and population of all the Presidencies of India, and estimated population of Native States.
—	219	Report of Sir C. Napier to the Duke of Wellington, on discipline of Indian army.
—	225	Reprint of appendix to report on Indian territories, 1853.
—	247	Extract of letter from Sir C. Napier to Duke of Wellington, June 14, 1850—Appendix to mutiny papers.
—	258	Amount to the credit of "Security Fund," of East India Company under statute 3 & 4 Wm. IV. cap. 85.
—	285	Statement of importations, 1853 to 1855.
—	295	Letter from the Court of Directors relative to the education of the Sonthals.
—	296	Measures taken relative to cotton since 1847.
—	322	Correspondence on the Levying Dues, Singapore.
—	341	Returns respecting titles of Land Commission in Bombay.
—	342	Returns relative to liberty of the press.
—	2217	Correspondence respecting relations with Persia.
—	2218	Treaty of Peace with Persia.
—	2252	Papers relating to mutinies in the East Indies.
—	2254	Appendix to papers relating to the mutinies in the East Indies.
—	2264	Supplement to papers relating to the mutinies in the East Indies.
—	2265	Appendix to papers on the mutinies in the East Indies.
—	2266	Further papers on the mutinies in the East Indies.
—	2277	Further papers on the mutinies in the East Indies.

APPENDIX A.

MR. FOX'S EAST INDIA BILLS.

First Bill. "*A Bill for vesting the Affairs of the East India Company in the hands of certain Commissioners, for the benefit of the Proprietors and the Public;*" *introduced into the House of Commons, in November,* 1783.

WHEREAS disorders of an alarming nature and magnitude have long prevailed, and do still continue and increase, in the management of the territorial possessions, the revenues, and the commerce of this kingdom in the East Indies, by means whereof the prosperity of the natives hath been greatly diminished, and the valuable interests of this nation in the said territorial possessions, revenues, and commerce have been materially impaired, and would probably fall into utter ruin if an immediate and fitting remedy were not provided:

S. 1. Be it therefore enacted by the King's Most Excellent Majesty, by and with the advice of the Lords Spiritual and Temporal, and the Commons, in this present Parliament assembled, and by the authority of the same, that the government and management of the territorial possessions, revenues, and commerce of the United Company of Merchants of England trading to the East Indies, by the Directors and Proprietors of the said Company, or either of them, and all and singular the powers and authorities of the said Directors and Proprietors, or of any special or general or other Court thereof, in the ordering and managing the said possessions, revenues, and commerce, and all elections of Directors of the said United Company, be, and are hereby declared to be, discontinued for and during the continuance of this Act, any charter, usage, law, or statute to the contrary notwithstanding. Fox's India Bills.

S. 2. And be it further enacted by the authority aforesaid, that for the better governing, ordering, and managing the said territorial possessions, revenues, and commerce, the Right Honourable William Earl Fitzwilliam, the Right Honourable Frederick Montagu, the Right Honourable George Legge, commonly called Lord Viscount Lewisham, the Honourable George Augustus North, Sir Gilbert Elliott, Baronet, Sir Henry Fletcher, Baronet, and Robert Gregory, Esquire, shall be and they are hereby constituted and appointed Directors of the said United Company, and shall be and they are hereby constituted members of the said Company; and that the said Directors hereby appointed, or any three of them, shall have, use, possess, and exercise all and singular the powers and authorities which have been at any time heretofore vested in, or lawfully exercised by, the said Directors hereby discontinued, or Proprietors, or by the General Court of Proprietors of the said United Company, and all such further and other powers and authorities, and under such directions, and subject to such limitations and restrictions as in this Act, or in any other Act, the provisions whereof are not hereby altered or repealed, are contained, for the government and management of the said territorial possessions, revenues, and commerce of the said United Company, or in anywise relative thereto.

S. 3. And be it further enacted by the authority aforesaid, that the said Directors hereby appointed shall, and they are hereby authorized and empowered, immediately and after the commencement of this Act, to enter into and upon and to possess themselves of all lands, tenements, houses, and warehouses, and other buildings whatever of or belonging to the said United Company; and also to take into their custody and

Fox's India Bills.

possession all books, records, documents, charters, acts, instruments, letters, and other papers whatsoever; and also all ships and vessels, goods, wares, merchandizes, money, securities for money, and all other effects whatsoever of or belonging to the said United Company, in trust for and for the benefit of the Proprietors thereof; and to have, hold, and possess the same in like manner as they were held and possessed by the Directors hereby discontinued, subject to such charges, claims, and demands as do or may affect the same; which Directors so discontinued, and all other officers and servants of the said United Company, are hereby enjoined, immediately upon the requisition of the said Directors hereby appointed, signified under their hands and seals, or the hands and seals of any three of them, to deliver to them, or to such person or persons as they shall for that purpose appoint, all such lands, tenements, houses, warehouses, buildings, books, records, documents, charters, acts, instruments, papers, ships, vessels, goods, wares, and merchandizes, money, securities for money, and all other effects whatsoever.

S. 4. And for the sole purpose of ordering and managing the commerce of the said United Company, under and subject to the orders and directions of the said Directors hereby appointed, be it further enacted by the authority aforesaid, that Thomas Cheap, Esquire, George Cuming, Esquire, Richard Hall, Esquire, John Harrison, Esquire, Joseph Sharp, Esquire, John Michie, Esquire, John Smith, Esquire, George Tatem, Esquire, and James Moffatt, Esquire, being Proprietors, each of them two thousand pounds capital stock in the said United Company at least, shall be Assistant Directors for the purpose aforesaid; and shall from time to time, without requisition, and also as often as they shall be thereunto required, render an account of their proceedings to the said Directors hereby appointed, and in all matters and things whatsoever shall pursue and follow such orders and directions as they shall from time to time receive from such Directors.

S. 5. And be it further enacted by the authority aforesaid, that in case any vacancy or vacancies shall happen in the office of the said Directors hereby appointed, by death, resignation, removal, or otherwise, such vacancy or vacancies shall be filled by His Majesty, under his Sign Manual, within twenty days after notice of such vacancy or vacancies shall have been given to one of His Majesty's principal Secretaries of State.

Fox's India Bills.

S. 6. And be it further enacted by the authority aforesaid, that in case any vacancy or vacancies shall happen in the office of the said Assistant Directors, by death, resignation, removal, or otherwise, such vacancy or vacancies shall be filled by the majority of the Proprietors of the said United Company, qualified in the manner required by an Act of the thirteenth year of his present Majesty, intituled "An Act for establishing certain Regulations for the better Management of the Affairs of the East India Company, as well in India as in Europe;" which Proprietors, at such election of any Assistant Director, shall not vote by ballot, or in any other covert or concealed manner, but in an open court, for that purpose only specially summoned; and every such Proprietor, by giving his or her vote, shall subscribe his or her name in a book to be prepared for that purpose, under the name of the person for whom he or she shall vote.

S. 7. And be it further enacted by the authority aforesaid, that if five of the said Directors hereby appointed, who shall be present at any meeting, shall, upon inquiry, and after examination into the conduct and behaviour of the said Assistant Directors, find that any of them is guilty of neglect or misdemeanor in the execution of his said office, or of wilful disobedience of any order or orders of the said Directors hereby appointed, they are hereby authorized and empowered to remove and displace such Assistant Directors; entering in their journals their reasons respectively for removing or displacing such Assistant Director, signed with their respective names.

S. 8. And be it further enacted by the authority aforesaid,

Fox's India Bills.

that the said William, Earl Fitzwilliam, shall be, during his continuance as a Director by virtue of this Act, Chairman of the Board of Directors, and the said Right Honourable Frederick Montagu, Deputy-chairman thereof; and if the said Chairman shall die, resign, or be removed from such office of Director, at any time during the continuance of this Act, then and in that case the said Deputy-chairman shall succeed to the office of Chairman of the said Board of Directors; and if the said Deputy-chairman, being become Chairman of the said Board of Directors, shall also die, resign or be removed from the said office of a Director, then and in that case, and also in every other case of a vacancy in the office of a Chairman of the said Board of Directors, the said Directors hereby appointed shall choose and elect one of themselves to supply such vacancy; and if a vacancy, either by succession, or otherwise, shall at any time happen in the said office of Deputy-chairman of the said Board of Directors, established by this Act, the said Directors hereby appointed shall, in like manner, choose and elect one of themselves to supply such vacancy.

S. 9. And be it further enacted by the authority aforesaid, that the said Chairman of the said Board of Directors, or, in his absence, the said Deputy-chairman, shall have power to call or summons any extraordinary meeting of the said Directors hereby appointed, at such time or times as he shall think expedient; and may, at any meeting whatever of such Directors, if he shall think fit, propose the business to be first considered by such Directors at such meeting; and in case of an equal division of voices on any question whatever before the said Board of Directors, shall have the casting voice; provided always, that nothing herein contained shall prevent the majority of such Directors present at any meeting from adjourning their meetings to such time or times as they shall think proper.

S. 10. And be it further enacted by the authority aforesaid, that it shall not be lawful for the said Directors hereby appointed, or any of them, upon any question whatever, to vote by ballot, or in any other covert manner; and that in any difference of opinion, except as to the election to offices of persons not having before been in the service of the said United Company, the said Directors (as well the majority as those who shall dissent) shall each of them enter, on the journals of the said Directors, his reasons for his vote, signed with his name, or his adherence to the reasons entered by any other Director. Fox's India Bills.

S. 11. And be it further enacted by the authority aforesaid, that no person furnishing the said United Company with shipping, or with any article of their investment outwards, either from Great Britain, or from such ports and places as the Company's ships have occasion to touch at in their way to India, or with any naval or military stores, or concerned in buying and selling any commodity of the said United Company's importation, shall be capable of being a Director or Assistant Director for the execution of this Act.

S. 12. And be it also enacted by the authority aforesaid, that no person shall be capable of being a Director or Assistant Director for the execution of this Act, against whom the charge of any corrupt practice, peculation, or oppression in India, doth or shall appear in the records of the said United Company, within the space of two years before the time of his nomination; or shall be made upon oath before the said Directors, hereby appointed within the space of two years before his nomination, until such Directors, or three of them, shall have examined into the same, and shall have severally declared that they have examined into the said charge, and do in their conscience believe such person not guilty of the said charge; or that they do, upon the said examination, find the said charge not of sufficient importance to exclude the said person from the said office of Director, or Assistant Director, as the case may be; and that they have entered upon their journals their reasons for such their opinion.

S. 13. And be it further enacted by the authority aforesaid, that no person who hath been, now is, or shall hereafter be, in the service of the said United Company in India, shall be capable of being a Director, or Assistant Director, for the execution

Fox's India Bills.

of this Act, within the space of two years from the time of his last return from India.

S. 14. And be it further enacted by the authority aforesaid, that the said Directors hereby appointed shall, once in every six months, lay before the Proprietors of the said United Company, in a General Court to be for that purpose assembled, an exact state of the debts and credits of the said United Company; the first cost and charges of their investments, outward and inward; with the sums of money in India applicable to an investment, according to the last accounts received therefrom; an account of the shipping; an account of the produce of the sales; and the state of the warehouses at home and abroad.

S. 15. And be it further enacted by the authority aforesaid, that the said Directors hereby appointed shall, within twenty days after the commencement of every session of Parliament, lay before the Lords Commissioners of His Majesty's Treasury (who are hereby authorized and required, without loss of time, to lay the same before both Houses of Parliament) an account of the produce of the territorial and other revenues of the said United Company in India; and also estimates of the civil, military, and naval establishments there; together with a state of the bond and other debts due from the said United Company in India, distinguishing what belongs to each of the principal Presidencies and Settlements of the said United Company in India; and also the state of the trade, laid by the said Directors before the said Proprietors at their then last General Court.

S. 16. And be it further enacted by the authority aforesaid, that the said Directors hereby appointed, or the major part of them, shall have full power and authority to remove, displace, suspend, appoint, confirm or restore, all and every person or persons whatsoever, from or to any office, station or capacity whatsoever, civil or military, in the service of the said United Company, or within the limits of the said United Company's charters, or any of them, or any way concerned in the management of their affairs within this kingdom, or in India, whether any such person or persons shall have been nominated or appointed in and by any Act or Acts of Parliament, or however otherwise nominated or appointed; except as herein provided and established, as to the appointment and removal of such Directors themselves, and of the said Assistant Directors. Fox's India Bills.

S. 17. And for the more speedy and effectual punishment of offences committed in India by persons employed in the service of the said Company, be it enacted by the authority aforesaid, that whenever any charge of corruption, peculation, oppression, extortion, receipt of presents, usury, breach of orders, or other grievous offence, shall be exhibited or made before the Governor-General and Council of Bengal, or the President and Council of any of the Presidencies or Settlements abroad of the said United Company, and transmitted from thence to the Court of Directors hereby discontinued, or to the said Directors hereby appointed, against any of the said Governors, Presidents or Members of the Council of any of the said Presidencies or Settlements of the said United Company, or others, in any office, station or employment, civil or military, in the said United Company's Service; or which shall be exhibited or made by any of the Native Princes dependent upon, or under the protection of the said United Company, against any such person or persons; the said Directors hereby appointed shall, within twenty days after the same shall be received, enter into an examination of such charge; and if, upon or in consequence of such examination, such Directors shall not think proper either to recall or order a prosecution against such person so charged, each and every such Director, making such examination as aforesaid into such charge, shall enter in writing, and subscribe with his name, in the journals of such Directors, his opinion on the validity and importance of such charge, with his specific reasons, on the particular case, for not recalling the person so charged, or for not ordering a prosecution upon such charge.

S. 18. And be it further enacted by the authority aforesaid,

Fox's India Bills.

that before any person or persons whatsoever, in the employment, civil or military, of the said United Company in any of their Presidencies, and against whom any charge shall appear upon any of the Company's records, or shall have been made to the said Court of Directors hereby discontinued, or General Court of Proprietors, or shall be made or exhibited to the said Directors hereby appointed, shall be permitted by the said Directors hereby appointed to return to any part of India, either in the same or in any other office, station or employment, in the service of the said United Company; and also, before the said Directors hereby appointed shall confirm the appointment, or suffer the departure from Great Britain for India, of any person or persons who may have been, or shall be, appointed to any office, station or employment whatsoever, in the service of the said United Company, and against whom any such charge shall appear, or shall have been made, or shall be made as aforesaid; and also before the said Directors hereby appointed shall themselves appoint any person, having before been in the service of the said United Company, to any office, station or employment whatsoever, in the said United Company's Service, and against whom any such charge shall appear, or shall have been made, or shall be made as aforesaid, the said Directors hereby appointed shall, and they are hereby required to make a full and particular examination and inquiry into the conduct of every such person relative to the said service, and the subject-matter of such charge; and shall enter on their journals their reasons for permitting any such person to return, or confirming the appointment, and permitting the departure of any such person, or for themselves appointing any such person (as the case may be) notwithstanding such charge.

S. 19. And be it further enacted by the authority aforesaid, that in case of any disputes, differences or controversies whatsoever, which have arisen and are depending, or may hereafter arise, between the Governor-General and Council of Bengal, or between any of the Presidents of any other of

Fox's India Bills.

the Settlements of the said United Company and their respective Councils; or between the government of one Settlement and the government of any other Settlement, or between any of the Governors or presiding powers of any of the subordinate Settlements; the said Directors hereby appointed shall, within twenty days after the receipt of any official account of such dispute, difference, or controversy, enter upon an examination and inquiry into the same, and shall, within three months thereafter, either come to a definitive decision thereupon, or enter upon their journals their reasons, signed with their respective names, for not coming to such definitive decision.

S. 20. And be it further enacted by the authority aforesaid, that if at any time the Governor-General and Council of Bengal, or the President and Council of any of the principal or subordinate Settlements, shall require the direction or opinion of the said Directors hereby appointed, on any matter whatsoever for the government of such Governor-General and Council, or President and Council, or for the settlement or accommodation of any matter in dispute, or likely to come into dispute between or among them, or any of them; the said Directors shall return an answer, opinion, or direction, to such requisition, within three months after receiving the letter or letters containing the same, or enter upon their journals their reasons, signed with their respective names, for not sending the same within the time aforesaid.

S. 21. And be it enacted by the authority aforesaid, that if at any time complaint shall be made of any breach of treaty, injury, wrong, or grievance, done or committed against any Native Prince in India, by any of the governments of the said United Company's Settlements, or any officer or other person, civil or military, in the service of the said United Company; or if any such breach of treaty, injury, wrong, or grievance, shall (without complaint being made thereof) appear upon any part of the correspondence relating to the said United Company's affairs, the said Directors hereby appointed shall, as speedily as may be, inquire into such breach

Fox's India Bills.

of treaty, injury, wrong, or grievance, and shall begin their examination into the same by reading and considering any treaties, agreements or assurances, subsisting between the said United Company and such Native Prince, or any way relative to him, if any such there shall be, or any orders which may have been given by the Court of Directors hereby discontinued, or General Court of Proprietors relating to such Native Prince; and the said Directors hereby appointed shall do full and complete justice to such Native Prince, for such breach of treaty, injury, wrong or grievance, and on every material article and head of charge (if there be more than one) specifically, and not upon the whole of such charge in gross.

S. 22. And be it further enacted by the authority aforesaid, that three, and not less, of the said Directors shall form a board for executing this Act, or any of the powers thereof, or any other powers vested in or committed to, or which shall be vested in or committed to, such Directors; and the major part of the said Directors present shall determine, except where the voices shall be equally divided, and then the Chairman, or in his absence the Deputy-chairman, shall have two voices, or the casting voice.

S. 23. And be it further enacted by the authority aforesaid, that all the correspondence of the said Directors hereby appointed, with all persons whatsoever in the service of the said United Company, shall be signed by the Secretary of such Directors, by order of the Board.

S. 24. And whereas, by virtue of the charter of the said Company, and the regulations which have from time to time been made for the better government of the said Company, it is required that certain acts should be done or consented to, and that certain accounts should be signed by a particular number of the Directors hereby discontinued: Be it therefore enacted by the authority aforesaid, that in all cases whatsoever where any act, matter or thing is directed to be done or consented to, or any accounts or writing to be signed by the Directors hereby discontinued, or to be done or consented to or signed by any particular number of such Directors, such act, matter or thing shall, from and after the commencement of this Act, be done or consented to, and such accounts or writing shall be signed by three of the Directors hereby appointed. Fox's India Bills.

S. 25. And be it further enacted by the authority aforesaid, that the said Directors hereby appointed and Assistant Directors, and each and every of them, during the continuance of this Act, shall be utterly incapable of taking, holding or exercising any office, station or employment whatsoever in the service of the said United Company, and shall also be incapable of taking, holding, or exercising any other place of profit from the Crown during pleasure.

S. 26. And be it further enacted by the authority aforesaid, that it shall and may be lawful for His Majesty to remove any of the said Directors hereby appointed or Assistant Directors, upon an address of either House of Parliament.

S. 27. And whereas a doubt may arise whether the place of Director, when the same shall be held by any person to be appointed by His Majesty in manner hereinbefore provided, be not within the provision of an Act of the sixth year of the reign of Queen Anne, intituled "An Act for the Security of Her Majesty's Person and Government, and of the Succession to the Crown of Great Britain in the Protestant Line," although the said place shall have been created and erected by authority of Parliament: Be it therefore enacted and declared by the authority aforesaid, that such office shall not be deemed and taken to be within the intent and purview of the said Act, nor shall any person accepting and holding the same, by an appointment from His Majesty under his Royal Sign Manual, be thereby disqualified from being elected, or sitting and voting as a Member of the House of Commons.

S. 28. And be it further enacted by the authority aforesaid, that there shall be allowed and paid for and to each of the Assistant Directors, for so long time as he shall continue in the office, a clear yearly salary of five hundred pounds,

Fox's India Bills. payable by half-yearly payments, and that the respective payments of the said salaries shall be stated and allowed in the account of the disbursements for the management of the affairs of the said United East India Company.

S. 29. And be it further enacted by the authority aforesaid, that this Act, and all the provisions herein contained, shall commence and take effect from and immediately after this Act shall have received His Majesty's Royal Assent, and shall continue and be in full force for and during the space of four years.

Second Bill.

"A Bill for the better Government of the Territorial Possessions and Dependencies in India."

WHEREAS great disorders have prevailed in the government of the British territorial possessions and dependencies thereof in India, and the laws and lawful authority of this kingdom have not been duly obeyed by divers of the servants of the United Company of Merchants trading to the East Indies:

S. 1. For remedy whereof in future, be it declared and enacted, and it is hereby declared and enacted by the King's Most Excellent Majesty, by and with the advice and consent of the Lords Spiritual and Temporal, and Commons, in this present Parliament assembled, and by the authority of the same, that there is not, nor hath been, any privilege, authority, power, pre-eminence, or jurisdiction granted, or meant or intended to be granted, in and by an Act of the thirteenth year of his present Majesty, intituled "An Act for establishing certain Regulations for the better Management of the Affairs of the East India Company, as well in India as in Europe," or in and by any other Act or Acts whatsoever, or in and by any law or usage whatsoever, for the Governor-General and Council of Bengal, or either or any of them, collectively or individually, or any other person whatsoever in the service of the said United Company, which doth or shall in any manner exempt him or them, in the exercise of any powers or authorities whatsoever, from a strict and faithful obedience to the orders and directions which have been issued to or for them from the late or any other Court of Directors, or which shall or may be issued to or for them by the Commissioners named and appointed in an Act of this session of Parliament, to manage and govern the affairs of the said United Company, instead of the said Court of Directors and General Court of Proprietors, or such other Commissioners as shall or may be lawfully appointed for exercising the powers given them in and by the said Act.

Fox's India Bills.

S. 2. And be it further declared and enacted, that all general or special orders of the Court of Directors of the said United Company for the regulation of the conduct of the Governor-General and Council of Bengal, or of any other President and Council, or of any other person or persons, in any other station, office, employment or capacity whatsoever, in the service of the said United Company, shall be, and are hereby declared to be, rules by which the persons hereinbefore described shall be governed and directed, until notice shall be given by the said Commissioners, of any alteration, revocation or repeal of them, or any of them.

S. 3. And whereas pretences have been used to evade the salutary regulations of the said Act of the thirteenth year of His Majesty's reign, relative to rules, ordinances and regulations, as if the provisions contained in the said Act, relative thereto, were confined to certain forts and factories; whereby a power subject to no control has been exercised throughout the provinces of Bengal, Bahar and Orissa; be it therefore declared and enacted, that all rules, ordinances and regulations, which by the said Act it is made lawful for the Governor-General and Council of Fort William, to issue, for the good order and civil government of the said Settlement, under certain restrictions and provisions in the said Act contained, are not meant nor intended to be confined only to such rules, ordinances and regulations, as are made or issued for the government of, or relative to forts and factories, or other subordinate places in the said Settlement only; but shall,

Fox's India Bills.

and all such restrictions and provisions are hereby expressly declared to extend, without any exception or limitation whatsoever, to all rules, ordinances and regulations, as are made or issued for the government of, or relative to forts and factories, or other subordinate places, in the said Settlement only; but shall, and all such restrictions and provisions are hereby expressly declared to extend, without any exception or limitation whatsoever, to all rules, ordinances and regulations, made and issued by the said Governor-General and Council of Fort William, in whatever place, or wheresoever, or over whatsoever class or description of persons, the same are to operate.

S. 4. And be it further enacted by the authority aforesaid, that any such rule, ordinance or regulations, shall not only be duly registered and published in the Supreme Court of Judicature, but an account or abstract of the true effect and substance thereof, and of every clause and provision thereof, in the Persian and Hindostan languages, shall be registered and published, and affixed up in some commodious and conspicuous place, in each and every provincial court within the provinces of Bengal, Bahar, and Orissa, or within the territory to which it relates.

S. 5. And be it enacted by the authority aforesaid, that no delegation whatsoever of the powers of Governor-General and Council of Bengal, or of any President and Council of any other of the said Settlements, shall be made or given to the said Governor-General or President, or any other person or persons whatsoever; and in case the said Governor-General, or any Member of the Council of Bengal, or any President or Member of the Council of any other of the said Settlements, or any other person or persons whatsoever, shall be employed in the execution of any special commission, the proceedings thereupon shall not be finally approved and confirmed until a full report of the same shall be made to the said Governor-General and Council, or President and Council, respectively; and the person or persons so employed shall, upon the requisition of the Governor-General or President, or any Member of the said Council, deliver into Council his documents or vouchers in support of any particular fact or facts alleged by him to have happened in the execution of such commission, and in support of which documents or vouchers might have been had.

S. 6. And be it further enacted by the authority aforesaid, that all correspondence and communication whatsoever, of or by any resident, agent or other person employed at the Court of any Native Prince or State, or of or by any such Native Prince or State, or any Agent or Minister of such Native Prince or State, or of or by any Chief and Council of any Factory or subordinate Settlement, or any of them, or of or by any Collector of Revenue, shall be addressed to the Governor-General or President respectively; and all correspondence and communication whatsoever of or by any such person or persons, whether addressed to the said Governor-General or his Secretary, or to any Member of the Council or his Secretary, shall be laid before the Council after the same shall be received.

S. 7. And be it enacted by the authority aforesaid, that the Governor-General of Bengal and the President of any other of the said principal Settlements in India, may, by his own authority, adjourn or postpone the consideration of any question whatsoever, in the respective Councils in which they preside, for the space of . . . . . . * and no longer: Provided always, that such Governor-General or President shall not have power to adjourn or postpone the same question more than . . . . *

S. 8. And be it enacted by the authority aforesaid, that neither the Governor-General and Council of Bengal, nor President and Council of any other of the said United Company's Presidencies or Settlements in India, shall have power to cede to, or exchange with, any Native Prince or State whatsoever, any territory which was in the possession of the said United Company, or of any of its dependent Princes or States, in or immediately before the year . . . . . . * nor shall

* Blanks left in the Bill.

Fox's India Bills.

make or accept any acquisition whatsoever, whereby the territory of the said United Company shall be increased or extended, without orders or directions expressly for that purpose, transmitted by the said Commissioners appointed in and by an Act of this present session of Parliament, for managing the affairs of the said United Company.

S. 9. And be it enacted by the authority aforesaid, that it shall not be lawful for the said Governor-General and Council of Bengal to invade, or enter with any armed force, or in any hostile or offensive manner, into the territory of any Native independent Prince or State in India, except upon intelligence, the credibility and importance of which shall be allowed by a majority in Council, and so declared to be, in minutes subscribed by each Member composing such majority, upon the records of the said Council, that such Prince or State is about to attack and make war upon, or actually making preparations to attack and make war upon the territories of the said United Company, or of some of the Princes or States dependent thereupon.

S. 10. And be it further enacted by the authority aforesaid, that neither the said Governor-General and Council of Bengal, nor the President and Council of any other of the said Presidencies or Settlements, shall have power to make any offensive alliance whatsoever, for the purpose of dividing or sharing any country or territory whatsoever between or with the said United Company and any Native Prince or State in India, without the express orders and directions, for that purpose, of the Commissioners aforesaid.

S. 11. And be it further enacted by the authority aforesaid, that the said Governor-General and Council of Bengal, or any President and Council of any other of the said Presidencies or Settlements, shall not make or enter into any treaty or agreement whatsoever, to hire out to any Native Prince or State in India, any part of the British or native troops serving in India under the orders of the said United Company; nor shall make or enter into any new treaty or agreement whatsoever, to or for the keeping up of any body of such troops in any of the countries or territories of any of the independent Princes or States in India. Fox's India Bills.

S. 12. And be it further enacted by the authority aforesaid, that the said Governor-General and Council of Bengal, or any other of the Presidents or Councils of the said Presidencies or Settlements in India, shall not appoint to, or employ in any office, place or station whatsoever, any person whatsoever, native or British, who hath been, or shall be, removed from any office, station or place whatsoever, for any misdemeanor or other offence, without authority for that purpose first had and obtained from the said Commissioners.

S. 13. And be it further enacted by the authority aforesaid, that it shall not be lawful for the said Governor-General and Council of Bengal, or any President and Council of any other of the said Presidencies or Settlements in India, or any Collector of Revenue, or Chief or other Member of any provincial or subordinate Settlement in India, to let or rent any farm of land or other thing whatsoever, to any banian, native steward or other native servant whatsoever, of any Governor-General, President or Member of any Council, Collector of Revenue, or of any officer in the army, or of any Judge in the Supreme Court, or of any civil servant of the said United Company; and all contracts and agreements made contrary to this Act, with any such banian, native steward or native servant, for the purpose of letting or renting any farm of land, or of other thing whatsoever, shall be deemed and taken to be for the account of the principal or person in whose service such banian, native steward or native servant is; and such banian, native steward or native servant, shall account to the said United Company for the profits made by such farm of land or other thing; which profits shall and may be recovered from such principal or person in whose service such banian, native steward or native servant was at the time when such contract or agreement was made or entered into.

S. 14. And be it further enacted by the authority aforesaid, that from and after . . . . . all monopolies, or pre-

Fox's India Bills.

ferences, by any authority, or upon any pretence whatsoever, of any commodities or goods in any of the said United Company's Settlements in India, shall be, and are hereby declared to be, contrary to law and void.

S. 15. And be it further enacted by the authority aforesaid, that no debt or balance exceeding . . . in consequence of any advance to be made for the making of any manufacture, or for the purchase of materials by any person making the same, or to any husbandman or actual cultivator of land for any raw commodity, shall be recoverable in any court, or by any action or suit at law, or by any compulsory or other process or means whatsoever, after the space of . . . . from the time of making the said advances; and that it shall not be lawful to imprison in any common prison, or in any private house or out-house, any person whatsoever, for or by reason of any such advances, at any time whatsoever.

S. 16. And whereas in and by the said Act of the thirteenth year of the reign of his present Majesty, it is enacted, that every present, gift, gratuity, donation or reward, accepted, taken or received, contrary to the true intent and meaning of the said Act, shall be deemed and construed to have been received and taken to and for the sole use of the said United Company. And whereas the said provision hath been attended with inconvenience, inasmuch as it has been pretended that the servants of the Company have liberty to take and receive presents, accounting to the said United Company for the same: Be it therefore enacted by the authority aforesaid, that every such present, gift, gratuity, donation or reward, accepted, taken or received, if the same shall not be corruptly given to obtain any place or other object to which the person giving the same shall not be entitled, shall be returned or re-delivered to the person giving the same, or his representatives, according to the custom of the country; and such person, or his representatives, shall and may recover the same by any suit, action or bill, or other mode of proceeding whatsoever in use in the place where such gift, gratuity, donation or reward, shall be accepted, taken or received, brought at any time against the person to whom the same was given, or his representatives; and if the same was corruptly given to obtain any place, or other object, in or any way relating to the said United Company's Service, then and in that case the person giving shall not be entitled to recover the same, but the same shall be to and for the sole use of the said United Company, as heretofore. Fox's India Bills.

S. 17. And whereas it may happen that neither the person giving such present, gift, gratuity, donation or reward, nor the said United Company, may sue for the same; be it therefore enacted, that in case the person giving the same, or the said United Company, shall not sue for the same within . . . . months, then the same shall and may be sued for, and recovered, in manner aforesaid, by any person or persons whatsoever, to and for his and their sole use and benefit.

S. 18. And be it further enacted by the authority aforesaid, that if any person, from and after . . . . shall, contrary to the said Act of the thirteenth year of the reign of his present Majesty, accept, receive or take, directly or indirectly, by himself or any other person or persons, on his behalf or for his use or benefit, of and from any of the Indian Princes or powers, or their Ministers or Agents, or any of the natives of Asia, any present, gift, donation, gratuity or reward, pecuniary or otherwise, upon any account or on any pretence whatsoever, or any promise or engagement for any present, gift, donation, gratuity or reward, and shall be therefor legally convicted in the Supreme Court at Calcutta, or in the Mayor's Court in any other of the said United Company's Settlements, or in any court of competent jurisdiction, to try such offence in this kingdom, such person shall thereupon . . . . . .

S. 19. And whereas some of the servants of the said United Company have raised the rents paid by landholders to the said United Company, and have farmed out the lands at new rents, by means of which practices several ancient families have been dispossessed of lands long in their occupation,

Fox's India Bills.

and have been reduced to indigence and distress; for remedy whereof, be it enacted and declared by the authority aforesaid, and it is hereby enacted and declared, that all lands and tenements within the provinces of Bengal, Bahar, and Orissa, or in any territories in which the receipt and management of the revenues is or shall be under the immediate administration of the said United Company, or their servants or agents, not in the actual occupation of the said United Company, or by them leased or farmed out, in or immediately before the year . . . . shall be deemed and taken to be the estate and inheritance of the native landholders and families who then had and held the same, unless dispossessed by judgment of some competent Court for some crime or misdemeanor or non-payment of their rent, and shall be from henceforward enjoyed by them and their heirs and descendants, according to the custom of the country of or relating to the same, or where the same is had and held, without any molestation, interruption or disturbance whatsoever of or by the said United Company, their Governors, Council, Ministers or servants.

S. 20. Provided always, that nothing herein contained shall be construed to deprive the said United Company of the rent or tribute which shall be due or payable to them from such native landholders, their families or descendants, for or on account of any such land, or to prevent the said United Company from having or taking any means, according to the laws and usages of the said countries, for recovering and obtaining payment of such rent or tribute.

S. 21. And for quieting the minds of the said native Princes, and preventing the corrupt practices which may arise from arbitrary alterations of rent or tribute: be it enacted by the authority aforesaid, that the rent, tribute, service or payment paid or agreed to be paid by the said native landholders, in the provinces or territories aforesaid, to the said United Company, in or immediately before the year . . . . shall remain and be the fixed and permanent rent, tribute, payment or service which shall be payable to the said United

Company by the said native landholders, their families, heirs and descendants; and that it shall not be lawful for the Governor-General and Council of Bengal, or the Governor and Council of any other principal Settlement, or the Chief and Council of any subordinate Settlement, or any other servant or agent of the said United Company, to alter such rent, tribute, service or payment upon any pretence whatsoever, or to exact from or impose upon any such native landholder, his family, heirs or descendants, any further or greater rent, tribute, service or payment, or any other charge than is herein provided. Fox's India Bills.

S. 22. And be it further enacted by the authority aforesaid, that it shall and may be lawful for the Governor-General and Council of Bengal to restore, and they are hereby authorized and required to restore, to every native landholder, his heirs or descendants, according to the usage of the country, who shall have been removed or dispossessed of his land or territory, the actual possession thereof, upon the rent, tribute, service or payment hereinbefore provided, if such native landholder shall be willing or desirous to repossess his land or territory; subject, nevertheless, to such farm or leases thereof as shall or may have been made before the . . . . and shall be still existing; and if such native landholder shall have quitted or been dispossessed of his land or territory for or upon condition of receiving any pension or appointment in lieu thereof, and shall prefer such pension or appointment, the same shall on no account or upon no pretence be discontinued, withheld, diminished or taken away, but shall be regularly paid to such native landholder, his family, heirs or descendants, according as the land or territory was held, and to the terms and stipulations made with such native landholder.

S. 23. And be it further enacted by the authority aforesaid, that all Native Princes and States in India, who, having the management of their own revenues, are engaged, by treaty or otherwise, to furnish or keep up a body of troops for the defence or service of the said United Company, or to pay

Fox's India Bills.

any tribute or sum of money in lieu thereof, or to keep up or pay any body of English troops, or to pay any tribute or sum of money in lieu thereof, or who pay any tribute or sum of money for the protection of the said United Company, are under the protection of His Majesty, and shall not be disturbed or molested by any of the servants of the said United Company, in the enjoyment of their rights, according to the laws and usage of the country.

S. 24. And whereas some of the servants of the said United Company have heretofore committed unwarrantable acts, in and relative to the territories and revenues of the Native Princes and States under the said United Company's protection; be it further enacted by the authority aforesaid, that all and every of the servants of the said United Company, civil and military, shall be and are hereby declared to be amenable to the said Commissioners appointed to manage the affairs of the said United Company, and in and to all courts of justice (both in India and in Great Britain) of competent jurisdiction to try offences committed in India, for all acts, injuries, wrongs, oppressions, trespasses, misdemeanors, crimes, and offences whatsoever, by them or any of them done or committed in any of the lands or territories of such protected Native Princes or States, or against their persons or properties, or the persons or properties of any of their subjects or people; whether the same were committed under pretence of the order of any Native protected Prince, or otherwise, howsoever, in the manner as if the same had been done or committed within the territories directly subject to and under the British Government in India.

S. 25. And be it further enacted by the authority aforesaid, that no civil or military servant in the said United Company's Service, or person in the service of His Majesty, shall, by himself, or any agent for him, take upon himself to collect or farm, or be in any way concerned, directly or indirectly, in collecting or farming of any of the revenues of such protected Native Princes or States.

S. 26. And be it further enacted by the authority aforesaid,

that if any officer, civil or military, of the said United Company, shall invade or make war upon, or enter with an armed force, in a hostile or offensive manner, any of the territories of the Native Princes or States in India, not under the protection of His Majesty and the said United Company, without express orders in writing from the Governor-General and Council of Bengal, such person, upon conviction thereof in the Supreme Court of Calcutta, or in any Mayor's Court in any other of the said principal Settlements, or in the Court of King's Bench, or in any other court which shall have jurisdiction to try offences committed in India, shall be . . . . Fox's India Bills.

S. 27. And be it further enacted by the authority aforesaid, that none of the said protected Native Princes or States shall have any other Native Prince or State dependent upon him or them, any further or otherwise than as such other Native Prince or State shall have stood bound or engaged to such protected Native Prince or State, on or before the year . . for the payment of any sum or sums of money, rent or tribute, or for furnishing or supplying some definite quota of troops, which troops shall not be required or called for without the orders of the Governor-General and Council of Bengal, or President and Council of some other principal Settlement.

S. 28. And be it further enacted by the authority aforesaid, that the succession of the said protected Native Princes shall be directed and disposed of according to the laws of the country, or to such treaties as shall have or contain any stipulation concerning the same; and that such succession shall not be altered or disposed of by will, or in any other manner, contrary to the laws of the country and the faith of such treaties.

S. 29. And be it further enacted by the authority aforesaid, that such protected Native Princes or States shall not be permitted to rent or take, or have any farm or lease of any lands whatsoever, of or from the said United Company.

And be it further enacted by the authority aforesaid, that no such protected Native Prince shall be permitted to reside for more than . . . in any of the said United Company's Settlements, unless, being expelled from or driven out

Fox's India Bills.

of his dominions, he shall take refuge in the said United Company's territories.

S. 30. And be it enacted by the authority aforesaid, that from and after . . it shall not be lawful for any servant, civil or military, of the said United Company, to have or be engaged in the borrowing or lending of any money, or in any money transaction whatsoever, or in the farming of any lands or revenues, or in the buying or selling of any goods or commodities whatsoever, or in any other transaction of commerce or business whatsoever, with any such protected or other Native Prince or State; and all such transactions, and all contracts and engagements of or relating to the same, are hereby declared . . . and any person or persons guilty of any such offence, and thereof convicted in the manner hereinbefore last mentioned, shall be . . . . .

S. 31. And be it further enacted by the authority aforesaid, that it shall not be lawful for the said protected Native Princes or States to remove or dispossess any Zemindar, or other Native Prince or landholder, nor to increase his rent or tribute beyond that which was paid by such Zemindar or Native Prince in the year . . . . nor to farm any land at any higher or greater rent or tribute than the same was farmed at or for in the said year . . . . nor to resume any jaghire granted at any time before the year . . . . . .

S. 32. And be it further enacted by the authority aforesaid, that all Zemindars and Native Princes and States, who shall have been dispossessed of their lands and territories by . . at any time since . . shall be restored to the possession and enjoyment of the same.

S. 33. And be it further enacted by the authority aforesaid, that the Nabob of Arcot, the Rajah of Tanjore, or any other protected Native Prince in India, shall not assign, mortgage or pledge any territory or land whatsoever, or the produce or revenue thereof, to any British subject whatsoever; neither shall it be lawful for any British subject whatsoever to take or receive any such assignment, mortgage or pledge; and the same are hereby declared . . . and all payments or deliveries of produce or revenue, under any such assignment, shall and may be recovered back by such Native Prince paying or delivering the same, from the person or persons receiving the same, or his or their representatives. Fox's India Bills.

S. 34. And be it further enacted by the authority aforesaid, that it shall not be lawful for any British subject whatsoever to have, receive or take any payment of money, produce, revenue, goods, commodities or effects whatsoever, of or from any such native protected Prince, or any agent or servant thereof, for or on account of any debt now due, or claimed to be due, from such protected Native Prince, except such debts as were consolidated in the year . . . . and allowed by the Court of Directors, and by them ordered to be recovered, without proof first made, to the satisfaction of the said Commissioners, or such person or persons as they shall appoint, that such debt was fairly and *bonâ fide* contracted for money lent, or goods sold and delivered, or in some open and avowed course of trade and commerce, and not as or for a reward for any service done or performed, by any such British subject, to or for any such native protected Prince, or for any other matter forbidden or prohibited to be made or done by any law or laws now in force, or hereafter to be in force, or by any order or orders of the said United Company, or any order or orders to be made by the said Commissioners appointed to manage the affairs thereof; and an entry, with the nature and particulars of the claim, and of the evidence in support thereof, shall be made in the journal of the said Commissioners, or in the minutes of such person or persons as they shall for those purposes appoint, with the opinion of the said Commissioners, or such person or persons thereon.

S. 35. And be it further enacted by the authority aforesaid, that all disputes and differences whatsoever, now actually subsisting between the Nabob of Arcot and the Rajah of Tanjore, shall be examined and considered, as soon as may be, by the said Commissioners appointed to manage the affairs of the said United Company, who shall, and they are

Fox's India Bills. hereby required, as soon as they shall have sufficiently examined and considered the same, to send and transmit such orders as shall appear to them best calculated for the quiet and final adjustment and termination of such disputes and differences, according to the principles of, and the terms and stipulations contained in, the treaty of 1762, between the said Nabob of Arcot and the Rajah of Tanjore, and to the orders and instructions of the Court of Directors given to George Lord Pigot, late Governor of Fort St. George, and to the arrangements made relative to such dispute and differences by the said George Lord Pigot.

S. 36. And be it further enacted, that the said Commissioners shall, and they are hereby directed and required to send and transmit to the Governor-General and Council of Bengal, or the President and Council of Fort St. George, or to or by such other person or persons as they shall for that purpose specially nominate and appoint, full and explicit orders and directions, not only to settle and terminate the said differences and disputes, but also to take into consideration and examine the present state of the affairs, revenues and debts of the said Nabob of Arcot and of the Rajah of Tanjore, and to inquire into and ascertain the origin, nature and amount of all claims whatsoever on them by British subjects, and immediately to make a full report thereupon to the said Commissioners; and to adopt, propose or suggest such ways or means for the liquidation and settlement of such debts as shall appear to be well founded and contracted *bonâ fide* (and not by any illicit dealing, or in consequence of any breach or disobedience of the said United Company's orders), and for the payment and discharge thereof by such instalments, and at such times and in such manner as shall be consistent with justice, to the creditors of the Nabob and Rajah, and to the service of the said United Company, and as shall occasion the least difficulty and inconvenience to the said Nabob and Rajah; and, as speedily as may be, to make a full report of all their proceedings touching the said matters, to the said Commissioners.

S. 37. And be it further enacted by the authority aforesaid, that all polygars which shall or may have been dispossessed or driven out of their lands or territories at any time since the year . . shall be restored to the possession of the same, and hold the same at and for the same, and no greater rent or tribute as such polygars paid or were liable to pay, on or immediately before . . . . . . Fox's India Bills.

S. 38. And whereas it is enacted in and by the Act of the thirteenth year of the reign of his present Majesty, that the said Governor-General and Council, or the major part of them, shall have power of superintending and controlling the government and management of the Presidencies of Madras, Bombay and Bencoolen respectively, so far as it shall not be lawful for any President and Council of Madras, Bombay or Bencoolen, for the time being, to make any orders for commencing hostilities, or declaring or making war against any Indian Princes or Powers, or for negotiating or concluding any treaty of peace or other treaty with any such Indian Princes or Powers, without the consent and approbation of the said Governor-General and Council first had and obtained (except in the cases of imminent necessity and of special orders from the said United Company), with power to the said Governor-General and Council to suspend any President and Council offending in any of the cases aforesaid; and whereas great disputes have at different times arisen respecting the extent of the said controlling power given to the said Governor-General and Council, to the embarrassment and injury of the said United Company's Service; for remedy whereof, be it enacted and declared, that the said power given to the Governor-General and Council of Fort William, of superintending and controlling the government and management of the Presidencies of Madras, Bombay and Bencoolen respectively, doth and shall extend to all negotiations and cases whatsoever, which, though they shall not in themselves be the commencement, or orders for the commencement, of hostilities, or the declaring or making war against any Indian Princes or Powers, shall nevertheless be of any unwar-

Fox's India Bills.

rantable nature or tendency against such Indian Princes or Powers, or shall be of a nature and tendency to create dissatisfaction and alarm among any of them, and, consequently, provoke to, bring on, and occasion hostilities and war, without directly importing or leading to the same; and in all such cases the said Governor-General and Council shall have all the powers of suspending given them in and by the said Act of the thirteenth year of the reign of his present Majesty; and shall enter on their Minutes of Consultation at large, the whole nature of the case in which, and the reasons for which, they exercise the said powers, and shall transmit the same, by the first opportunity, to the said Commissioners appointed for the management of the affairs of the said United Company; and if the case in which the said superintending, controlling and suspending powers, or any of them, are exercised, be such as creates a reasonable doubt whether the said powers apply to it, the Governments and Presidencies of Madras, Bombay and Bencoolen are nevertheless hereby required to submit and yield obedience to the Acts of the said Governor-General and Council, and to lay the case before the said Commissioners, for the determination thereof.

S. 39. And be it further enacted by the authority aforesaid, that it shall and may be lawful to and for the Government and Presidency of Bombay, whenever and as often as any war against the said United Company, their possessions or dependencies, shall be actually commenced, or the danger thereof is impending and imminent, in the north-west and western coasts of India, or in the territories adjoining thereto and in the neighbourhood thereof, or in any part of the territories of the states of the Mahrattas, to make and conclude any treaty or terms of peace, truce or cessation of arms with any of such Indian Princes or States actually at war, or about to make war, or for the amity, assistance or alliance of any other Indian Prince or State, the better to defend the possessions of the said United Company against such war commenced or impending: Provided always, that the said

Government and Presidency of Bombay do and shall insert, or cause to be inserted, in all and every such treaty hereinbefore mentioned a clause or provision that the same shall be null and void, unless it shall be approved and ratified (within a certain reasonable time therein to be named) by the Governor-General and Council of Fort William; and the said Government and Presidency shall, and they are hereby required to enter on their minutes of consultation, at full length, the occasion of a necessity for such proceedings, with the reasons upon which they have acted, and the documents or vouchers (if any such there shall be), for the facts alleged; and shall transmit the same from time to time, as they shall arise or happen, and all propositions relative to the same, as they shall be made, to the said Governor-General and Council of Fort William, and to the said Commissioners appointed to manage the affairs of the said United Company respectively; and shall obey and follow, under the pain of suspension, all such orders and directions thereupon as they shall receive from the said Governor-General of Fort William, until the same shall be altered or corrected by the said Commissioners. Fox's India Bills.

S. 40. And be it further enacted by the authority aforesaid, that the Government and Presidency of Madras shall have the like powers and authorities, under the same limitations and restrictions, in case of war against the said United Company, their possessions or dependencies, actually commenced, or the danger thereof impending and imminent, on the coast of Coromandel, from . . . . . to . . . . . . on the coast of Malabar, or in the territories adjoining thereto, and in the neighbourhood thereof.

S. 41. And be it further enacted by the authority aforesaid, that no Governor-General, Council or President, Member of Council, or other officer, civil or military, in the service of the said United Company in India (whether such person shall be actually in the execution of his office in India, or shall be absent therefrom in Great Britain, or in any other place), or any agent in Great Britain or India of any pro-

Fox's India Bills.

tected or other Native Prince in India, shall be capable of being a Member of or of sitting and voting in the House of Commons: Provided that every such person, actually a Member of the House of Commons at the time of passing this Act, shall and may sit and vote for and during the remainder of the present Parliament.

S. 42. And be it further enacted by the authority aforesaid, that no person having been in the civil and military service of the said United Company, and who hath resigned or quitted the same, shall be capable of being elected into or of sitting or voting in the House of Commons, at any time within . . . . after he shall have been returned to and resident in Great Britain, or whilst any proceedings in Parliament or any other public prosecution shall be depending against him for any crimes or offences alleged to have been committed by him whilst he was in the said service: Provided always, that such proceedings or public prosecution shall have been commenced before the expiration of the said space of . . . . . after the return of such person, and shall be finally determined within the space of . . . . after the . . . . . . after the commencement thereof, otherwise the same shall not operate to disable such person from being elected into or from sitting or voting in the House of Commons, unless the delay in such proceedings or public prosecution shall be at the request or through the default of the party prosecuted.

S. 43. And be it further enacted, that all crimes and offences against this Act may be prosecuted in the Supreme Court at Calcutta, or in the Mayor's Court in any other of the principal Settlements in India, or in the Court of King's Bench, or any other Court in this kingdom which shall be established for taking cognizance of crimes and offences committed in India; and all the powers and authorities given to the said Court of King's Bench in and by the said Act of the thirteenth year of the reign of his present Majesty, and not herein otherwise provided for, are hereby declared to be extended to all the crimes and offences committed against this Act; and in all cases where the punishment is not herein appointed, the Court in which the conviction shall take place shall appoint such fine or imprisonment, or both, as they shall think proper, provided the fine shall not exceed . . . . . . nor the imprisonment . . . . . . and may, in their discretion, superadd the incapacity of serving the said United Company.

Fox's India Bills.

APPENDIX B.

DRAFT OF PROPOSED TREATY BETWEEN THE EAST INDIA COMPANY AND THE KING OF OUDE, AND PROCLAMATION ISSUED ON THE NON-ACCEPTANCE THEREOF.

Whereas, in the year 1801, a Treaty was concluded between the Honourable East India Company and His Excellency the Nawab Vizier, Saadut Alee Khan Bahadoor; and whereas the sixth Article of the said Treaty requires that the Ruler of Oude, always advising with, and acting in conformity to the counsel of, the officers of the Honourable Company, shall "establish, in his reserved dominions, such a system of administration, to be carried into effect by his own officers, as shall be conducive to the prosperity of his subjects, and be calculated to secure the lives and property of the inhabitants;" and whereas the infraction of this essential engagement of the Treaty, by successive Rulers of Oude, has been continued and notorious; and whereas its long toleration of such infraction of the Treaty on the part of the Rulers of Oude has exposed the British Government to the reproach of having failed to fulfil the obligations it assumed towards the people of that country; and whereas it has now become the imperative duty of the British Government to take effectual measures for securing, permanently, to the people of Oude such a system of just and beneficent administration as the Treaty of 1801 was intended, but has failed, to provide: the following Treaty, consisting of seven Articles, is concluded, on the one part, by the Most Noble the Marquis of Dalhousie, K.T., Governor-General in Council, appointed by the Honourable Company to direct and control all their affairs in the East Indies, through Major-General Outram, C.B., Resident at Lucknow, under full powers vested in him by the said Governor-General; and, on the other part, by His Majesty Abool Munsoor, Nasir-ood-deen, Sikundur Jah, Mahommed Wajid Alee Shah, King of Oude, for himself and his heirs, through, &c.

Art. I. It is hereby stipulated and agreed, that the sole and exclusive administration of the Civil and Military Government of the territories of Oude shall be henceforth vested, for ever, in the Honourable East India Company, together with the full and exclusive right to the revenues thereof; the said Company hereby engaging to make ample provision for the maintenance of the Royal dignity, as hereinafter mentioned, and for the due improvement of the said territories.

Art. II. It is stipulated and agreed that the sovereign title of "King of Oude" shall be retained by His Majesty, and that it shall descend, in continual succession, to the heirs male of his body born in lawful wedlock.

Art. III. It is stipulated and agreed that His Majesty the King, and his successors, shall be treated, upon all occasions, with the attention, respect, and honour which are due to a Sovereign Prince.

Art. IV. It is further stipulated and agreed that, notwithstanding the provisions of the first Article of the present Treaty, His Majesty the King of Oude, and his successors, shall retain full and exclusive jurisdiction within the precincts of the Palace at Lucknow, as well as within the Dil Khosha and Beebeepore Parks, provided always that the punishment of death shall not be inflicted by the order of the King, or within the limits of the palace and garden parks aforesaid, unless with the previous consent of the Governor-General in Council.

Art. V. Whereas it is expedient and right that the Crown of His Majesty the King of Oude should be upheld in fitting dignity and honour, it is hereby stipulated and agreed that the Honourable East India Company shall pay to His Majesty the said Mahommed Wajid Alee Shah, from out of the revenues of Oude, twelve lakhs of Company's rupees per annum; and that the said Company shall further maintain, for His Majesty, a body of palace-guards, at a cost not exceeding three lakhs of Company's rupees per annum.

To each of His Majesty's successors it is agreed that the said Company shall pay twelve lakhs of Company's rupees per annum.

Art. VI. In order that nothing may be wanting to the full measure of liberal endowment which the Honourable East India Company desires to secure to His Majesty the King of Oude, it is hereby agreed that the said Company shall take upon itself the maintenance of all collateral members of the Royal family, for whom provision is now made by His Majesty the King.

Art. VII. All former treaties between the Honourable East India Company and the Rulers of Oude which are now in force, and which are not contrary to the tenor of this engagement, are confirmed by it.

Inclosure 6 *in No.* 4.

DRAFT OF PROCLAMATION.

(B.)

By a treaty concluded in the year 1801, the Honourable East India Company engaged to protect the Sovereign of Oude against foreign and domestic enemies, while the Sovereign of Oude, upon his part, bound himself to establish "such a system of admininistration, to be carried into effect by his own officers, as should be conducive to the prosperity of his subjects, and calculated to secure the lives and property of the inhabitants."

The obligations which the Treaty imposed upon the Honourable East India Company have been observed by it for more than half a century, faithfully, constantly, and completely.

In all that time, though the British Government has itself been engaged in frequent wars, no foreign foe has ever set his foot on the soil of Oude; no rebellion has ever threatened the stability of its throne. British troops have been stationed in close proximity to the King's person, and their aid has never been withheld whenever his power was wrongfully defied.

On the other hand, one chief and vital stipulation of the treaty has been wholly disregarded by every successive ruler of Oude, and the pledge which was given for the establishment of such a system of administration as should secure the lives and property of the people of Oude, and be conducive to their prosperity, has, from first to last, been deliberately and systematically violated.

By reason of this violation of the compact made, the British Government might long since have justly declared the Treaty void, and might have withdrawn its protection from the Rulers of Oude. But it has hitherto been reluctant to have recourse to measures which would be fatal to the power and authority of a royal race who, whatever their faults towards their own subjects, have ever been faithful and true to their friendship with the English nation.

Nevertheless, the British Government has not failed to labour, during all that time, earnestly and perseveringly, for the deliverance of the people of Oude from the grievous oppression and misrule under which they have suffered.

Many years have passed since the Governor-General, Lord William Bentinck, perceiving that every previous endeavour to ameliorate the condition of the people of Oude had been thwarted or evaded, made formal declaration to the Court of Lucknow that it would become necessary that he should proceed to assume the direct management of the Oude territories.

The words and the menace which were then employed by Lord William Bentinck were, eight years ago, repeated, in person, by Lord Hardinge to the King. The Sovereign of Oude was, on that day, solemnly bid remember that, whatever might now happen, "it would be manifest to all the world" that he "had received a friendly and timely warning."

But the friendly intentions of the British Government have been wholly defeated, by the obstinacy or incapacity, or apathy, of the Viziers and Kings of Oude. Disinterested counsel and indignant censure, alternating, through more than fifty years, with repeated warning, remonstrance, and threats, have all proved ineffectual and vain. The chief condition of the Treaty remains unfulfilled, the promises of the King rest unperformed, and the people of Oude are still the victims of incompetency, corruption, and tyranny, without remedy, or hope of relief.

It is notorious throughout the land that the King, like most of his predecessors, takes no real share in the direction of public affairs.

The powers of government throughout his dominions are, for the most part, abandoned to worthless favourites of the court, or to violent and corrupt men, unfit for their duties, and unworthy of trust.

The Collectors of the revenue hold sway over their districts with uncontrolled authority, extorting the utmost payment from the people, without reference to past or present engagements.

The King's troops, with rare exceptions, undisciplined and disorganized, and defrauded of their pay by those to whom it is entrusted, are permitted to plunder the villages for their own support, so that they have become a lasting scourge to the country they are employed to protect.

Gangs of freebooters infest the districts; law and justice are unknown; armed violence and bloodshed are daily events; and life and property are nowhere secure for an hour.

The time has come when the British Government can no longer tolerate in Oude these evils and abuses, which its position under the treaty serves indirectly to sustain; or continue to the Sovereign that protection which alone upholds the power whereby such evils are inflicted.

Fifty years of sad experience have proved that the Treaty of 1801 has wholly failed to secure the happiness and prosperity of Oude, and have conclusively shown that no effectual security can be had for the release of the people of that country from the grievous oppression they have long endured, unless the exclusive administration of the territories of Oude shall be permanently transferred to the British Government.

To that end, it has been declared, by the special authority and consent of the Honourable the Court of Directors, that the Treaty of 1801, disregarded and violated by each succeeding Sovereign of Oude, is henceforth wholly null and void.

His Majesty Wajid Alee Shah was invited to enter into a new engagement, whereby the government of the territories of Oude should be vested, exclusively and for ever, in the Honourable East India Company; while ample provision should be made for the dignity, affluence, and honour of the King and of his family.

But His Majesty the King refused to enter into the amicable agreement which was offered for his acceptance.

Inasmuch, then, as His Majesty Wajid Alee Shah, in common with all his predecessors, has refused, or evaded, or neglected, to fulfil the obligations of the Treaty of 1801, whereby he was bound to establish within his dominions such a system of administration as should be conducive to the prosperity and happiness of his subjects; and inasmuch as the Treaty he thereby violated has been declared to be null and void; and inasmuch as His Majesty has refused to enter into other agreements which were offered to him in lieu of such Treaty; and inasmuch as the terms of that Treaty, if it had still been maintained in force, forbade the employment of British officers in Oude, without which no efficient system of administration could be established there, it is manifest to all that the British Government had but one alternative before it.

Either it must altogether desert the people of Oude, and deliver them up helpless to oppression and tyranny, which, acting under the restrictions of Treaty, it has already too long appeared to countenance; or it must put forth its own great power on behalf of a people for whose happiness it, more than fifty years ago, engaged to interpose, and must at once assume to itself the exclusive, and permanent, administration of the territories of Oude.

The British Government has had no hesitation in choosing the latter alternative.

Wherefore, proclamation is hereby made that the government of the territories of Oude is henceforth vested, exclusively and for ever, in the Honourable East India Company.

All Amils, Nazims, Chuckledars, and other servants of the Durbar; all officers, civil and military; the soldiers of the state; and all the inhabitants of Oude, are required to render, henceforth, implicit and exclusive obedience to the officers of the British Government.

If any officer of the Durbar,—Jageerdar, Zemindar, or other person,—shall refuse to render such obedience,—if he shall withhold the payment of revenue, or shall otherwise dispute or defy the authority of the British Government, he shall be declared a rebel, his person shall be seized, and his jageers or lands shall be confiscated to the State.

To those who shall immediately and quietly submit themselves to the authority of the British Government—whether Amils or public officers, Jageerdars, Zemindars, or other inhabitants of Oude—full assurance is hereby given of protection, consideration, and favour.

The revenue of the districts shall be determined on a fair and settled basis.

The gradual improvement of the Oude Territories shall be steadily pursued.

Justice shall be measured out with an equal hand.

Protection shall be given to life and property; and every man shall enjoy henceforth his just rights, without fear of molestation.

APPENDIX C.

REGULATIONS FOR THE EXAMINATION OF CANDIDATES FOR THE CIVIL SERVICE.

1. ANY natural-born subject of Her Majesty who shall be desirous of entering the Civil Service of the Company, will be entitled to be examined at such examination, provided he shall, on or before the 1st of May, 1855, have transmitted to the Board of Commissioners:—

- (*a*) A certificate of his age being above eighteen years and under twenty-three years.
- (*b*) A certificate, signed by a physician or surgeon, of his having no disease, constitutional affection, or bodily infirmity, unfitting him for the Civil Service of the Company.
- (*c*) A certificate of good moral character, signed by the head of the school or college at which he has last received his education; or, if he has not received education at any school or college since the year 1852, then such proof of good moral character as may be satisfactory to the Board of Commissioners.
- (*d*) A statement of those branches of knowledge hereinafter enumerated in which he desires to be examined.

2. The examination will take place only in the following branches of knowledge:

English Language and Literature:—	MARKS.
Composition	500
English Literature and History, including that of the Laws and Constitution .	1,000
	1,500
Language, Literature, and History of Greece	750
" " " Rome	750
" " " France	375
" " " Germany	375
" " " Italy	375
Mathematics, pure and mixed . .	1,000
Natural Science, that is, Chemistry, Electricity and Magnetism, Natural History, Geology, and Mineralogy . .	500
Moral Sciences, that is, Logic, Mental, Moral, and Political Philosophy .	500
Sanscrit Language and Literature . .	375
Arabic Language and Literature . .	375
	6,875

3. The merit of the persons examined will be estimated by Marks, according to the ordinary system in use at several of the Universities, and the numbers set opposite to each branch in the preceding paragraph denote the greatest number of Marks that can be obtained in respect of it.

4. No Candidate will be allowed any Marks in respect of any subject of examination unless he shall, in the opinion of the Examiners, possess a competent knowledge of that subject.

5. The examination will be conducted by means of printed questions and written answers, and by *vivâ voce* examination, as the Examiners may deem necessary.

6. After the examination shall have been completed, the Examiners shall add up the Marks obtained by each Candidate in respect of each of the subjects in which he shall have been examined, and shall set forth, in order of merit, the names of the twenty Candidates who shall have obtained a greater

number of Marks than any of the remaining Candidates; and such twenty Candidates shall be deemed to be selected Candidates for the Civil Service of the East India Company. Their choice of the Presidency in India to which they shall be appointed shall be determined by the order in which they stand on such list.

7. In August, 1856, and August, 1857, further examinations of the selected Candidates will take place by Examiners appointed by the Board of Commissioners for the Affairs of India in the following subjects:—

	MARKS.
Law, including the ordinary rules of taking Evidence, and the Mode of conducting civil and criminal trials . . .	1,000
The History of India . . .	400
Political Economy	400
Any Language of India in which the selected Candidate shall have given notice of his desire to be examined . . .	200

and such further examinations will be conducted in the same manner as that above described. (The numbers set opposite to each subject denote the greatest number of Marks which can be obtained in respect of such subjects.)

8. Each selected Candidate, desirous of being examined at either of the further examinations of 1856 and 1857, shall, two months previously to such examination, transmit to the Board of Commissioners for the Affairs of India a statement mentioning the language or languages of India in which he is desirous of being examined.

9. Any selected Candidate who, having been examined at the further examination of 1856, shall not have passed, may, nevertheless, be again examined at the further examination of 1857.

10. Any selected Candidate who shall not have passed at one or the other of the further examinations of 1856 and 1857, shall be struck off the list of selected Candidates.

11. The selected Candidates, who, at either of such further examinations, shall be deemed by the Examiners to have a

competent knowledge of law, the history of India, political economy, and at least one language of India, shall be adjudged to have passed and to be entitled to be appointed to the Civil Service of the East India Company; and the names of the selected Candidates who shall have so passed shall be placed in a list in the order of their merit in such examinations, estimated as above by the total number of Marks which they shall have obtained in respect of all the subjects in which they shall have been examined at such examination.

12. The seniority in the Civil Service of the East India Company of the selected Candidates, shall be determined by the date of the further examination at which they shall be adjudged to have passed; and, as between those who passed at the same further examination, their seniority in such Civil Service shall be determined according to the order in which they stand on the list resulting from such examination.

13. No person will, even after such examination, be allowed to proceed to India unless he shall comply with the regulations in force at the time for the Civil Service of the East India Company, and shall be of sound bodily health and good moral character.

India Board, 26th January, 1855.

REGULATIONS FOR THE EXAMINATION OF CADETS RECEIVING DIRECT APPOINTMENTS IN THE MILITARY SERVICE.

Resolution of Court, —Dated 22nd January, 1851.

THE following are the points upon which Candidates are to be examined before they are passed as Cadets:—

1. Each Candidate will be required to write English correctly from dictation.

2. He should possess a competent knowledge of the ordinary Rules of Arithmetic, including the Rule of Three,

Compound Proportion, Simple and Compound Interest, Vulgar and Decimal Fractions, and the extraction of the Square Root. He should also have read the first three Books of Euclid.

3. In Languages he should be able to translate into English passages from Cæsar's Commentaries, or from the first four Books of Virgil's Æneid; and he will be, further, expected to parse, and show his knowledge of Grammar and Syntax.

The Candidate will be required to translate from French into English an extract from one of the following works, viz. Telemachus, Charles the Twelfth, and Peter the Great. But the Candidate will have the option of being examined in the Hindustani, in lieu of the French Language; and in that case he will be required to translate from Hindustani into English an extract from one of the following works, viz. Bagh-o-Buhar, Tota Kuhanee.

4. In History he should be prepared to pass an examination in Keightley's Histories of Greece and Rome, in Gleig's History of England, and in the History of British India, contained in Vols. I. and II. of the Edinburgh Cabinet Library.

5. In Geography he should possess a competent knowledge of the modern Divisions of the World; the principal Nations in Europe and Asia; the Names of the Capital of each Nation in Europe, and of the chief Cities of Hindostan; and the Names and Situations of the principal Rivers and Mountains in the World.

6. In Fortification he should have read some elementary work on the subject (Straith's Introductory Essay to the Study of Fortification, or Macaulay's Field Fortification), and have received some instruction in Drawing.

Resolution of Court, —Dated 15th January, 1852.

The evidence to be required from Candidates of their having acquired "some knowledge of drawing," is, that they shall trace correctly upon paper, in presence of the Examiners, a front of fortification according to Vauban's first system, and also the profile of a rampart and parapet.

The examination of the Candidates will take place before a Board of Examiners to be convened for that purpose at the Military College at Addiscombe, near Croydon.

If not found qualified on their first examination, they may be allowed a second trial within the next ensuing twelve months; and if not then found qualified, their nominations will revert to their patrons, and they will be deemed ineligible for another nomination for a direct appointment. Resolution of Court,—Dated 9th August, 1854, and 13th May, 1856.

Candidates who have passed the prescribed examinations at Sandhurst for commissions in Her Majesty's cavalry or infantry, within one year from the date of their being presented to the Political and Military Committee as Cadets, and have not failed at the final examination at Addiscombe, are eligible to appointments as Cadets in the Company's Army, on producing certificates from the Professors at Sandhurst of their having duly passed the prescribed examination in the several subjects, without being required to pass an examination at Addiscombe. Resolution of Court, 24th December, 1856.

If the Candidate has been confirmed as a member of the Church of England, he will be required to make a declaration to that effect. If not so confirmed, or if not a member of the Church of England, he will be required to produce a certificate from a minister stating that he has been well instructed in the principles of the religion in which he has been brought up. Resolution of Court,—Dated 5th February, 1851.

The Candidate will also be required to produce testimonials of good moral conduct, under the hand of the principal or superior authority of the college or public institution in which he may have been educated, or under the hand of the private instructor to whose care he may have been confided,—and the said testimonials shall have reference to his conduct during the two years immediately preceding his presentation for admission.

A Candidate must have attained the age of sixteen years. He is not eligible to be appointed a Cadet after having attained the age of twenty-two years, unless he shall have been, for the space of one year at least, a Commissioned Resolution of Court,—Dated 7th December, 1808.

Act 33 Geo. III. c. 52, s. 60. Officer in Her Majesty's Service, or in the Militia or Fencible Corps when embodied, and hath been called into actual service, or shall have been in the Company of Cadets of the Royal Regiment of Artillery. Such persons are eligible for the appointment of Cadet in the Company's Service, provided their age does not exceed twenty-five years. [A Commission in the Guernsey Militia, or in other Corps similarly circumstanced, is not a qualification. (Resolution of Court 3rd April, 1844.)]

Resolution of Court,—Dated 31st July, 1821. A Candidate who has been so employed must produce his Commission, together with a Certificate from the War Office or Commanding Officer of his Regiment, of his having actually joined and done duty with the regiment for the full term of one year and upwards; and that he was neither dismissed nor resigned his regiment in consequence of any misconduct.

Resolution of Court,—Dated 19th June, 1833. No person who has been dismissed or obliged to retire from the Army or Navy, the Royal Military College at Sandhurst, the Royal Military Academy at Woolwich, or from any other Public Institution, on account of immoral or ungentlemanly conduct, can be appointed a Cadet.

INDEX.

ABKARRY, Revenue, 132; Regulations and Acts concerning, 194, 198, 206, 210, 221.

Acheen, first Expedition to, 6.

Acts, of Governor-General in India first so called, 23; List of, 181; of Imperial Parliament, relating to India, list of, 226.

Adawlut, Sudder Dewanny, Regulations and Acts concerning, 182, 183, 186, 189, 190, 191, 192, 194, 201, 207, 212; Nizamut, 186, 187, 192, 194, 199, 201, 207.

Addiscombe, 67; Rules for admission to, 67; Papers relating to Education at, 248.

Aden, Treaty concerning, 160; Act concerning, 211.

Affghanistan invaded, 25.

Agra, 20.

Ajmeer, Factory established at, 6; district round, annexed, 21.

Allahabad, Treaty of, 15; ceded to Great Britain, 19.

Amherst, Lord, administration of, 21.

Arab Tribes, Treaties with, 157, 162, 164.

Area and Population of British India, 3; of Native States, 138.

Arracan, &c., ceded, 21; Act concerning, 215.

Assam, Treaty concerning, 146; Acts concerning, 203, 216.

Assaye, Battle of, 20.

Auckland, Lord, Administration of, 24.

Aumeens, Sudder and Principal Sudder, functions and salaries of, 87; Regulations and Acts concerning, 198, 203, 205, 207, 208, 209, 211, 212.

Ava, Treaties with King of, 147, 158.

BANTAM, Factory established at, 6.

Baroda, Dispatches relating to, 243.

Barristers, English, Scotch, and Irish, who have received judicial appointments in India, 238.

Bassein, Treaty of, 148, 149.

Behar, Civil Government of, 15; Treaty concerning, 142; Regulations concerning, 181, 182.

Benares, Treaty concerning, 142, 144; Regulation concerning, 183.

Bengal, Civil Government of, 15; Treaty concerning, 142; Regulations, list of, page 181.

Bentinck, Lord William, administration of, 22.

Berar, 19; Annexed, 25; Treaties with, 149, 151.

Bhopal, Treaty with, 156.

Bhurtpore, 22; Treaties concerning, 149, 150.

Bishop, the first, 20; Madras and Bombay, 24.

Board of Control, 18, 28; how administered, 35; present Constitution of, 36; Departments of, 37; how conducted, 38.

Bombay, acquired, 9; Government of, 52, *et seq.*; Marine service, 68; Supreme Court of Judicature, 84; Land Revenues in, 119; University, 165; Colleges, 169.

Bootan, Treaty with Rajah of, 144.

British subjects in India, 73.

Bundelcund, 20; Regulation concerning, 193.

Burdwan, acquired, 15; Treaties concerning, 141, 143.

Burmah, war with, 21; Papers relating to, 237, 246.

CABOOL, acquired by Nadir Shah,

14; Treaties concerning, 152, 160.
Cabot, Sebastian, 5.
Calcutta, jurisdiction of Supreme Court at, 77; Treaty for free tenure of, 140; University, 165; Acts concerning, 222, 223.
Canals, &c., 170.
Canara, 19.
Carnatic ceded, 19.
Cavendish, 5.
Chancellor, 5.
Charles II., Charters granted by, 8, 9, 73, 74.
Charters granted, 6, 8, 9, 10, 73, 74, 75.
China, trade with, 20, 22.
Chittagong, acquired, 15; Treaty concerning, 141.
Christianity in India, Parliamentary papers relating to, 236, 238, 239, 242, 247.
Cis-Sutlej Territories annexed, 25.
Civil Service, 55.
Clive, Lord, administration of, 15.
Cochin, relations of, with British Government, 138; Treaties concerning, 146, 152.
Coffee Planting, Reports relating to, 240.
Coimbatoor, 19.
Coinage, Regulations and Acts concerning, 191, 192, 196, 202, 203, 204, 205, 208.
Collegiate Institutions, 168.
Commander-in-Chief, Act concerning, 27.
Commissioners, Board of, appointed, 18; remodelled, 22.
Committee of Inquiry on Indian Affairs and Territories appointed, 16, 17, 234, 235, 242; Secret, of Court of Directors, 33.
Companies, Indo-European Trading, enumerated, 4.
Company, East Indian, charter to, first granted, 6; renewed, 6: amalgamated with "Assada Merchants," 7; Charter granted by Cromwell, 8; renewed by Charles II., 8; renewed, 9; incorporated with a Competitive Company under the title of "General Society trading to East Indies," 10; designated as "United Company of Merchants Trading to East Indies," and now amalgamated, 11; Corporate capacity recognised, 12; privileges continued, 14; Territories and Revenues guaranteed, 15; assumed absolute Government of Bengal, 16; Financial Difficulties, 16; Privileges continued, 17, 19, 20, 22; Military Establishment, 65, 66.
Company, Turkey, 5.
Contingents of Native States, numbers of, 66, 67.
Control, Board of, 18, 28; how administered, 35; present Constitution of, 36; Departments of, 37; how conducted, 38.
Cornwallis, Lord, Administration of, 18; Proclamation of Permanent Settlement of Bengal, 108; Treaty with the Nizam, 146.
Cotton, cultivation of, 172, *et seq.* Minute by Governor-General; Returns and Reports relating to, 238, 239, 240.
Council, Supreme, constitution of, 46; how transact business, 47.
Court of Directors, first instituted, 12; twenty-four Directors, election of, 16; Appointments vested in, 24, 25; Remodelled, 26; how administered, 30, *et seq.*; Patronage of, 32; Business, how transacted, 38; Correspondence with, 48.
Courts of Justice, civil, 85, 86; and criminal, 85; Moonsiffs, 86; Zillah, 87, 88, 89; Sudder Dewanny Adawlut, 89; Nizamut Adawlut, 93; Foujdary Adawlut, 93.
Covenanted and Uncovenanted Services, distinction between, 55; List of, 244.
Criminal Courts, jurisdictions of, 85.
Cromwell, Charter granted by, 8.
Customs and Duties, 130; Treaties concerning, 162, 163, 164; Regulations and Acts concerning, 191, 192, 193, 194, 195, 197, 200, 208, 210, 211, 219.
Cutch, treaties concerning, 152, 157, 159, 164.
Cuttack, 20; Acts concerning, 189, 191, 196, 197.

DACOITS, Special Police for, 95; Regulations and Acts concerning, 188, 189, 199, 201, 208, 210.
Dalhousie, Lord, Administration of, 25.
Debt, Indian, Origin of, 10.
Deccan, Boundaries of, 4; under Mahratta rule, 14.
Delhi, 20; Regulation concerning Administration of, 202.
Dioceses of Calcutta, Madras, Bombay, Establishment of, 20.
Directors, Court of, first established, 12; twenty-four Directors, election of, 16; Appointments vested in, 24, 25; Remodelled, 26; present Constitution of, 30: Patronage of, 32; Mode of transacting Business, 38; Correspondence with, 48.
Doab, Part of the, ceded, 19, 20.
Drake, 5.
Dudley, Sir Robert, 5.

ECCLESIASTICAL Establishment, 69, 70.
Educational Institutions, 165; Government Institutions, 168; Papers relating to, 240, 241, 245.
Ellenborough, Lord, Administration of, 25.
Elphinstone Code, 86.
Embassy to Delhi, Mr. Hamilton, 13.
Emigration, Acts relating to, 205, 208, 209, 212, 218.

FINANCE, Arrangements of, 16.
Fort William established, 10.
Fox's, Mr., Indian Bills, text of, 17.
French, War with, 14.
Furruckabad, Treaties concerning, 147, 148.

GARRISONS, composed of, 13.
General Court, 34.
George I., Charter granted by, 74.
George II., Charter granted by, 75.
George III., Charter granted by, 75.
Ghauts, district of, 19.
Golab Sing, Relations with British Government, 138.
Government of British India, how begun and modified, 5; Parliamentary resolution concerning, 16; Statutes concerning, 18, 19; Natives first employed in, 22; Changes in, 22; Local government of, 45.
Governor General, First appointed, 16; Powers of, 45, *et seq.*; Staff of, 47; Appointments made by, 50; Salary of, 51.
Guicowar, relations of, with British Government, 138; Treaties with, 155, 156.
Guzerat, 19; Treaties concerning, 148, 149.

HAILEYBURY, Act for abolition of, 28.
Hamilton, Mr., Embassy, 13.
Hardinge, Lord, Administration of, 25.
Hastings, Lord, Administration of, 20.
——— Warren, Administration of, 17.
Herat, Treaty concerning, 160
Hindoo Law, 71; exceptions respecting, 81; codified, 99; College, 168; Regulations and Acts concerning, 182, 187, 200, 206, 207, 220; correspondence relating to temples, 239.
Hindostan Proper, comprises, 4.
Hindustanee language, 68, 73.
Holkar, 19; relations with British Government, 138; Treaties with, 150, 156.
Holland, Treaty with, 7, 141; Order in Council concerning, 224.
Home Government, existing, 30.
Hooghly Factory, 8.
Hospital, 169.
Hyder Ali, 14; Treaty with, 144.
Hydrabad, Treaty of, 150; Regulations concerning, 159, 161.

IDOLATRY in India; Papers relating to the connection of the Government with, 236, 239, 241.
Inams, 122.
Indigo, Regulations and Acts respecting, 184, 193, 198, 201, 203, 204.
Infanticide, Proclamation concerning, 159, 162, 164; Regulations and Acts concerning, 184, 187, 189; Papers relating to, 239.
Insolvent Debtors, Court for relief of, 76.
Iron Works, 176.

Irrigation, Documents relating to, 242.

JAFFIER, Ali Khan, Treaties with, 140, 142.
Jhansi, Treaty concerning, 155.
"Jumma," definition of, 186.

KATTYWAR, Treaty with Ranee of, 143.
Kazis, the, Acts concerning, 182, 184, 188.
Kolapore, relations with, of British Government, 138.
Kotah, Treaty with, 156, 160.

LAHORE, Treaty of, 25; Regulations and Acts concerning, 150, 152, 159, 160, 163.
La-Khiraj Lands, 122; Regulations and Acts concerning, 182, 184, 188, 196, 199, 200.
Lancaster, Expedition of, to India, 5.
Land Revenue, various systems of Assessment, 105; in Bengal, 112: in North-West Provinces, 113; in Madras, 116; in Bombay, 119; in the Punjaub, 120; lands exempted from, 122; Fifth Report of Committee on, 236.
Law Commission, appointment of, 24; recommendations of, 95, *et seq.*; Penal Code prepared by, 238; Reports of, 239, 247.
Local Administration of India, 45.

MADRAS, constituted distinct Presidency, 8; government of, 52; Supreme Court of Judicature of, 83; Land Revenue in, 116; University, 165; Schools and Colleges, 170; Assessment and Survey of, 247.
Mahomedan Dynasties, 4; Law, 71, 81; Criminal Law codified, 99; College at Calcutta, 168; Regulations and Acts concerning Mahomedans, 182, 185, 186, 200-7.
Mahomedanism, Papers relating to the connection of the Government with, 236-9, 241.
Mahrattas, war with, 10, 19; subdued, 20; Treaties with, 140, 145, 152.
Malacca acquired, 20; Regulations and Acts concerning, 220, 221, 222, 223.
Malwa, Treaty concerning, 153.
Marine, Bombay, 68.
Masulipatam, Treaty for cession of, 141.
Mayor's Court in Calcutta, established, 74; abolished, 75.
Medical College at Calcutta, 169.
Midnapore, acquired, 15; Treaty concerning, 141.
Military Force, East India Company's Native, 65; European, 66; Queen's troops in India, 66; Contingents of Native States, 66, 67; Military Service, rules of admission to, 67, and Appendix C.; Regulations and Acts concerning Cantonments and Courts-Martial, 191, 192, 197, 205, 206, 207, 222, 223; Articles of War, 210, 211, 220.
Mints, established at Bombay, 9; Act concerning, 185; Returns relating to, 248.
Missionaries, existing Societies in India, 168; Parliamentary Papers relating to, 236, 247; Dispatch concerning Memorial of, 248.
Mofussil, Regulations and Acts relating to the, 206, 207, 212.
Mogul, Imperial Firman from, 6; Pensioned by Great Britain, 20.
Moonsiffs, powers and salaries of, 86; Regulations and Acts concerning, 194, 203, 205, 207, 209, 211, 212, 214.
Moultan acquired by Nadir Shah, 14.
Mutiny of Vellore, 20; of 1857, Papers relating to, 249, 250.
Mysore, 19; relations with British Government, 138; Treaties with, 147, 149, 151, 159.

NADIR SHAH, 14.
Napier (Sir C.), correspondence, &c., with Duke of Wellington on state of Indian Army, 249; Papers relating to Resignation of, 244.
Native Princes, Territories of, 3.
Native States, Administration of, 135; summary of relations with Great Britain, 138; total area and Population of, 138; list of Treaties and engagements with, 140.

Navy, Indian, 68; Act concerning, 216.
Nazim, Acts concerning the, 182, 189, 190.
Nepaul, acquired, 20; relations with British Government, 138; Treaties with, 146, 148, 155, 164; Papers relating to War with, 237.
Nizam, relations of, with British Government, 138; Treaties with, 146, 147, 148 149, 158, 159, 164.
Non-Regulation Provinces, 1; Appointments in, 46.
Northern Circars acquired, 15; Treaty concerning, 143.
North-Western Provinces, Lieutenant-Governor of, 25, 27; Colleges and Schools in, 169; Sudder Courts in, 201, 202; Act for Settlement of, 209.

Opium Revenue, 223, *et seq.*; Acts concerning, 195, 196, 200, 212, 222; Returns relating to, 248.
Orders in Council, first regulating trade to East Indies, 7; uniting the two Companies, 11; list of, relating to British India, 224.
Orissa, Act concerning, 181; Civil Government of, 15; Treaty concerning, 142, 143.
Oude, half of Territory ceded, 19; finally annexed, 29; Treaties concerning, 145, 153, 154, 155, 158, 159, 160; Draft of Treaty proposed in 1856, Appendix B.
Oudeypore, Treaty with, 156.

Patna, Treaty concerning, 151.
Patronage, Report of Committee on, 236; Returns relating to, 243.
Patteedary tenure, definition of, 108.
Pegu, Conquest of, 25.
Pensions to Native Princes first given, 15.
Pepper, Treaties relating to, 140, 141, 146.
Persia, Treaties with, 148, 151, 152, 153, 154, 158, 159, 160, 161, 164; War of 1856, Papers relating to, 248-9.
Pindarrees, 19.
Pitt, India Bill, 18.
Plassey, Battle of, 15.
Police, authority of, 92; Regulations and Acts concerning, 184, 185, 189, 191, 192, 195, 202, 204, 212, 220; Dispatch relating to, in Bengal, 248.
Poonah, Peishwah of, deposed, 20.
Population of British India, 3.
Post Office, 132; Acts, 205, 214; Returns, 240, 241.
Presidencies, three British, first organized, 12.
Previous Communication, meaning of phrase, 39.
Prince of Wales' Island, or Penang, 20; Treaty concerning, 145, 146; Acts concerning, 220, 221, 222.
Printing, Acts concerning, 203, 222.
Proprietors, Court of, Constitution of, 34.
Provinces, Regulation and Non-Regulation, 1.
Public Works, 170; Acts concerning, 184, 190, 192, 201, 211, 215, 218; Returns relating to, 241, 243.
Punchayat, Constitution of, 88, 94.

Queda, Treaty for cession of, 148.
Queen's Troops in India, 66.

Railways, 171; Act relating to, 214; Papers relating to, 239, 248, 249.
Rajpoot States, Relations with British Government, 138.
Regulations for Admission to Indian Services, Appendix C.
Requests, Court of, 75.
Residencies in Native States, 2, 138.
Revenue, existing system of, 104; Sources of, 104; Collection of, 105; Boards of, 105; Opium, 123, *et seq.*; Salt, 127; Customs' duties, 130; Subsidies from Native States, 130; other sources, 132; Annual accounts of, 235, *et seq.*
Rewah, Treaties with, 154.
Roads, 171.
Rohilcund, 19; Treaty with Rohillas, 147.
Roman Catholics, three Bishops and seventy-eight Priests; Salaries of, 70; Parliamentary Papers relating to, 236; Treaties, Acts and Ordinances relating to, 240.
Runjeet Singh, defeated, 21; Treaty with, 160, 238.

Ryotwar tenure, definition of, 112

SALARIES of first Civil Servants, 12; of Moonsiffs, 87; of Directors of East India Company, 34; of Presidents of Board of Control, 38; Ecclesiastical, 70; of Governor-General and Members of Council, 51; of Judges of Sudder Courts, 91.
Saltpetre, Treaties relating to, 140; Acts concerning, 193, 215, 218.
Salt, Revenues, 127; Agencies, 128; Acts concerning, 188, 197, 199, 203, 205, 208, 210, 212; Report on monopoly of, 238.
Sanskrit College, 168.
Sattara, lapsed, 25; Treaty concerning, 157; Proclamation by Rajah of, 162; Papers relating to, 240, 242, 245.
Saugur, Treaty concerning, 156, 157; Act concerning, 187.
Sayer, Acts concerning, 182, 192.
Schools, Statistical table of, 167; connected with Missionary Societies, 168.
Secret Committee, 23; Constitution of, 33.
Sepoys first employed by E. I. Company, 13.
Seringapatam, 19.
Shujah-al-Dowlah, Treaty with, 143, 144.
Siam, Treaty with, 158.
Sinde, acquired by Nadir Shah, 14: conquered by British, 25; Treaty with, 140, 141; Acts concerning, 152, 157, 160, 161; Correspondence relating to Treaties with Ameers, 239.
Sindia, 19; Relations with, 138; Treaties with, 149, 150, 155, 156.
Singapore, purchased, 21; Acts concerning, 220, 221, 222, 223.
Sirhind, Treaty with, 152, 153.
Slave Trade, Treaties concerning, 156, 157; Agreements for abolition of African, 163, 164, 192, 202.
Somnauth, Proclamation relating to the Gates of, 239.
Stamps, Revenue, 131
St. Helena, 24.
Statistical Papers, 241.
Steam Communication with India, Papers relating to, 238.
Straits Settlements, formed, 21; Act concerning, 217, 223.
Subordinate Governments, Madras, Bombay, North-West Provinces, 51, *et seq.*
Subsidies from Native States, 130.
Sudder Courts, Regulations and Acts concerning, 201, 202, 206, 207, 211, 216; Dewanny Adawlut, 89, 182, *et seq.*; Nizamut Adawlut, 93, 186, *et seq.*; Foujdarry Adawlut, 93.
Sugar, Acts concerning, 204, 207; Reports relating to, 240.
Supreme Council, 45.
Supreme Courts, 16; Jurisdiction of, 75; Law administered by, 80; Courts of Madras or Bombay, 83–85.
Surat, Factory established at, 6; Treaty relating to, 141, 147.
Survey of India; Papers relating to, 241.
Suttee, Treaty concerning, 161, 162; Acts concerning, 201; Papers relating to, 237.

TANJORE, 19; Treaty concerning, 144, 146, 147.
Teignmouth, Lord; Administration of, 19.
Telegraphs, 171; Act concerning, 216.
Territories of Native Princes under British protection, 1; Law concerning, 71.
Thugs, special police for, 95; Acts concerning, 204, 205, 208, 209, 210.
Tinnevelly, Treaty concerning, 148.
Tippoo Saib's powers reduced, 19; Treaties with, 145, 146.
Transportation of criminals, 7; Regulations and Acts concerning, 192, 193, 200, 218.
Travancore, relations of, with British Government, 138; Treaties with Rajah of, 146, 147, 150.
Turkey Company, 5.

UNCOVENANTED Civil Service, 62.
Universities, 165.

VELLORE mutiny ; Note, page 20.
Village communities, definition of, 106.

WARDS, Court of ; Regulations and Acts concerning, 182, 183, 185, 186, 188, 197, 218.
Wellesley, Lord, Administration of, 19.

YANDABU, Treaty of, 21.

ZEMINDAR, Definition of, 106 ; Regulation concerning, 191.
Zemindary tenure, Definition of, 111.
Zillah Courts and Judges, powers of, 87, 88, 89 ; Regulations and Acts concerning, 181, 183, 185, 189, 190, 194, 195, 196, 199, 200, 201, 202, 203, 204, 205, 208, 211.